Drug Tales

Drug Tales

Edited by
DUNCAN FALLOWELL

ST. MARTIN'S PRESS
NEW YORK

Copyright © 1979 by Duncan Fallowell
All rights reserved. For information, write:
St. Martin's Press, Inc. 175 Fifth Ave., New York, N.Y. 10010
Manufactured in the United States of America

Library of Congress Cataloging in Publication Data

Main entry under title:

Drug tales.

   1. Drugs—Fiction. 2. Short stories, English.
3. Short stories, American. I. Fallowell, Duncan.
PZ1.D6546 1980   [PR1309.D78]   823′.01   79-22918
ISBN 0-312-21977-6

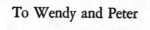

To Wendy and Peter

Contents

Acknowledgements

Acknowledgements are due to the Estate of the late Arthur Machen for 'The Novel of the White Powder'; to the Estate of the late Sir Max Beerbohm for 'Enoch Soames'; to Peter Owen Ltd., Publishers, London, for Anna Kavan's 'Julia and the Bazooka'; to Allied Publishers Private Ltd., New Delhi, for 'The Fabled Nizam' from *Maharaja* by Jarmani Dass; to A.D. Peters Ltd., for 'The Heat Closing In' from *Dead Fingers Talk* by William Burroughs; to the Sterling Lord Agency, Inc., for 'The Blood of a Wig' from *Red-Dirt Marijuana and Other Tales* © 1967 by Terry Southern; to the author for 'Cable Street' from *The White Room* © 1968 by Lee Harwood; to Deborah Rogers Ltd., for 'A Night on the Town' from *Fear and Loathing in Las Vegas* © 1971 by Hunter S. Thompson, published in the United Kingdom by Paladin Books; to Mohammed Mrabet for his stories 'The Doctor from the Chemel' and 'The Canebreak', taped and translated from the Moghrebi by © 1969 Paul Bowles; to Dylan Hyatt for 'Randel' by Mark Hyatt © 1979 Dylan Hyatt, and to Duncan Fallowell for Peter Riviera's 'Rome' © 1979.

A*

Introduction

DUNCAN FALLOWELL

I

IN FACT, I have nursed no special restlessness for the opportunity to make a collection of stories on this theme. But in 1977, while working on something altogether different, I was asked to review *The Film Addict's Archive,* a volume of fiction and poems about the cinema, published by a division of Hamish Hamilton Ltd. The dust cover mentioned a 'series'. *The Cricket Addict's Archive, The Antique Addict's Archive*—where could this be leading? I was in bed at the time, hoping that the coffee, etc, would soon take grip on a thick, slowly churning fog of viscous half-thoughts and incomplete hypnagogic images laced now and again with an enlivening flash of paranoia. Then very gradually the answer began to rise up through this somnolent plankton until it burst sunlike across the high plateau of a clear mind, the conclusion to which films, cricket and antiques had only been indications . . . *The Drug Addict's Archive.* I goose-pimpled violently. Next thing, there was a powerful physical sensation as of a wave sucking backwards just before it breaks forward on the shore, and suddenly I realised I was out of bed. A quick squirt of eyedrops was enormously helpful in adjusting my vision to this new perspective. The same day a letter was sent to the publishers who wrote back and confirmed the idea, but for a book independent of the *Archive* series.

II

The telephone rang. It was a friend of mine who wanted to start up a magazine, which we did. It had a very consuming effect on the people involved. What, for example, is an ozalid? It became essential to know. As for *Drug Tales*, this new outburst shredded the original contents list completely.

III

Any attempt to be 'representative' now seemed more than futile. It seemed unattractive. With a sigh of relief all the obvious dead wood could go—De Quincey, Aldous Huxley, Jack Kerouac, Baudelaire's Hashish Club, etc. And the clinical approach could go too. Bring in alcohol, aspirins, cigarettes, attendants to the profession of letters for so long that one is hard put to find a writer who is pill-free, teetotal, a non-smoker, and still worth reading. Of the few first-round choices that survived, Poe could stay in, but not on account of his bogus flirtation with opium—drink was Poe's indulgence. Burroughs would stay in for giving the subject a contemporary mythology that is sharp, Hunter Thompson for giving it one that is hilarious. And Peter Riviera because nobody knows about him yet. Which left plenty of room for newcomers. Balzac was a brief thought because of his staggering addiction to coffee (which has recently been said to have remarkable chromosome-splitting properties—it would be interesting to search for signs of this in his work), but I decided to streamline further by dropping all translations—with the exception of those from the Moghrebi language. This had the fortunate side-effect of eliminating several contentious copyright problems on over-rated material. I went further and shed poetry. It was slovenly not to have realised from the start what a nostalgic gesture its presence would have been. With one quasi-exception. Lee Harwood's *Cable Street*, apart from its comprehensive internal melancholia, is interesting because it shows prose actually in the act of swallowing up the purpose of poetry. Which, if one wonders where poetry has gone, must be what has happened to it (incidentally, this collection is among other things a map of the evolution of English prose from the Regency to the post-present). The extraordinary use to which Le Fanu put green tea came out of thin air one night and made sense. And having opened up the theme in this way, other eccentric substances became available: Hawthorne's elixir of youth, Machen's white powder, Terry Southern's syringe of blood from a Chinese schizophrenic. With the catchment thus enlarged and deepened, it was possible without any loss of coherence to take up several stories which intruded themselves naturally, if less explicitly, into the overall weirdness. Beerbohm's character, Enoch Soames, would have been a junky later on, but at the time had to make do with absinthe and the devil. *The Fabled Nizam,* pure non-fiction by intent, is here nonetheless because it has the unearthly and phantasmagorical iridescence of an hallucination, in which the Nizam's addiction to cigarettes is only one bizarre component of a personality whose ultimate addiction was to jewels.

IV

By the time this encompassing process had reached its limit I was more than ever behind schedule, with a mass of material lying around (I never did find anything decent on aspirin), notes and an introduction to write. Does anyone ever read introductions? A common practice is to pass the job on to an academic. Perhaps one of them had written a study called *The Stoned Literatus*—no. Besides it is peculiar strategy to begin a book with an exhaustive version of the worst thing in it. Introductions should be short. The telephone rang. The publishers were being reasonable to an embarrassing degree. It was time to clench up. That very day I cancelled all appointments, heaped all the books and papers into one room, closed the door, sat down at the desk, opened a bottle of gin, swallowed a few pills, lit a cigarette and began.

The Dinner

THOMAS LOVE PEACOCK

THE SUN WAS NOW terminating his diurnal course, and the lights were glittering on the festal board. When the ladies had retired, and the Burgundy had taken two or three tours of the table, the following conversation took place:

SQUIRE HEADLONG. Push about the bottle: Mr Escot, it stands with you. No heeltaps. As to skylight, liberty-hall.

MR MAC LAUREL. Really, Squire Headlong, this is the vara nactar itsel. Ye hae saretainly discovered the tarrestrial paradise, but it flows wi' a better leecor than milk an' honey.

THE REVEREND DOCTOR GASTER. Hem! Mr Mac Laurel! there is a degree of profaneness in that observation, which I should not have looked for in so staunch a supporter of church and state. Milk and honey was the pure food of the antediluvian patriarchs, who knew not the use of the grape, happily for them—(*Tossing off a bumper of Burgundy.*)

MR ESCOT. Happily, indeed! The first inhabitants of the world knew not the use either of wine or animal food; it is, therefore, by no means incredible that they lived to the age of several centuries, free from war, and commerce, and arbitrary government, and every other species of desolating wickedness. But man was then a very different animal to what he now is: he had not the faculty of speech; he was not encumbered with clothes; he lived in the open air; his first step out of which, as Hamlet truly observes, is *into his grave.** His first dwellings, of course, were the hollows of trees and rocks.

* See Lord Monboddo's *Ancient Metaphysics.*

In process of time he began to build: thence grew villages; thence grew cities. Luxury, oppression, poverty, misery, and disease kept pace with the progress of his pretended improvements, till, from a free, strong, healthy, peaceful animal, he has become a weak, distempered, cruel, carnivorous slave.

THE REVEREND DOCTOR GASTER. Your doctrine is orthodox, in so far as you assert that the original man was not encumbered with clothes, and that he lived in the open air; but, as to the faculty of speech, that, it is certain, he had, for the authority of Moses—

MR ESCOT. Of course, sir, I do not presume to dissent from the very exalted authority of that most enlightened astronomer and profound cosmogonist, who had, moreover, the advantage of being inspired; but when I indulge myself with a ramble in the fields of speculation, and attempt to deduce what is probable and rational from the sources of analysis, experience, and comparison, I confess I am too often apt to lose sight of the doctrines of that great fountain of theological and geological philosophy.

SQUIRE HEADLONG. Push about the bottle.

MR FOSTER. Do you suppose the mere animal life of a wild man, living on acorns, and sleeping on the ground, comparable in felicity to that of a Newton, ranging through unlimited space, and penetrating into the arcana of universal motion—to that of a Locke, unravelling the labyrinth of mind—to that of a Lavoisier, detecting the minutest combinations of matter, and reducing all nature to its elements—to that of a Shakespeare, piercing and developing the springs of passion—or of a Milton, identifying himself, as it were, with the beings of an invisible world?

MR ESCOT. You suppose extreme cases; but, on the score of happiness, what comparison can you make between the tranquil being of the wild man of the woods and the wretched and turbulent existence of Milton, the victim of persecution, poverty, blindness, and neglect? The records of literature demonstrate that Happiness and Intelligence are seldom sisters. Even if it were otherwise, it would prove nothing. The many are always sacrificed to the few. Where one man advances, hundreds retrograde; and the balance is always in favour of universal deterioration.

MR FOSTER. Virtue is independent of external circumstances. The exalted understanding looks into the truth of things, and, in its own peaceful contemplations, rises superior to the world. No philosopher would resign his mental acquisitions for the purchase of any terrestrial good.

MR ESCOT. In other words, no man whatever would resign his identity, which is nothing more than the consciousness of his perceptions, as the price of any acquisition. But every man, without exception, would willingly effect a very material change in his relative situation to other individuals. Unluckily for the rest of your argument, the understanding of literary people is for the most part *exalted*, as you express it, not so much by the love of truth and virtue, as by arrogance and self-sufficiency; and there is, perhaps, less disinterestedness, less liberality, less general benevolence, and more envy, hatred, and uncharitableness among them, than among any other description of men.

(*The eye of Mr Escot, as he pronounced these words, rested very innocently and unintentionally on Mr Gall.*)

MR GALL. You allude, sir, I presume, to my review.

MR ESCOT. Pardon me, sir. You will be convinced it is impossible I can allude to your review, when I assure you that I have never read a single page of it.

MR GALL, MR TREACLE, MR NIGHTSHADE, AND MR MAC LAUREL. Never read our review!!!

MR ESCOT. Never. I look on periodical criticism in general to be a species of shop, where panegyric and defamation are sold, wholesale, retail, and for exportation. I am not inclined to be a purchaser of these commodities, or to encourage a trade which I consider pregnant with mischief.

MR MAC LAUREL. I can readily conceive, sir, ye wou'd na wullinly encoorage ony dealer in panegeeric; but, frae the manner in which ye speak o' the first creetics an' scholars o' the age, I shou'd think ye wou'd have a little mair predilaction for deefamation.

MR ESCOT. I have no predilection, sir, for defamation. I make a point of speaking the truth on all occasions; and it seldom happens that the truth can be spoken without some stricken deer pronouncing it a libel.

MR NIGHTSHADE. You are perhaps, sir, an enemy to literature in general?

MR ESCOT. If I were, sir, I should be a better friend to periodical critics.

SQUIRE HEADLONG. Buz!

MR TREACLE. May I simply take the liberty to inquire into the basis of your objection?

MR ESCOT. I conceive that periodical criticism disseminates superficial knowledge, and its perpetual adjunct, vanity; that it checks in the youthful mind the habit of thinking for itself; that it delivers partial opinions, and thereby misleads the judgement; that it is never conducted with a view to the general interests of literature, but to serve the interested ends of individuals, and the miserable purposes of party.

MR MAC LAUREL. Ye ken, sir, a mon mun leeve.

MR ESCOT. While he can live honourably, naturally, justly, certainly: no longer.

MR MAC LAUREL. Every mon, sir, leeves according to his ain notions of honour an' justice: there is a wee defference amang the learned wi' respact to the defineetion o' the terms.

MR ESCOT. I believe it is generally admitted, that one of the ingredients of justice is disinterestedness.

MR MAC LAUREL. It is no admetted, sir, amang the pheelosophers of Edinbroo', that there is ony sic thing as desenterestedness in the warld, or that a mon can care for onything sae much as his ain sel: for ye mun observe, sir, every mon has his ain parteecular feelings of what is gude, an' beautifu', an' consentaneous to his ain indiveedual nature, an' desires to see everything aboot him in that parteecular state which is maist conformable to his ain notions o' the moral an' poleetical fetness o' things. Twa men, sir, shall purchase a piece o' grund atween 'em, and ae mon shall cover his half wi' a park—

MR MILESTONE. Beautifully laid out in lawns and clumps, with a belt of trees at the circumference, and an artificial lake in the centre.

MR MAC LAUREL. Exactly, sir: an' shall keep it a' for his ain sel: an' the other mon shall divide his half into leetle farms of two or three acres—

MR ESCOT. Like those of the Roman republic, and build a cottage on each of them, and cover his land with a simple, innocent, and smiling population, who shall owe, not only their happiness, but their existence, to his benevolence.

MR MAC LAUREL. Exactly, sir: an' ye will ca' the first mon selfish, an' the second desenterested; but the pheelosophical truth is semply this, that the ane is pleased wi' looking at trees, an' the other wi' seeing people happy an' comfortable. It is aunly a matter of indiveedual feeling. A paisant saves a mon's life for the same reason that a hero or a footpad cuts his thrapple: an' a pheelosopher delevers a mon frae a preson, for the same reason that a tailor or a prime menester puts him into it: because it is conformable to his ain parteecular feelings o' the moral an' poleetical fetness o' things.

SQUIRE HEADLONG. Wake the Reverend Doctor. Doctor, the bottle stands with you.

THE REVEREND DOCTOR GASTER. It is an error of which I am seldom guilty.

MR MAC LAUREL. Noo, ye ken, sir, every mon is the centre of his ain system, an' endaivours as much as possible to adapt everything aroond him to his ain parteecular views.

MR ESCOT. Thus, sir, I presume, it suits the particular views of a poet, at one time to take the part of the people against their oppressors, and at another, to take the part of the oppressors, against the people.

MR MAC LAUREL. Ye mun alloo, sir, that poetry is a sort of ware or commodity, that is brought into the public market wi' a' other descreptions of merchandise, an' that a mon is pairfectly justified in getting the best price he can for his article. Noo, there are three reasons for taking the part o' the people: the first is, when general leeberty an' public happiness are conformable to your ain parteecular feelings o' the moral an' poleetical fetness o' things: the second is, when they happen to be, as it were, in a state of exceetabeelity, an' ye think ye can get a gude price for your commodity, by flingin' in a leetle seasoning o' pheelanthropy an' republican speerit: the third is, when ye think ye can bully the menestry into gieing ye a place or a pansion to hau'd your din, an' in that case, ye point an attack against them within the pale o' the law; an' if they tak nae heed o' ye, ye open a stronger fire; an' the less heed they tak, the mair ye bawl; an' the mair factious ye grow, always within the pale o' the law, till they send a plenipotentiary to treat wi' ye for yoursel, an' then the mair popular ye happen to be, the better price ye fetch.

SQUIRE HEADLONG. Off with your heeltaps.

MR CRANIUM. I perfectly agree with Mr Mac Laurel in his definition of self-love and disinterestedness: every man's actions are determined by his own peculiar views, and those views are determined by the organisation of his skull. A man in whom the organ of benevolence is not developed, cannot be benevolent: he, in whom it is so, cannot be otherwise. The organ of self-love is prodigiously developed in the greater number of subjects that have fallen under my observation.

MR ESCOT. Much less, I presume, among savage than civilised men, who, *constant only to the love of self, and consistent only in their aim to deceive, are always actuated by the hope of personal advantage, or by the dread of personal punishment.**

MR CRANIUM. Very probably.

MR ESCOT. You have, of course, found very copious specimens of the organs of hypocrisy, destruction, and avarice.

MR CRANIUM. Secretiveness, destructiveness, and covetiveness. You may add, if you please, that of constructiveness.

MR ESCOT. Meaning, I presume, the organ of building; which I contend to be not a natural organ of the *featherless biped.*

MR CRANIUM. Pardon me: it is here.—(*As he said these words, he produced a skull from his pocket, and placed it on the table, to the great surprise of the company.*)—This was the skull of Sir Christopher Wren. You observe this protuberance.—(*The skull was handed round the table.*)

MR ESCOT. I contend that the original unsophisticated man was by no means constructive. He lived in the open air, under a tree.

THE REVEREND DOCTOR GASTER. The tree of life. Unquestionably. Till he had tasted the forbidden fruit.

MR JENKINSON. At which period, probably, the organ of constructiveness was added to his anatomy, as a punishment for his transgression.

MR ESCOT. There could not have been a more severe one, since the propensity which has led him to building cities has proved the greatest curse of his existence.

SQUIRE HEADLONG (*taking the skull*). *Memento mori.* Come, a bumper of Burgundy.

MR NIGHTSHADE. A very classical application, Squire Headlong. The Romans were in the practice of adhibiting skulls at their banquets, and sometimes little skeletons of silver, as a silent admonition to the guests to enjoy life while it lasted.

THE REVEREND DOCTOR GASTER. Sound doctrine, Mr Nightshade.

* Drummond's *Academical Questions.*

MR ESCOT. I question its soundness. The use of vinous spirit has a tremendous influence in the deterioration of the human race.

MR FOSTER. I fear, indeed, it operates as a considerable check to the progress of the species towards moral and intellectual perfection. Yet many great men have been of opinion that it exalts the imagination, fires the genius, accelerates the flow of ideas, and imparts to dispositions naturally cold and deliberative that enthusiastic sublimation which is the source of greatness and energy.

MR NIGHTSHADE. *Laudibus arguitur vini vinosus Homerus.**

MR JENKINSON. I conceive the use of wine to be always pernicious in excess, but often useful in moderation: it certainly kills some, but it saves the lives of others: I find that an occasional glass, taken with judgement and caution, has a very salutary effect in maintaining that equilibrium of the system, which it is always my aim to preserve; and this calm and temperate use of wine was, no doubt, what Homer meant to inculcate, when he said:

Παρ δε δεπας οινοιο, πιειν ότε θυμος ανωγοι.†

SQUIRE HEADLONG. Good. Pass the bottle. (*Un morne silence.*) Sir Christopher does not seem to have raised our spirits. Chromatic, favour us with a specimen of your vocal powers. Something in point.

Mr Chromatic, without further preface, immediately struck up the following

SONG

In his last binn SIR PETER lies,
    Who knew not what it was to frown:
Death took him mellow, by surprise,
    And in his cellar stopped him down.
Through all our land we could not boast
    A knight more gay, more prompt than he,
To rise and fill a bumper toast,
    And pass it round with THREE TIMES THREE.

---

* Homer is proved to have been a lover of wine by the praises he bestows upon it.
† A cup of wine at hand, to drink as inclination prompts.

None better knew the feast to sway,
　Or keep Mirth's boat in better trim;
For Nature had but little clay
　Like that of which she moulded him.
The meanest guest that graced his board
　Was there the freest of the free,
His bumper toast when PETER poured,
　And passed it round with THREE TIMES THREE.

He kept at true good humour's mark
　The social flow of pleasure's tide:
He never made a brow look dark,
　Nor caused a tear, but when he died.
No sorrow round his tomb should dwell:
　More pleased his gay old ghost would be,
For funeral song, and passing bell,
　To hear no sound but THREE TIMES THREE.

(Hammering of knuckles and glasses, and shouts of Bravo!)

MR PANSCOPE. (*suddenly emerging from a deep reverie.*) I have heard, with the most profound attention, everything which the gentleman on the other side of the table has thought proper to advance on the subject of human deterioration; and I must take the liberty to remark that it augurs a very considerable degree of presumption in any individual, to set himself up against the *authority* of so many great men, as may be marshalled in metaphysical phalanx under the opposite banners of the controversy; such as Aristotle, Plato, the scholiast on Aristophanes, St Chrysostom, St Jerome, St Athanasius, Orpheus, Pindar, Simonides, Gronovius, Hemsterhusius, Longinus, Sir Isaac Newton, Thomas Paine, Doctor Paley, the King of Prussia, the King of Poland, Cicero, Monsieur Gautier, Hippocrates, Machiavelli, Milton, Colley Cibber, Bojardo, Gregory, Nazianzenus, Locke, D'Alembert, Boccaccio, Daniel Defoe, Erasmus, Doctor Smollett, Zimmermann, Solomon, Confucius, Zoroaster, and Thomas-a-Kempis.

MR ESCOT. I presume, sir, you are one of those who value an *authority* more than a reason.

MR PANSCOPE. The *authority*, sir, of all these great men, whose works, as well as the whole of the *Encyclopaedia Britannica*, the entire series of the *Monthly Review*, the complete set of the

Variorum Classics, and the *Memoirs of the Academy of Inscriptions,* I have read through from beginning to end, deposes, with irrefragable refutation, against your ratiocinative speculations, wherein you seem desirous, by the futile process of analytical dialectics, to subvert the pyramidal structure of synthetically deduced opinions, which have withstood the secular revolutions of physiological disquisition, and which I maintain to be transcendentally self-evident, categorically certain, and syllogistically demonstrable.

SQUIRE HEADLONG. Bravo! Pass the bottle. The very best speech that ever was made.

MR ESCOT. It has only the slight disadvantage of being unintelligible.

MR PANSCOPE. I am not obliged, sir, as Dr Johnson observed on a similar occasion, to furnish you with an understanding.

MR ESCOT. I fear, sir, you would have some difficulty in furnishing me with such an article from your own stock.

MR PANSCOPE. 'Sdeath, sir, do you question my understanding?

MR ESCOT. I only question, sir, where I expect a reply; which, from things that have no existence, I am not visionary enough to anticipate.

MR PANSCOPE. I beg leave to observe, sir, that my language was perfectly perspicuous, and etymologically correct; and, I conceive, I have demonstrated what I shall now take the liberty to say in plain terms, that all your opinions are extremely absurd.

MR ESCOT. I should be sorry, sir, to advance any opinion that you would not think absurd.

MR PANSCOPE. Death and fury, sir—

MR ESCOT. Say no more, sir. That apology is quite sufficient.

MR PANSCOPE. Apology, sir?

MR ESCOT. Even so, sir. You have lost your temper, which I consider equivalent to a confession that you have the worst of the argument.

MR PANSCOPE. Lightning and devils! sir—

SQUIRE HEADLONG. No civil war!—Temperance, in the name of Bacchus!—A glee! a glee! *Music has charms to bend the knotted oak.* Sir Patrick, you'll join?

SIR PATRICK O'PRISM. Troth, with all my heart: for, by my soul, I'm bothered completely.

SQUIRE HEADLONG. Agreed, then: you, and I, and Chromatic. Bumpers!—bumpers! Come, strike up.

Squire Headlong, Mr Chromatic, and Sir Patrick O'Prism, each holding a bumper, immediately vociferated the following

GLEE

A heeltap! a heeltap! I never could bear it!
So fill me a bumper, a bumper of claret!
Let the bottle pass freely, don't shirk it nor spare it,
For a heeltap! a heeltap; I never could bear it!
No skylight! no twilight! while Bacchus rules o'er us:
No thinking! no shrinking! all drinking in chorus:
Let us moisten our clay, since 'tis thirsty and porous:
No thinking! no shrinking! all drinking in chorus!

GRAND CHORUS

By Squire Headlong, Mr Chromatic, Sir Patrick O'Prism, Mr Pan-scope, Mr Jenkinson, Mr Gall, Mr Treacle, Mr Nightshade, Mr Mac Laurel, Mr Cranium, Mr Milestone, and the Reverend Doctor Gaster.

A heeltap! a heeltap! I never could bear it!
So fill me a bumper, a bumper of claret!
Let the bottle pass freely, don't shirk it nor spare it,
For a heeltap! a heeltap! I never could bear it.

΄ΟΜΑΔΟΣ ΚΑΙ ΔΟΥΠΟΣ ΟΡΩΡΕΙ!΄

The little butler now waddles in with a summons from the ladies to tea and coffee. The squire was unwilling to leave his Burgundy. Mr Escot strenuously urged the necessity of immediate adjournment, observing, that the longer they continued drinking the worse they should be. Mr Foster seconded the motion, declaring the transition from the bottle to female society to be an indisputable amelioration of the state of the sensitive man. Mr Jenkinson allowed the squire and his two brother philosophers to settle the point between them, concluding that he was just as well in one place as another. The question of adjournment was then put, and carried by a large majority.

Dr Heidegger's Experiment

NATHANIEL HAWTHORNE

THAT VERY SINGULAR MAN, old Dr Heidegger, once invited four venerable friends to meet him in his study. There were three white-bearded gentlemen, Mr Medbourne, Colonel Killigrew, and Mr Gascoigne, and a withered gentlewoman, whose name was the Widow Wycherly. They were all melancholy old creatures who had been unfortunate in life, and whose greatest misfortune it was, that they were not long ago in their graves. Mr Medbourne, in the vigour of his age, had been a prosperous merchant, but had lost his all by a frantic speculation, and was now little better than a mendicant. Colonel Killigrew had wasted his best years and his health and substance, in the pursuit of sinful pleasures, which had given birth to a brood of pains, such as the gout, and divers other torments of soul and body. Mr Gascoigne was a ruined politician, a man of evil fame, or at least had been so, till time had buried him from the knowledge of the present generation, and made him obscure instead of infamous. As for the Widow Wycherly, tradition tells us that she was a great beauty in her day; but, for a long while past, she had lived in deep seclusion, on account of certain scandalous stories, which had prejudiced the gentry of the town against her. It is a circumstance worth mentioning, that each of these three old gentlemen, Mr Medbourne, Colonel Killigrew, and Mr Gascoigne, were early lovers of the Widow Wycherly, and had once been on the point of cutting each other's throats for her sake. And, before proceeding further, I will merely hint, that Dr Heidegger and all his four guests were sometimes thought to be a little beside themselves; as is not unfrequently the case with old people, when worried either by present troubles or woeful recollections.

'My dear old friends,' said Dr Heidegger, motioning them to be seated, 'I am desirous of your assistance in one of those little experiments with which I amuse myself here in my study.'

If all stories were true, Dr Heidegger's study must have been a very curious place. It was a dim, old-fashioned chamber, festooned with cobwebs, and besprinkled with antique dust. Around the walls stood several oaken bookcases, the lower shelves of which were filled with rows of gigantic folios, and black-letter quartos, and the upper with little parchment-covered duodecimos. Over the central bookcase was a bronze bust of Hippocrates, with which, according to some authorities, Dr Heidegger was accustomed to hold consultations, in all difficult cases of his practice. In the obscurest corner of the room stood a tall and narrow oaken closet, with its door ajar, within which doubtfully appeared a skeleton. Between two of the bookcases hung a looking-glass, presenting its high and dusty plate within a tarnished gilt frame. Among many wonderful stories related to this mirror, it was fabled that the spirits of all the doctor's deceased patients dwelt within its verge, and would stare him in the face whenever he looked thitherward. The opposite side of the chamber was ornamented with the full-length portrait of a young lady, arrayed in the faded magnificence of silk, satin, and brocade, and with a visage as faded as her dress. Above half a century ago, Dr Heidegger had been on the point of marriage with this young lady; but, being affected with some slight disorder, she had swallowed one of her lover's prescriptions, and died on the bridal evening. The greatest curiosity of the study remains to be mentioned; it was a ponderous folio volume, bound in black leather, with massive silver clasps. There were no letters on the back, and nobody could tell the title of the book. But it was well known to be a book of magic; and once, when a chambermaid had lifted it, merely to brush away the dust, the skeleton had rattled in its closet, the picture of the young lady had stepped one foot upon the floor, and several ghastly faces had peered forth from the mirror; while the brazen head of Hippocrates frowned, and said—'Forbear!'

Such was Dr Heidegger's study. On the summer afternoon of our tale, a small round table, as black as ebony, stood in the centre of the room, sustaining a cut-glass vase, of beautiful form and elaborate workmanship. The sunshine came through the window, between the heavy festoons of two faded damask curtains, and fell directly across this vase; so that a mild splendour was reflected from it on the ashen visages of the five old people who sat around. Four champagne glasses were also on the table.

'My dear old friends,' repeated Dr Heidegger, 'may I reckon on your aid in performing an exceedingly curious experiment?'

Now Dr Heidegger was a very strange old gentleman, whose eccentricity had become the nucleus for a thousand fantastic stories. Some of these fables, to my shame be it spoken, might possibly be traced back to mine own veracious self; and if any passages of the present tale should startle the reader's faith, I must be content to bear the stigma of a fiction-monger.

When the doctor's four guests heard him talk of his proposed experiment, they anticipated nothing more wonderful than the murder of a mouse in an air-pump, or the examination of a cobweb by the microscope, or some similar nonsense, with which he was constantly in the habit of pestering his intimates. But without waiting for a reply, Dr Heidegger hobbled across the chamber, and returned with the same ponderous folio, bound in black leather, which common report affirmed to be a book of magic. Undoing the silver clasps, he opened the volume, and took from among its black-letter pages a rose, or what was once a rose, though now the green leaves and crimson petals had assumed one brownish hue, and the ancient flower seemed ready to crumble to dust in the doctor's hands.

'This rose,' said Dr Heidegger, with a sigh, 'this same withered and crumbling flower, blossomed five and fifty years ago. It was given me by Sylvia Ward, whose portrait hangs yonder; and I meant to wear it in my bosom at our wedding. Five-and-fifty years it has been treasured between the leaves of this old volume. Now, would you deem it possible that this rose of half a century could ever bloom again?'

'Nonsense!' said the Widow Wycherly, with a peevish toss of her head. 'You might as well ask whether an old woman's wrinkled face could ever bloom again.'

'See!' answered Dr Heidegger.

He uncovered the vase, and threw the faded rose into the water which it contained. At first, it lay lightly on the surface of the fluid, appearing to imbibe none of its moisture. Soon, however, a singular change began to be visible. The crushed and dried petals stirred, and assumed a deepening tinge of crimson, as if the flower were reviving from a deathlike slumber; the slender stalk and twigs of foliage became green; and there was the rose of half a century, looking as fresh as when Sylvia Ward had first given it to her lover. It was scarcely full blown; for some of its delicate red leaves curled modestly around its moist bosom, within which two or three dew-drops were sparkling.

'That is certainly a very pretty deception,' said the doctor's friends; carelessly, however, for they had witnessed greater miracles at a conjuror's show; 'pray how was it effected?'

'Did you never hear of the "Fountain of Youth"?' asked Dr Heidegger, 'which Ponce de Leon, the Spanish adventurer, went in search of, two or three centuries ago?'

'But did Ponce de Leon ever find it?' said the Widow Wycherly.

'No,' answered Dr Heidegger, 'for he never sought it in the right place. The famous Fountain of Youth, if I am rightly informed, is situated in the southern part of the Floridian peninsula, not far from Lake Macaco. Its source is overshadowed by several gigantic magnolias, which, though numberless centuries old, have been kept as fresh as violets, by the virtues of this wonderful water. An acquaintance of mine, knowing my curiosity in such matters, has sent me what you see in the vase.'

'Ahem!' said Colonel Killigrew, who believed not a word of the doctor's story; 'and what may be the effect of this fluid on the human frame?'

'You shall judge for yourself, my dear colonel,' replied Dr Heidegger; 'and all of you, my respected friends, are welcome to so much of this admirable fluid as may restore to you the bloom of youth. For my own part, having had much trouble in growing old, I am in no hurry to grow young again. With your permission, therefore, I will merely watch the progress of the experiment.'

While he spoke, Dr Heidegger had been filling the four champagne glasses with the water of the Fountain of Youth. It was apparently impregnated with an effervescent gas, for little bubbles were continually ascending from the depths of the glasses, and bursting in silvery spray at the surface. As the liquor diffused a pleasant perfume, the old people doubted not that it possessed cordial and comfortable properties; and, though utter sceptics as to its rejuvenescent power, they were inclined to swallow it at once. But Dr Heidegger besought them to stay a moment.

'Before you drink, my respectable old friends,' said he, 'it would be well that, with the experience of a lifetime to direct you, you should draw up a few general rules for your guidance, in passing a second time through the perils of youth. Think what a sin and shame it would be, if, with your peculiar advantages, you should not become patterns of virtue and wisdom to all the young people of the age!'

The doctor's four venerable friends made him no answer, except by a feeble and tremulous laugh; so very ridiculous was the idea, that, knowing how closely repentance treads behind the steps of error, they should ever go astray again.

'Drink, then,' said the doctor, bowing: 'I rejoice that I have so well selected the subjects of my experiment.'

With palsied hands, they raised the glasses to their lips. The liquor, if it really possessed such virtues as Dr Heidegger imputed to it, could not have been bestowed on four human beings who needed it more woefully. They looked as if they had never known what youth or pleasure was, but had been the offspring of Nature's dotage, and always the grey, decrepit, sapless, miserable creatures, who now sat stooping round the doctor's table, without life enough in their souls or bodies to be animated even by the prospect of growing young again. They drank off the water, and replaced their glasses on the table.

Assuredly there was an almost immediate improvement in the aspect of the party, not unlike what might have been produced by a glass of generous wine, together with a sudden glow of cheerful sunshine, brightening over all their visages at once. There was a healthful suffusion on their cheeks, instead of the ashen hue that had made them look so corpse-like. They gazed at one another, and fancied that some magic power had really begun to smooth away the deep and sad inscriptions which Father Time had been so long engraving on their brows. The Widow Wycherly adjusted her cap, for she felt almost like a woman again.

'Give us more of this wondrous water!' cried they, eagerly. 'We are younger—but we are still too old! Quick—give us more!'

'Patience, patience!' quoth Dr Heidegger, who sat watching the experiment, with philosophic coolness. 'You have been a long time growing old. Surely, you might be content to grow young in half an hour! But the water is at your service.'

Again he filled their glasses with the liquor of youth, enough of which still remained in the vase to turn half the old people in the city to the age of their own grandchildren. While the bubbles were yet sparkling on the brim, the doctor's four guests snatched their glasses from the table, and swallowed the contents in a single gulp. Was it delusion? even while the draught was passing down their throats, it seemed to have wrought a change on their whole systems. Their eyes grew clear and bright; a dark shade deepened among their silvery locks; they sat around the table, three gentlemen of middle age, and a woman hardly beyond her buxom prime.

'My dear widow, you are charming!' cried Colonel Killigrew, whose eyes had been fixed upon her face, while the shadows of age were flitting from it like darkness from the crimson daybreak.

The fair widow knew of old that Colonel Killigrew's compliments were not always measured by sober truth; so she started up and ran to the mirror, still dreading that the ugly visage of an old woman would meet her gaze. Meanwhile, the three gentlemen behaved in such a manner, as proved that the water of the Fountain of Youth possessed some intoxicating qualities; unless, indeed, their exhilaration of spirits were merely a lightsome dizziness, caused by the sudden removal of the weight of years. Mr Gascoigne's mind seemed to run on political topics, but whether relating to the past, present, or future, could not easily be determined, since the same ideas and phrases have been in vogue these fifty years. Now he rattled forth full-throated sentences about patriotism, national glory, and the people's right; now he muttered some perilous stuff or other, in a sly and doubtful whisper, so cautiously that even his own conscience could scarcely catch the secret; and now, again, he spoke in measured accents, and a deeply deferential tone, as if a royal ear were listening to his well-turned periods. Colonel Killigrew all this time had been trolling forth a jolly bottle song, and ringing his glass in symphony with the chorus, while his eyes wandered toward the buxom figure of the Widow Wycherly. On the other side of the table, Mr Medbourne was involved in a calculation of dollars and cents, with which was strangely intermingled a project for supplying the East Indies with ice, by harnessing a team of whales to the polar icebergs.

As for the Widow Wycherly, she stood before the mirror courtesying and simpering to her own image, and greeting it as the friend whom she loved better than all the world beside. She thrust her face close to the glass, to see whether some long-remembered wrinkle or crow's foot had indeed vanished. She examined whether the snow had so entirely melted from her hair, that the venerable cap could be safely thrown aside. At last, turning briskly away, she came with a sort of dancing step to the table.

'My dear old doctor,' cried she, 'pray favour me with another glass!'

'Certainly, my dear madam, certainly!' replied the complaisant doctor; 'see! I have already filled the glasses.'

There, in fact, stood the four glasses, brimful of this wonderful water, the delicate spray of which, as it effervesced from the surface, resembled the tremulous glitter of diamonds. It was now so nearly sunset, that the chamber had grown duskier than ever; but a mild and moonlike splendour gleamed from within the vase, and rested alike on the four guests, and on the doctor's venerable figure. He sat in a high-backed, elaborately-carved, oaken arm-chair, with a grey dignity of aspect that might have well befitted that very Father Time, whose power had never been disputed, save by his fortunate company. Even while quaffing the third draught of the Fountain of Youth, they were almost awed by the expression of his mysterious visage.

But, the next moment, the exhilarating gush of young life shot through their veins. They were now in the happy prime of youth. Age, with its miserable train of cares, and sorrows, and diseases, was remembered only as the trouble of a dream, from which they had joyously awoken. The fresh gloss of the soul, so early lost, and without which the world's successive scenes had been but a gallery of faded pictures, again threw its enchantment over all their prospects. They felt like new-created beings, in a new-created universe.

'We are young! We are young!' they cried exultantly.

Youth, like the extremity of age, had effaced the strongly-marked characteristics of middle life, and mutually assimilated them all. They were a group of merry youngsters, almost maddened with the exuberant frolicsomeness of their years. The most singular effect of their gaiety was an impulse to mock the infirmity and decrepitude of which they had so lately been the victims. They laughed loudly at their old-fashioned attire, the wide-skirted coats and flapped waistcoats of the young men, and the ancient cap and gown of the blooming girl. One limped across the floor like a gouty grandfather; one set a pair of spectacles astride of his nose, and pretended to pore over the black-letter pages of the book of magic; a third seated himself in an arm-chair, and strove to imitate the venerable dignity of Dr Heidegger. Then all shouted mirthfully, and leaped about the room. The Widow Wycherly—if so fresh a damsel could be called a widow—tripped up to the doctor's chair, with a mischievous merriment in her rosy face.

'Doctor, you dear old soul,' cried she, 'get up and dance with me!' And then the four young people laughed louder than ever, to think what a queer figure the poor old doctor would cut.

'Pray excuse me,' answered the doctor quietly. 'I am old and rheumatic, and my dancing days were over long ago. But either of these gay young gentlemen will be glad of so pretty a partner.'

'Dance with me, Clara!' cried Colonel Killigrew.

'No, no, I will be her partner!' shouted Mr Gascoigne.

'She promised me her hand, fifty years ago!' exclaimed Mr Medbourne.

They all gathered round her. One caught both her hands in his passionate grasp—another threw his arm about her waist—the third buried his hand among the glossy curls that clustered beneath the widow's cap. Blushing, panting, struggling, chiding, laughing, her warm breath fanning each of their faces by turns, she strove to disengage herself, yet still remained in their triple embrace. Never was there a livelier picture of youthful rivalship, with bewitching beauty for the prize. Yet, by a strange deception, owing to the duskiness of the chamber, and the antique dresses which they still wore, the tall mirror is said to have reflected the figures of the three old, grey, withered grandsires, ridiculously contending for the skinny ugliness of a shrivelled grandam.

But they were young: their burning passions proved them so. Inflamed to madness by the coquetry of the girl-widow, who neither granted nor quite withheld her favours, the three rivals began to interchange threatening glances. Still keeping hold of the fair prize, they grappled fiercely at one another's throats. As they struggled to and fro, the table was overturned, and the vase dashed into a thousand fragments. The precious Water of Youth flowed in a bright stream across the floor, moistening the wings of a butterfly, which, grown old in the decline of summer, had alighted there to die. The insect fluttered lightly through the chamber, and settled on the snowy head of Dr Heidegger.

'Come, come, gentlemen!—come Madame Wycherly,' exclaimed the doctor, 'I really must protest against this riot.'

They stood still, and shivered; for it seemed as if grey Time were calling them back from their sunny youth, far down into the chill and darksome vale of years. They looked at old Dr Heidegger, who sat in his carved arm-chair, holding the rose of half a century, which he had rescued from among the fragments of the shattered vase. At the motion of his hand, the four rioters resumed their seats; the more readily, because their violent exertions had wearied them, youthful though they were.

'My poor Sylvia's rose!' ejaculated Dr Heidegger, holding it in the light of the sunset clouds; 'it appears to be fading again.'

And so it was. Even while the party were looking at it, the flower continued to shrivel up, till it became as dry and fragile as when the doctor had first thrown it into the vase. He shook off the few drops of moisture which clung to its petals.

'I love it as well thus, as in its dewy freshness,' observed he, pressing the withered rose to his withered lips. While he spoke, the butterfly fluttered down from the doctor's snowy head, and fell upon the floor.

His guests shivered again. A strange chillness, whether of the body or spirit they could not tell, was creeping gradually over them all. They gazed at one another, and fancied that each fleeting moment snatched away a charm, and left a deepening furrow where none had been before. Was it an illusion? Had the changes of a lifetime been crowded into so brief a space, and were they now four aged people, sitting with their old friend, Dr Heidegger?

'Are we grown old again, so soon?' cried they, dolefully.

In truth, they had. The Water of Youth possessed merely a virtue more transient than that of wine. The delirium which it created had effervesced away. Yes! they were old again. With a shuddering impulse, that showed her a woman still, the widow clasped her skinny hands before her face, and wished that the coffin lid were over it, since it could be no longer beautiful.

'Yes, friends, ye are old again,' said Dr Heidegger; 'and lo! the Water of Youth is all lavished on the ground. Well—I bemoan it not; for if the fountain gushed at my doorstep, I would not stoop to bathe my lips in it—no, though its delirium were for years instead of moments. Such is the lesson ye have taught me!'

But the doctor's four friends had taught no such lesson to themselves. They resolved forthwith to make a pilgrimage to Florida, and quaff at morning, noon, and night, from the Fountain of Youth.

B

The Cask of Amontillado

EDGAR ALLAN POE

THE THOUSAND INJURIES of Fortunato I had borne as I best could, but when he ventured upon insult I vowed revenge. You, who so well know the nature of my soul, will not suppose, however, that I gave utterance to a threat. *At length* I would be avenged; this was a point definitely settled—but the very definiteness with which it was resolved precluded the idea of risk. I must not only punish but punish with impunity. A wrong is unredressed when retribution overtakes the redresser. It is equally unredressed when the avenger fails to make himself felt as such to him who has done the wrong.

It must be understood that neither by word nor deed had I given Fortunato cause to doubt my good will. I continued, as was my wont, to smile in his face, and he did not perceive that my smile *now* was at the thought of his immolation.

He had a weak point—this Fortunato—although in other regards he was a man to be respected and even feared. He prided himself on his connoisseurship in wine. Few Italians have the true virtuoso spirit. For the most part their enthusiasm is adopted to suit the time and opportunity, to practise imposture upon the British and Austrian *millionaires*. In painting and gemmary, Fortunato, like his countrymen, was a quack, but in the matter of old wines he was sincere. In this respect I did not differ from him materially;—I was skilful in the Italian vintages myself, and bought largely whenever I could.

It was about dusk, one evening during the supreme madness of the carnival season, that I encountered my friend. He accosted me with excessive warmth, for he had been drinking much. The man wore motley. He had on a tight-fitting parti-striped dress, and his head was surmounted by the conical cap and bells. I was so pleased to see him that I thought I should never have done wringing his hand.

I said to him—'My dear Fortunato, you are luckily met. How remarkably well you are looking today. But I have received a pipe of what passes for Amontillado, and I have my doubts.'

'How?' said he. 'Amontillado? A pipe? Impossible! And in the middle of the carnival!'

'I have my doubts,' I replied; 'and I was silly enough to pay the full Amontillado price without consulting you in the matter. You were not to be found, and I was fearful of losing a bargain.'

'Amontillado!'

'I have my doubts.'

'Amontillado!'

'And I must satisfy them.'

'Amontillado!'

'As you are engaged, I am on my way to Luchresi. If anyone has a critical turn it is he. He will tell me——'

'Luchresi cannot tell Amontillado from Sherry.'

'And yet some fools will have it that his taste is a match for your own.'

'Come, let us go.'

'Whither?'

'To your vaults.'

'My friend, no; I will not impose upon your good nature. I perceive you have an engagement. Luchresi——'

'I have no engagement;—come.'

'My friend, no. It is not the engagement, but the severe cold with which I perceive you are afflicted. The vaults are insufferably damp. They are encrusted with nitre.'

'Let us go, nevertheless. The cold is merely nothing. Amontillado! You have been imposed upon. And as for Luchresi, he cannot distinguish Sherry from Amontillado.'

Thus speaking, Fortunato possessed himself of my arm; and putting on a mask of black silk and drawing a *roquelaure* closely about my person, I suffered him to hurry me to my palazzo.

There were no attendants at home; they had absconded to make merry in honour of the time. I had told them that I should not return until the morning, and had given them explicit orders not to stir from the house. These orders were sufficient, I well knew, to insure their immediate disappearance, one and all, as soon as my back was turned.

I took from their sconces two flambeaux, and giving one to Fortunato, bowed him through several suites of rooms to the archway that led into the vaults. I passed down a long and winding staircase, requesting him to be cautious as he followed. We came at length to the foot of the descent, and stood together upon the damp ground of the catacombs of the Montresors.

The gait of my friend was unsteady, and the bells upon his cap jingled as he strode.

'The pipe,' he said.

'It is farther on,' said I; 'but observe the white web-work which gleams from these cavern walls.'

He turned towards me, and looked into my eyes with two filmy orbs that distilled the rheum of intoxication.

'Nitre?' he asked, at length.

'Nitre,' I replied. 'How long have you had that cough?'

'Ugh! ugh! ugh!—ugh! ugh! ugh!—ugh! ugh! ugh!—ugh! ugh! ugh!—ugh! ugh! ugh!'

My poor friend found it impossible to reply for many minutes.

'It is nothing,' he said, at last.

'Come,' I said, with decision, 'we will go back; your health is precious. You are rich, respected, admired, beloved; you are happy, as once I was. You are a man to be missed. For me it is no matter. We will go back; you will be ill, and I cannot be responsible. Besides, there is Luchresi——'

'Enough,' he said; 'the cough is a mere nothing; it will not kill me. I shall not die of a cough.'

'True—true,' I replied; 'and, indeed, I had no intention of alarming you unnecessarily—but you should use all proper caution. A draught of this Medoc will defend us from the damps.'

Here I knocked off the neck of a bottle which I drew from a long row of its fellows that lay upon the mould.

'Drink,' I said, presenting him the wine.

He raised it to his lips with a leer. He paused and nodded to me familiarly, while his bells jingled.

'I drink,' he said, 'to the buried that repose around us.'

'And I to your long life.'

He again took my arm, and we proceeded.

'These vaults,' he said, 'are extensive.'

'The Montresors,' I replied, 'were a great and numerous family.'

'I forget your arms.'

'A huge human foot d'or, in a field azure; the foot crushes a serpent rampant whose fangs are imbedded in the heel.'

'And the motto?'

'*Nemo me impune lacessit.*'

'Good!' he said.

The wine sparkled in his eyes and the bells jingled. My own fancy grew warm with the Medoc. We had passed through long walls of piled skeletons, with casks and puncheons intermingling, into the inmost recesses of catacombs. I paused again, and this time I made bold to seize Fortunato by an arm above the elbow.

'The nitre!' I said; 'see, it increases. It hangs like moss upon the vaults. We are below the river's bed. The drops of moisture trickle among the bones. Come, we will go back ere it is too late. Your cough——'

'It is nothing,' he said; 'let us go on. But first, another draught of the Medoc.'

I broke and reached him a flagon of De Grâve. He emptied it at a breath. His eyes flashed with a fierce light. He laughed and threw the bottle upwards with a gesticulation I did not understand.

I looked at him in surprise. He repeated the movement—a grotesque one.

'You do not comprehend?' he said.

'Not I,' I replied.

'Then you are not of the brotherhood.'

'How?'

'You are not of the masons.'

'Yes, yes,' I said; 'yes, yes.'

'You? Impossible! A mason?'

'A mason,' I replied.

'A sign,' he said, 'a sign.'

'It is this,' I answered, producing from beneath the folds of my *roquelaure* a trowel.

'You jest,' he exclaimed, recoiling a few paces. 'But let us proceed to the Amontillado.'

'Be it so,' I said, replacing the tool beneath the cloak and again offering my arm. He leaned upon it heavily. We continued our route in search of the Amontillado. We passed through a range of low arches, descended, passed on, and descending again, arrived at a deep crypt, in which the foulness of the air caused our flambeaux rather to glow than flame.

At the most remote end of the crypt there appeared another less spacious. Its walls had been lined with human remains, piled to the vault overhead, in the fashion of the great catacombs of Paris. Three sides of this interior crypt were still ornamented in this manner. From the fourth side the bones had been thrown down, and lay promiscuously upon the earth, forming at one point a mound of some size. Within the wall thus exposed by the displacing of the bones, we perceived a still interior crypt or recess, in depth about four feet, in width three, in height six or seven. It seemed to have been constructed for no especial use within itself, but formed merely the interval between two of the colossal supports of the roof of the catacombs, and was backed by one of their circumscribing walls of solid granite.

It was in vain that Fortunato, uplifting his dull torch, endeavoured to pry into the depth of the recess. Its termination the feeble light did not enable us to see.

'Proceed,' I said; 'herein is the Amontillado. As for Luchresi——'

'He is an ignoramus,' interrupted my friend, as he stepped unsteadily forward, while I followed immediately at his heels. In an instant he had reached the extremity of the niche, and finding his progress arrested by the rock, stood stupidly bewildered. A moment more and I had fettered him to the granite. In its surface were two iron staples, distant from each other about two feet, horizontally. From one of these depended a short chain, from the other a padlock. Throwing the links about his waist, it was but the work of a few seconds to secure it. He was too much astounded to resist. Withdrawing the key I stepped back from the recess.

'Pass your hand,' I said, 'over the wall; you cannot help feeling the nitre. Indeed, it is *very* damp. Once more let me *implore* you to return. No? Then I must positively leave you. But I must first render you all the little attentions in my power.'

'The Amontillado!' ejaculated my friend, not yet recovered from his astonishment.

'True,' I replied; 'the Amontillado.'

As I said these words I busied myself among the pile of bones of which I have before spoken. Throwing them aside, I soon uncovered a quantity of building stone and mortar. With these materials and with the aid of my trowel, I began vigorously to wall up the entrance to the niche.

I had scarcely laid the first tier of the masonry when I discovered that the intoxication of Fortunato had in a great measure worn off. The earliest indication I had of this was a low moaning cry from the depth of the recess. It was *not* the cry of a drunken man. There was then a long and obstinate silence. I laid the second tier, and the third, and the fourth, and then I heard the furious vibrations of the chain. The noise lasted for several minutes, during which, that I might hearken to it with the more satisfaction, I ceased my labours and sat down upon the bones. When at last the clanking subsided, I resumed the trowel, and finished without interruption the fifth, the sixth, and the seventh tier. The wall was now nearly upon a level with my breast. I again paused, and holding the flambeaux over the mason-work, threw a few feeble rays upon the figure within.

A succession of loud and shrill screams, bursting suddenly from the throat of the chained form, seemed to thrust me violently back. For a brief moment I hesitated, I trembled. Unsheathing my rapier, I began to grope with it about the recess; but the thought of an instant reassured me. I placed my hand upon the solid fabric of the catacombs, and felt satisfied. I reapproached the wall; I replied to the yells of him who clamoured. I re-echoed, I aided, I surpassed them in volume and in strength. I did this, and the clamourer grew still.

It was now midnight, and my task was drawing to a close. I had completed the eighth, the ninth, and the tenth tier. I had finished a portion of the last and the eleventh; there remained but a single stone to be fitted and plastered in. I struggled with its weight; I placed it partially in its destined position. But now there came from out the niche a low laugh that erected the hairs upon my head. It was succeeded by a sad voice, which I had difficulty in recognising as that of the noble Fortunato. The voice said—

'Ha! ha! ha!—he! he! he!—a very good joke, indeed—an excellent jest. We shall have many a rich laugh about it at the palazzo—he! he! he!—over our wine—he! he! he!'

'The Amontillado!' I said.

'He! he! he!—he! he! he!—yes, the Amontillado. But is it not getting late? Will not they be awaiting us at the palazzo, the Lady Fortunato and the rest? Let us be gone.'

'Yes,' I said, 'let us be gone.'

'For the love of God, Montresor!'

'Yes,' I said, 'for the love of God!'

But to these words I hearkened in vain for a reply. I grew impatient. I called aloud—

'Fortunato!'

No answer. I called again—

'Fortunato!'

No answer still. I thrust a torch through the remaining aperture and let it fall within. There came forth in return only the jingling of the bells. My heart grew sick; it was the dampness of the catacombs that made it so. I hastened to make an end of my labour. I forced the last stone into its position; I plastered it up. Against the new masonry I re-erected the old rampart of bones. For half of a century no mortal has disturbed them. *In pace requiescat!*

Green Tea

SHERIDAN LE FANU

Prologue: Martin Hesselius, the German Physician

THOUGH CAREFULLY EDUCATED in medicine and surgery, I have never practised either. The study of each continues, nevertheless, to interest me profoundly. Neither idleness nor caprice caused my seccession from the honourable calling which I had just entered. The cause was a very trifling scratch inflicted by a dissecting knife. This trifle cost me the loss of two fingers, amputated promptly, and the more painful loss of my health, for I have never been quite well since, and have seldom been twelve months together in the same place.

In my wanderings I became acquainted with Dr Martin Hesselius, a wanderer like myself, like me a physician, and like me an enthusiast in his profession. Unlike me in this, that his wanderings were voluntary, and he a man, if not of fortune, as we estimate fortune in England, at least in what our forefathers used to term 'easy circumstances.' He was an old man when I first saw him; nearly five-and-thirty years my senior.

In Dr Martin Hesselius, I had found my master. His knowledge was immense, his grasp of a case was an intuition. He was the very man to inspire a young enthusiast, like me, with awe and delight. My admiration has stood the test of time and survived the separation of death. I am sure it was well-founded.

For nearly twenty years I acted as his medical secretary. His immense collection of papers he has left in my care, to be arranged, indexed and bound. His treatment of some of these cases is curious. He writes in two distinct characters. He describes what

B*

he saw and heard as an intelligent layman might, and when in his style of narrative he had seen the patient either through his own hall-door, to the light of day, or through the gates of darkness to the caverns of the dead, he returns upon the narrative, and in the terms of his art and with all the force of originality of genius, proceeds to the work of analysis, diagnosis and illustration.

Here and there a case strikes me as of a kind to amuse or horrify a lay reader with an interest quite different from the peculiar one which it may possess for an expert. With slight modifications, chiefly of language, and of course a change of names, I copy the following. The narrator is Dr Martin Hesselius. I find it among the voluminous notes of cases which he made during a tour in England about sixty-four years ago.

It is related in series of letters to his friend Professor Van Loo of Leyden. The professor was not a physician, but a chemist, and a man who read history and metaphysics and medicine, and had, in his day, written a play.

The narrative is therefore, if somewhat less valuable as a medical record, necessarily written in a manner more likely to interest an unlearned reader.

These letters, from a memorandum attached, appear to have been returned on the death of the professor, in 1819, to Dr Hesselius. They are written, some in English, some in French, but the greater part in German. I am a faithful, though I am conscious, by no means a graceful translator, and although here and there I omit some passages, and shorten others, and disguise names, I have interpolated nothing.

1 *Dr Hesselius Relates how He Met the Rev Mr Jennings*

The Rev Mr Jennings is tall and thin. He is middle-aged, and dresses with a natty, old-fashioned, high church precision. He is naturally a little stately, but not at all stiff. His features, without being handsome, are well formed, and their expression extremely kind, but also shy.

I met him one evening at Lady Mary Heyduke's. The modesty and benevolence of his countenance are extremely prepossessing.

We are but a small party, and he joined agreeably enough in the conversation. He seems to enjoy listening very much more than contributing to the talk; but what he says is always to the purpose and well said. He is a great favourite of Lady Mary's, who it seems, consults him upon many things, and thinks him the most happy and blessed person on earth. Little knows she about him.

The Rev Mr Jennings is a bachelor, and has, they say sixty thousand pounds in the funds. He is a charitable man. He is most anxious to be actively employed in his sacred profession, and yet though always tolerably well elsewhere, when he goes down to his vicarage in Warwickshire, to engage in the actual duties of his sacred calling, his health soon fails him, and in a very strange way. So says Lady Mary.

There is no doubt that Mr Jennings' health does break down in, generally, a sudden and mysterious way, sometimes in the very act of officiating in his old and pretty church at Kenlis. It may be his heart, it may be his brain. But so it has happened three or four times, or oftener, that after proceeding a certain way in the service, he has on a sudden stopped short, and after a silence, apparently quite unable to resume, he has fallen into solitary, inaudible prayer, his hands and his eyes uplifted, and then pale as death, and in the agitation of a strange shame and horror, descended trembling, and got into the vestry-room, leaving his congregation, without explanation, to themselves. This occurred when his curate was absent. When he goes down to Kenlis now, he always takes care to provide a clergyman to share his duty, and to supply his place on the instant should he become thus suddenly incapacitated.

When Mr Jennings breaks down quite, and beats a retreat from the vicarage, and returns to London, where, in a dark street off Piccadilly, he inhabits a very narrow house, Lady Mary says that he is always perfectly well. I have my own opinion about that. There are degrees of course. We shall see.

Mr Jennings is a perfectly gentlemanlike man. People, however, remark something odd. There is an impression a little ambiguous. One thing which certainly contributes to it, people I think don't remember; or, perhaps, distinctly remark. But I did, almost immediately. Mr Jennings has a way of looking sidelong upon the carpet, as if his eye followed the movements of something there. This, of course, not always. It occurs now and then. But often enough to give a certain oddity, as I have said, to his manner, and in this glance travelling along the floor there is something both shy and anxious.

A medical philosopher, as you are good enough to call me, elaborating theories by the aid of cases sought out by himself, and by him watched and scrutinised with more time at command, and consequently infinitely more minuteness than the ordinary practitioner can afford, falls insensibly into habits of observation, which accompany him everywhere, and are exercised, as some people would say, impertinently, upon every subject that presents itself with the least likelihood of rewarding inquiry.

There was a promise of this kind in the slight, timid, kindly, but reserved gentleman, whom I met for the first time at this agreeable little evening gathering. I observed, of course, more than I here set down; but I reserve all that borders on the technical for a strictly scientific paper.

I may remark, that when I here speak of medical science, I do so, as I hope some day to see it more generally understood, in a much more comprehensive sense than its generally material treatment would warrant. I believe the entire natural world is but the ultimate expression of that spiritual world from which, and in which alone, it has its life. I believe that the essential man is a spirit, that the spirit is an organised substance, but as different in point of material from what we ordinarily understand by matter, as light or electricity is; that the material body is, in the most literal sense, a vesture, and death consequently no interruption of the living man's existence, but simply his extrication from the natural body—a process which commences at the moment of what we term death, and the completion of which, at further a few days later, is the resurrection 'in power'.

The person who weighs the consequences of these positions will probably see their practical bearing upon medical science. This is, however, by no means the proper place for displaying the proofs and discussing the consequences of this too generally unrecognised state of facts.

In pursuit of my habit, I was covertly observing Mr Jennings, with all my caution—I think he perceived it—and I saw plainly that he was as cautiously observing me. Lady Mary happening to address me by my name, as Dr Hesselius, I saw that he glanced at me more sharply, and then became thoughtful for a few minutes.

After this, as I conversed with a gentleman at the other end of the room, I saw him look at me more steadily, and with an interest which I thought I understood. I then saw him take an opportunity of chatting with Lady Mary, and was, as one always is, perfectly aware of being the subject of a distant inquiry and answer.

This tall clergyman approached me by-and-by; and in a little time we had got into conversation. When two people, who like reading, and know books and places, having travelled, wish to converse, it is very strange if they can't find topics. It was not accident that brought him near me, and led him into conversation. He knew German and had read my Essays on Metaphysical Medicine which suggest more than they actually say.

This courteous man, gentle, shy, plainly a man of thought and reading, who moving and talking among us, was not altogether of us, and whom I already suspected of leading a life whose transactions and alarms were carefully concealed, with an impenetrable reserve from, not only the world, but his best beloved friends— was cautiously weighing in his own mind the idea of taking a certain step with regard to me.

I penetrated his thoughts without his being aware of it, and was careful to say nothing which could betray to his sensitive vigilance my suspicions respecting his position, or my surmises about his plans respecting myself.

We chatted upon indifferent subjects for a time; but at last he said:

'I was very much interested by some papers of yours, Dr Hesselius, upon what you term Metaphysical Medicine—I read them in German, ten or twelve years ago—have they been translated?'

'No, I'm sure they have not—I should have heard. They would have asked my leave, I think.'

'I asked the publishers here, a few months ago, to get the book for me in the original German; but they tell me it is out of print.'

'So it is, and has been for some years; but it flatters me as an author to find that you have not forgotten my little book, although,' I added, laughing, 'ten or twelve years is a considerable time to have managed without it; but I suppose you have been turning the subject over again in your mind, or something has happened lately to revive your interest in it.'

At this remark, accompanied by a glance of inquiry, a sudden embarrassment disturbed Mr Jennings, analogous to that which makes a young lady blush and look foolish. He dropped his eyes, and folded his hands together uneasily, and looked oddly, and you would have said, guiltily, for a moment.

I helped him out of his awkwardness in the best way, by appearing not to observe it, and going straight on, I said: 'Those revivals of interest in a subject happen to me often; one book suggests another, and often sends me back on a wild-goose chase over an interval of twenty years. But if you will care to possess a copy, I shall be

only too happy to provide you; I have still got two or three by me
—and if you allow me to present one I shall be very much honoured.'

'You are very good indeed,' he said, quite at his ease again, in a
moment: 'I almost despaired—I don't know how to thank you.'

'Pray don't say a word; the thing is really so little worth that I am
only ashamed of having offered it, and if you thank me any more
I shall throw it into the fire in a fit of modesty.'

Mr Jennings laughed. He inquired where I was staying in London,
and after a little more conversation on a variety of subjects, he took
his departure.

2   *The Doctor Questions Lady Mary, and She Answers*

'I like your vicar so much, Lady Mary,' said I, as soon as he was
gone. 'He has read, travelled, and thought, and having also suffered,
he ought to be an accomplished companion.'

'So he is, and, better still, he is a really good man,' said she. 'His
advice is invaluable about my schools, and all my little undertakings
at Dawlbridge, and he's so painstaking, he takes so much trouble
—you have no idea—wherever he thinks he can be of use; he's so
good-natured and so sensible.'

'It is pleasant to hear so good an account of his neighbourly
virtues. I can only testify to his being an agreeable and gentle companion, and in addition to what you have told me, I think I can tell
you two or three things about him,' said I.

'Really!'

'Yes, to begin with, he's unmarried.'

'Yes, that's right—go on.'

'He has been writing, that is he *was*, but two or three years perhaps he has not gone on with his work, and the book was upon
some rather abstract subject—perhaps theology.'

'Well, he was writing a book, as you say; I'm not quite sure what
it was about, but only that it was nothing that I cared for; very
likely you are right, and he certainly did stop—yes.'

'And although he only drank a little coffee here tonight, he likes
tea, at least, did like it extravagantly.'

'Yes, that's *quite* true.'

'He drank green tea, a good deal, didn't he?' I pursued.

'Well, that's very odd! Green tea was a subject on which we used
almost to quarrel.'

'But he has quite given that up,' said I.

'So he has.'

'And, now, one more fact. His mother or his father, did you know them?'

'Yes, both; his father is only ten years dead, and their place is near Dawlbridge. We knew them very well,' she answered.

'Well, either his mother or his father—I should rather think his father, saw a ghost,' said I.

'Well, you really are a conjuror, Dr Hesselius.'

'Conjuror or no, haven't I said right?' I answered merrily.

'You certainly have, and it *was* his father; he was a silent, whimsical man, and he used to bore my father about his dreams, and at last he told him a story about a ghost he had seen and talked with, and a very odd story it was. I remember it particularly, because I was so afraid of him. This story was long before he died—when I was quite a child—and his ways were so silent and moping, and he used to drop in sometimes, in the dusk, when I was alone in the drawing-room, and I used to fancy there were ghosts about him.'

I smiled and nodded.

'And now, having established my character as a conjuror, I think I must say good-night,' said I.

'But how *did* you find it out?'

'By the planets, of course, as the gipsies do,' I answered, and so, gaily, we said goodnight.

Next morning I sent the little book he had been inquiring after, and a note to Mr Jennings, and on returning late that evening, I found that he had called at my lodgings, and left his card. He asked whether I was at home, and asked at what hour he would be most likely to find me.

Does he intend opening his case, and consulting me 'professionally', as they say? I hope so. I have already conceived a theory about him. It is supported by Lady Mary's answers to my parting questions. I should like much to ascertain from his own lips. But what can I do consistently with good breeding to invite a confession? Nothing. I rather think he meditates one. At all events, my dear Van L, I shan't make myself difficult of access; I mean to return his visit tomorrow. It will be only civil in return for his politeness, to ask to see him. Perhaps something may come of it. Whether much, little, or nothing, my dear Van L, you shall hear.

3   *Dr Hesselius Picks Up Something in Latin Books*

Well, I have called at Blank Street.

On inquiring at the door, the servant told me that Mr Jennings was engaged very particularly with a gentleman, a clergyman from Kenlis, his parish in the country. Intending to reserve my privilege, and to call again, I merely intimated that I should try another time, and had turned to go, when the servant begged my pardon, and asked me, looking at me a little more attentively than well-bred persons of his order usually do, whether I was Dr Hesselius; and, on learning that I was, he said, 'Perhaps then, sir, you would allow me to mention it to Mr Jennings, for I am sure he wishes to see you.'

The servant returned in a moment, with a message from Mr Jennings, asking me to go into his study, which was in effect his back drawing-room, promising to be with me in a very few minutes.

This was really a study—almost a library. The room was lofty, with two tall slender windows, and rich dark curtains. It was much larger than I had expected, and stored with books on every side, from floor to the ceiling. The upper carpet—for to my tread it felt that there were two or three—was a Turkey carpet. My steps fell noiselessly. The bookcases standing out, placed the windows, particularly narrow ones, in deep recesses. The effect of the room was, although extremely comfortable, and even luxurious, decidedly gloomy, and aided by the silence, almost oppressive. Perhaps, however, I ought to have allowed something for association. My mind had connected peculiar ideas with Mr Jennings. I stepped into this perfectly silent room, of a very silent house, with a peculiar foreboding; and its darkness, and solemn clothing of books, for except where two narrow looking-glasses were set in the wall, they were everywhere, helped this sombre feeling.

While awaiting Mr Jennings' arrival, I amused myself by looking into some of the books with which his shelves were laden. Not among these, but immediately under them, with their backs upward, on the floor, I lighted upon a complete set of Swedenborg's *Arcana Cælestia*, in the original Latin, a very fine folio set, bound in the natty livery which theology affects, pure vellum, namely, gold letters, and carmine edges. There were paper markers in several of these volumes. I raised and placed them, one after the other upon the table, and opening where these papers were placed, I read in the solemn Latin phraseology, a series of sentences indicated by a pencilled line at the margin. Of these I copy here a few, translating them into English.

'When man's interior sight is opened, which is that of his spirit, then there appears the things of another life, which cannot possibly be made visible to the bodily sight . . .'

'By the internal sight it has been granted to me to see the things that are in the other life, more clearly than I see those that are in the world. From these considerations, it is evident that external vision exists from interior vision, and this from a vision still more interior, and so on . . .'

'There are with every man at least two evil spirits . . .'

'With wicked genii there is also a fluent speech, but harsh and grating. There is also among them a speech which is not fluent, wherein the dissent of the thoughts is perceived as something secretly creeping along within it . . .'

'The evil spirits associated with man are indeed from the hells, but when with man they are not then in hell, but are taken out thence. The place where they then are, is in the midst between heaven and hell, and is called the world of spirits—when the evil spirits who are with man, are in that world, they are not in any infernal torment, but in every thought and affection of man, and so, in all that the man himself enjoys. But when they are remitted into their hell, they return to their former state . . .'

'If evil spirits could perceive that they were associated with man, and yet that they were spirits separate from him, and if they could flow in into the things of his body, they would attempt by a thousand means to destroy him; for they hate man with a deadly hatred . . .'

'Knowing, therefore, that I was a man in the body, they were continually striving to destroy me, not as to the body only, but especially as to the soul; for to destroy any man or spirit is the very delight of the life of all who are in hell; but I have been continually protected by the Lord. Hence it appears how dangerous it is for man to be in a living consort with spirits unless he be in the good of faith . . .'

'Nothing is more carefully guarded from the knowledge of associate spirits than their being thus conjoint with a man, for if they knew it they would speak to him, with the intention to destroy him . . .'

'The delight of hell is to do evil to man, and to hasten his eternal ruin.'

A long note, written with a very sharp and fine pencil, in Mr Jennings' neat hand, at the foot of the page, caught my eye. Expecting his criticism upon the text, I read a word or two, and stopped, for it was something quite different, and began with these words, *Deus misereatur mei*—'May God compassionate me'. Thus warned of its private nature, I averted my eyes, and shut the book, replacing all the volumes as I had found them, except one which interested me, and in which, as men studious and solitary in their habits will do, I grew so absorbed as to take no cognisance of the outer world, nor to remember where I was.

I was reading some pages which refer to 'representatives' and 'correspondents', in the technical language of Swedenborg, and had arrived at a passage, the substance of which is, that evil spirits, when seen by other eyes than those of their infernal associates, present themselves, by 'correspondence', in the shape of the beast *(fera)* which represents their particular lust and life, in aspect direful and atrocious. This is a long passage, and particularises a number of those bestial forms.

4   *Four Eyes were Reading the Passage*

I was running the head of my pencil-case along the line as I read it, and something caused me to raise my eyes.

Directly before me was one of the mirrors I have mentioned, in which I saw reflected the tall shape of my friend, Mr Jennings, leaning over my shoulder, and reading the page at which I was busy, and with a face so dark and wild that I should hardly have known him.

I turned and rose. He stood erect also, and with an effort laughed a little, saying:

'I came in and asked you how you did, but without succeeding in awaking you from your book; so I could not restrain my curiosity, and very impertinently, I'm afraid, peeped over your shoulder. This is not the first time of looking into those pages. You have looked into Swedenborg, no doubt, long ago?'

'Oh dear, yes! I owe Swedenborg a great deal; you will discover traces of him in the little book on Metaphysical Medicine, which you were so good as to remember.'

Although my friend affected a gaiety of manner, there was a

slight flush in his face, and I could perceive that he was inwardly much perturbed.

'I'm scarcely yet qualified, I know so little of Swedenborg. I've only had them a fortnight,' he answered, 'and I think they are rather likely to make a solitary man nervous—that is, judging from the very little I have read—I don't say that they have made me so,' he laughed; 'and I'm so very much obliged for the book. I hope you got my note?'

I made all proper acknowledgments and modest disclaimers.

'I never read a book that I go with, so entirely, as that of yours,' he continued. 'I saw at once there is more in it than is quite unfolded. Do you know Dr Harley?' he asked, rather abruptly.

In passing, the editor remarks that the physician here named was one of the most eminent who had ever practised in England.

I did, having had letters to him, and had experienced from him great courtesy and considerable assistance during my visit to England.

'I think that man one of the very greatest fools I ever met in my life,' said Mr Jennings.

This was the first time I had ever heard him say a sharp thing of anybody, and such a term applied to so high a name a little startled me.

'Really! and in what way?' I asked.

'In his profession,' he answered.

I smiled.

'I mean this,' he said: 'he seems to me, one half, blind—I mean one half of all he looks at is dark—preternaturally bright and vivid all the rest; and the worst of it is, it seems *wilful*. I can't get him —I mean he won't—I've had some experience of him as a physician, but I look on him as, in that sense, no better than a paralytic mind, an intellect half dead. I'll tell you—I know I shall some time—all about it,' he said, with a little agitation. 'You stay some months longer in England. If I should be out of town during your stay for a little time, would you allow me to trouble you with a letter?'

'I should be only too happy,' I assured him.

'Very good of you. I am so utterly dissatisfied with Harley.'

'A little leaning to the materialistic school,' I said.

'A *mere* materialist,' he corrected me; 'you can't think how that sort of thing worries one who knows better. You won't tell anyone —any of my friends you know—that I am hippish; now, for

instance, no one knows—not even Lady Mary—that I have seen Dr
Harley, or any other doctor. So pray don't mention it; and, if I
should have any threatening of an attack, you'll kindly let me write,
or, should I be in town, have a little talk with you.'

I was full of conjecture, and unconsciously I found I had fixed
my eyes gravely on him, for he lowered his for a moment, and he
said:

'I see you think I might as well tell you now, or else you are
forming a conjecture; but you may as well give it up. If you were
guessing all the rest of your life, you will never hit on it.'

He shook his head smiling, and over that wintry sunshine a black
cloud suddenly came down, and he drew his breath in, through his
teeth as men do in pain.

'Sorry, of course, to learn that you apprehend occasion to consult
any of us; but, command me when and how you like, and I need
not assure you that your confidence is sacred.'

He then talked of quite other things, and in a comparatively
cheerful way and after a little time, I took my leave.

5 Dr Hesselius is Summoned to Richmond

We parted cheerfully, but he was not cheerful, nor was I. There
are certain expressions of that powerful organ of spirit—the human
face—which, although I have seen them often, and possess a doctor's
nerve, yet disturb me profoundly. One look of Mr Jennings haunted
me. It had seized my imagination with so dismal a power that I
changed my plans for the evening, and went to the opera, feeling
that I wanted a change of ideas.

I heard nothing of or from him for two or three days, when a
note in his hand reached me. It was cheerful, and full of hope.
He said that he had been for some little time so much better—
quite well, in fact—that he was going to make a little experiment,
and run down for a month or so to his parish, to try whether a little
work might not quite set him up. There was in it a fervent religious
expression of gratitude for his restoration, as he now almost hoped
he might call it.

A day or two later I saw Lady Mary, who repeated what his note
had announced, and told me that he was actually in Warwickshire,
having resumed his clerical duties at Kenlis; and she added, 'I begin
to think that he is really perfectly well, and that there never was
anything the matter, more than nerves and fancy; we are all nervous,

but I fancy there is nothing like a little hard work for that kind of weakness, and he has made up his mind to try it. I should not be surprised if he did not come back for a year.'

Notwithstanding all this confidence, only two days later I had this note, dated from his house off Piccadilly:

DEAR SIR, I have returned disappointed. If I should feel at all able to see you, I shall write to ask you kindly to call. At present, I am too low, and, in fact, simply unable to say all I wish to say. Pray don't mention my name to my friends. I can see no one. By-and-by, please God, you shall hear from me. I mean to take a run into Shropshire, where some of my people are. God bless you! May we, on my return, meet more happily than I can now write.

About a week after this I saw Lady Mary at her own house, the last person, she said, left in town, and just on the wing for Brighton, for the London season was quite over. She told me that she had heard from Mr Jennings' niece, Martha, in Shropshire. There was nothing to be gathered from her letter, more than that he was low and nervous. In those words, of which healthy people think so lightly, what a world of suffering is sometimes hidden!

Nearly five weeks had passed without any further news of Mr Jennings. At the end of that time I received a note from him. He wrote:

'I have been in the country, and have had change of air, change of scene, change of faces, change of everything—and in everything—but *myself*. I have made up my mind, so far as the most irresolute creature on earth can do it, to tell my case fully to you. If your engagements will permit, pray come to me today, tomorrow, or the next day; but, pray defer as little as possible. You know not how much I need help. I have a quiet house at Richmond, where I now am. Perhaps you can manage to come to dinner, or to luncheon, or even to tea. You shall have no trouble in finding me out. The servant at Blank Street, who takes this note, will have a carriage at your door at any hour you please; and I am always to be found. You will say that I ought not to be alone. I have tried everything. Come and see.'

I called up the servant, and decided on going out the same evening, which accordingly I did.

He would have been much better in a lodging-house, or hotel, I thought, as I drove up through a short double row of sombre elms to a very old-fashioned brick house, darkened by the foliage of these trees, which overtopped, and nearly surrounded it. It was a perverse choice, for nothing could be imagined more triste and silent. The house, I found, belonged to him. He had stayed for a day or two in town, and, finding it for some cause insupportable, had come out here, probably because being furnished and his own, he was relieved of the thought and delay of selection, by coming here.

The sun had already set, and the red reflected light of the western sky illuminated the scene with the peculiar effect with which we are all familiar. The hall seemed very dark, but, getting to the back drawing-room, whose windows command the west, I was again in the same dusky light.

I sat down, looking out upon the richly-wooded landscape that glowed in the grand and melancholy light which was every moment fading. The corners of the room were already dark; all was growing dim, and the gloom was insensibly toning my mind, already prepared for what was sinister. I was waiting alone for his arrival, which soon took place. The door communicating with the front room opened, and the tall figure of Mr Jennings, faintly seen in the ruddy twilight, came, with quiet stealthy steps, into the room.

We shook hands, and, taking a chair to the window, where there was still light enough to enable us to see each other's faces, he sat down beside me, and, placing his hand upon my arm, with scarcely a word of preface began his narrative.

6 *How Mr Jennings Met his Companion*

The faint glow of the west, the pomp of the then lonely woods of Richmond, were before us, behind and about us the darkening room, and on the stony face of the sufferer—for the character of his face, though still gentle and sweet, was changed—rested that dim, odd glow which seems to descend and produce, where it touches, lights, sudden though faint, which are lost, almost without gradation, in darkness. The silence, too, was utter: not a distant wheel, or bark, or whistle from without; and within, the depressing stillness of an invalid bachelor's house.

I guessed well the nature, though not even vaguely the particulars of the revelations I was about to receive, from that fixed face of suffering that so oddly flushed stood out, like a portrait of Schalken's, before its background of darkness.

'It began,' he said, 'on the 15th of October, three years and eleven weeks ago, and two days—I keep very accurate count, for every day is torment. If I leave anywhere a chasm in my narrative, tell me.

'About four years ago I began a work, which had cost me very much thought and reading. It was upon the religious metaphysics of the ancients.'

'I know,' said I, 'the actual religion of educated and thinking paganism, quite apart from symbolic worship? A wide and very interesting field.'

'Yes, but not good for the mind—the Christian mind, I mean. Paganism is all bound together in essential unity, and, with evil sympathy, their religion involves their art, and both their manners, and the subject is a degrading fascination and the Nemesis sure. God forgive me!

'I wrote a great deal; I wrote late at night. I was always thinking on the subject, walking about, wherever I was, everywhere. It thoroughly infected me. You are to remember that all the material ideas connected with it were more or less of the beautiful, the subject itself delightfully interesting, and I, then, without a care.'

He sighed heavily.

'I believe that every one who sets about writing in earnest does his work, as a friend of mine phrased it, *on* something—tea, or coffee, or tobacco. I suppose there is a material waste that must be hourly supplied in such occupations, or that we should grow too abstracted, and the mind, as it were, pass out of the body, unless it were reminded often enough of the connection by actual sensation. At all events, I felt the want, and I supplied it. Tea was my companion—at first the ordinary black tea, made in the usual way, not too strong; but I drank a good deal, and increased its strength as I went on. I never experienced an uncomfortable symptom from it.

'I began to take a little green tea. I found the effect pleasanter, it cleared and intensified the power of thought so, I had come to take it frequently, but not stronger than one might take it for pleasure. I wrote a great deal out here, it was so quiet, and in this room. I used to sit up very late, and it became a habit with me to sip my tea—green tea—every now and then as my work proceeded. I had a little kettle on my table, that swung over a lamp, and made tea two or three times between eleven o'clock and two or three in the morning, my hours of going to bed.

'I used to go into town every day. I was not a monk, and, although I spent an hour or two in a library, hunting up authorities and looking out lights upon my theme, I was in no morbid state as far as I can judge. I met my friends pretty much as usual and enjoyed their society, and, on the whole, existence had never been, I think, so pleasant before.

'I had met with a man who had some odd old books, German editions in mediæval Latin, and I was only too happy to be permitted access to them. This obliging person's books were in the City, a very out-of-the-way part of it. I had rather out-stayed my intended hour, and, on coming out, seeing no cab near, I was tempted to get into the omnibus which used to drive past this house. It was darker than this by the time the 'bus had reached an old house, you may have remarked, with four poplars at each side of the door, and there the last passenger but myself got out. We drove along rather faster. It was twilight now. I leaned back in my corner next the door ruminating pleasantly.

'The interior of the omnibus was nearly dark. I had observed in the corner opposite to me at the other side, and at the end next the horses, two small circular reflections, as it seemed to me of a reddish light. They were about two inches apart, and about the size of those small brass buttons that yachting men used to put upon their jackets. I began to speculate, as listless men will, upon this trifle, as it seemed. From what centre did that faint but deep red light come, and from what—glass beads, buttons, toy decorations —was it reflected? We were lumbering along gently, having nearly a mile still to go. I had not solved the puzzle, and it became in another minute more odd, for these two luminous points, with a sudden jerk descended nearer and nearer the floor, keeping still their relative distance and horizontal position, and then, as suddenly they rose to the level of the seat on which I was sitting and I saw them no more.

'My curiosity was now really excited, and, before I had time to think, I saw again these two dull lamps, again together near the floor; again they disappeared, and again in their old corner I saw them.

'So, keeping my eyes upon them, I edged quietly up my own side, towards the end at which I still saw these tiny discs of red.

'There was very little light in the 'bus. It was nearly dark. I leaned forward to aid my endeavour to discover what these little circles really were. They shifted position a little as I did so. I began now to perceive an outline of something black, and I soon saw, with

tolerable distinctiveness, the outline of a small black monkey, pushing its face forward in mimicry to meet mine; those were its eyes,
and I now dimly saw its teeth grinning at me.

'I drew back, not knowing whether it might not meditate a
spring. I fancied that one of the passengers had forgot this ugly
pet, and wishing to ascertain something of its temper, though not
caring to trust my fingers to it, I poked my umbrella softly towards
it. It remained immovable—up to it—*through* it! For through it,
and back and forward it passed, without the slightest resistance.

'I can't, in the least, convey to you the kind of horror I felt.
When I had ascertained that the thing was an illusion, as I then
supposed, there came a misgiving about myself and a terror that
fascinated me in impotence to remove my gaze from the eyes of the
brute for some moments. As I looked, it made a little skip back,
quite into the corner, and I, in a panic found myself at the door,
having put my head out, drawing deep breaths of the outer air, and
staring at the lights and trees we were passing, too glad to reassure
myself of reality.

'I stopped the 'bus and got out. I perceived the man look oddly
at me as I paid him. I dare say there was something unusual in my
looks and manner, for I had never felt so strangely before.'

7 *The Journey: First Stage*

'When the omnibus drove on, and I was alone upon the road, I
looked carefully round to ascertain whether the monkey had followed me. To my indescribable relief I saw it nowhere. I can't
describe easily what a shock I had received, and my sense of genuine
gratitude on finding myself, as I supposed, quite rid of it.

'I had got out a little before we reached this house, two or three
hundred steps. A brick wall runs along the footpath, and inside
the wall is a hedge of yew, or some dark evergreen of that kind,
and within that again the row of fine trees which you may have
remarked as you came.

'This brick wall is about as high as my shoulder, and happening
to raise my eyes I saw the monkey, with that stooping gait, on all
fours, walking or creeping, close beside me, on top of the wall. I
stopped, looking at it with a feeling of loathing and horror. As I
stopped so did it. It sat up on the wall with its long hands on its
knees looking at me. There was not light enough to see it much
more than in outline, nor was it dark enough to bring the peculiar

light of its eyes into strong relief. I still saw, however, that red
foggy light plainly enough. It did not show its teeth, nor exhibit
any sign of irritation, but seemed jaded and sulky, and was observing me steadily.

'I drew back into the middle of the road. It was an unconscious
recoil, and there I stood, still looking at it; it did not move.

'With an instinctive determination to try something—anything,
I turned about and walked briskly towards town with askance look,
all the time, watching the movements of the beast. It crept swiftly
along the wall, at exactly my pace.

'Where the wall ends, near the turn of the road, it came down,
and with a wiry spring or two brought itself close to my feet, and
continued to keep up with me, as I quickened my pace. It was at
my left side, so close to my leg that I felt every moment as if I
should tread upon it.

'The road was quite deserted and silent, and it was darker every
moment. I stopped dismayed and bewildered, turning as I did so,
the other way—I mean, towards this house, away from which I had
been walking. When I stood still, the monkey drew back to a distance of, I suppose, about five or six yards, and remained stationary,
watching me.

'I had been more agitated than I have said. I had read, of course,
as everyone has, something about "spectral illusions", as you physicians term the phenomena of such cases. I considered my situation,
and looked my misfortune in the face.

'These affections, I had read, are sometimes transitory and sometimes obstinate. I had read of cases in which the appearance, at first
harmless, had, step by step, degenerated into something direful and
insupportable, and ended by wearing its victim out. Still as I stood
there, but for my bestial companion, quite alone, I tried to comfort
myself by repeating again and again the assurance, "the thing is
purely disease, a well-known physical affection, as distinctly as
small-pox or neuralgia. Doctors are all agreed on that, philosophy
demonstrates it. I must not be a fool. I've been sitting up too late,
and I daresay my digestion is quite wrong, and, with God's help, I
shall be all right, and this is but a symptom of nervous dyspepsia."
Did I believe all this? Not one word of it, no more than any other
miserable being ever did who is once seized and riveted in this
satanic captivity. Against my convictions, I might say my knowledge, I was simply bullying myself into a false courage.

'I now walked homeward. I had only a few hundred yards to go. I had forced myself into a sort of resignation, but I had not got over the sickening shock and the flurry of the first certainty of my misfortune.

'I had made up my mind to pass the night at home. The brute moved close beside me, and I fancied there was the sort of anxious drawing toward the house, which one sees in tired horses or dogs, sometimes as they come toward home.

'I was afraid to go into town. I was afraid of anyone's seeing and recognising me. I was conscious of an irrepressible agitation in my manner. Also, I was afraid of any violent change in my habits, such as going to a place of amusement, or walking from home in order to fatigue myself. At the hall door it waited till I mounted the steps, and when the door was opened entered with me.

'I drank no tea that night. I got cigars and some brandy-and-water. My idea was that I should act upon my material system, and by living for a while in sensation apart from thought, send myself forcibly, as it were, into a new groove. I came up here to this drawing-room. I sat just there. The monkey then got upon a small table that then stood *there*. It looked dazed and languid. An irrepressible uneasiness as to its movements kept my eyes always upon it. Its eyes were half closed, but I could see them glow. It was looking steadily at me. In all situations, at all hours, it is awake and looking at me. That never changes.

'I shall not continue in detail my narrative of this particular night. I shall describe, rather, the phenomena of the first year, which never varied, essentially. I shall describe the monkey as it appeared in daylight. In the dark, as you shall presently hear, there are peculiarities. It is a small monkey, perfectly black. It had only one peculiarity—a character of malignity—unfathomable malignity. During the first year it looked sullen and sick. But this character of intense malice and vigilance was always underlying that surly languor. During all that time it acted as if on a plan of giving me as little trouble as was consistent with watching me. Its eyes were never off me. I have never lost sight of it, except in my sleep, light or dark, day or night, since it came here, excepting when it withdraws for some weeks at a time, unaccountably.

'In total dark it is visible as in daylight. I do not mean merely its eyes. It is *all* visible distinctly in a halo that resembles a glow of red embers, and which accompanies it in all its movements.

'When it leaves me for a time, it is always at night, in the dark, and in the same way. It grows at first uneasy, and then furious, and then advances towards me, grinning and shaking, its paws clenched, and, at the same time, there comes the appearance of fire in the grate. I never have any fire. I can't sleep in the room where there is any, and it draws nearer and nearer to the chimney, quivering, it seems, with rage, and when its fury rises to the highest pitch, it springs into the grate, and up the chimney, and I see it no more.

'When first this happened, I thought I was released. I was now a new man. A day passed—a night—and no return, and a blessed week—a week—another week. I was always on my knees. Dr Hesselius, always, thanking God and praying. A whole month passed of liberty, but on a sudden, it was with me again.'

8 *The Second Stage*

'It was with me, and the malice which before was torpid under a sullen exterior, was now active. It was perfectly unchanged in every other aspect. This new energy was apparent in its activity and its looks, and soon in other ways.

'For a time, you will understand, the change was shown only in an increased vivacity, and an air of menace, as if it were always brooding over some atrocious plan. Its eyes, as before, were never off me.'

'Is it here now?' I asked.

'No,' he replied, 'it has been absent exactly a fortnight and a day—fifteen days. It has sometimes been away so long as nearly two months, once for three. Its absence always exceeds a fortnight, although it may be but by a single day. Fifteen days having past since I saw it last, it may return now at any moment.'

'Is its return,' I asked, 'accompanied by any peculiar manifestation?'

'Nothing—no,' he said. 'It is simply with me again. On lifting my eyes from a book, or turning my head, I see it, as usual, looking at me, and then it remains, as before, for its appointed time. I have never told so much and so minutely before to any one.'

I perceived that he was agitated, and looking like death, and he repeatedly applied his handkerchief to his forehead; I suggested that he might be tired, and told him that I would call, with pleasure, in the morning, but he said:

'No, if you don't mind hearing it all now. I have got so far, and

I should prefer making one effort of it. When I spoke to Dr Harley, I had nothing like so much to tell. You are a philosophic physician. You give spirit its proper rank. If this thing is real—'

He paused, looking at me with agitated inquiry.

'We can discuss it by-and-by, and very fully. I will give you all I think,' I answered, after an interval.

'Well—very well. If it is anything real, I say, it is prevailing, little by little, and drawing me more interiorly into hell. Optic nerves, he talked of. Ah! well—there are other nerves of communication. May God Almighty help me! You shall hear.

'Its power of action, I tell you, had increased. Its malice became, in a way aggressive. About two years ago, some questions that were pending between me and the bishop having been settled, I went down to my parish in Warwickshire, anxious to find occupation in my profession. I was not prepared for what happened, although I have since thought I might have apprehended something like it. The reason of my saying so is that——'

He was beginning to speak with a great deal more effort and reluctance, and sighed often, and seemed at times nearly overcome. But at this time his manner was not agitated. It was more like that of a sinking patient, who has given himself up.

'Yes, but I will first tell you about Kenlis, my parish.

'It was with me when I left this place for Dawlbridge. It was my silent travelling companion, and it remained with me at the vicarage. When I entered on the discharge of my duties, another change took place. The thing exhibited an atrocious determination to thwart me. It was with me in the church—in the reading-desk— in the pulpit—within the communion rails. At last, it reached this extremity, that while I was reading to the congregation, it would spring upon the book and squat there, so that I was unable to see the page. This happened more than once.

'I left Dawlbridge for a time. I placed myself in Dr Harley's hands. I did everything he told me. He gave my case a great deal of thought. It interested him, I think. He seemed successful. For nearly three months I was perfectly free from a return. I began to think I was safe. With his full assent I returned to Dawlbridge.

'I travelled in a chaise. I was in good spirits. I was more—I was happy and grateful. I was returning, as I thought, delivered from a dreadful hallucination, to the scene of duties which I longed to enter upon. It was a beautiful sunny evening, everything looked serene and cheerful, and I was delighted. I remember looking out of the window to see the spire of my church at Kenlis among the trees, at the point where one has the earliest view of it. It is exactly where the little stream that bounds the parish passes under the road by a culvert, and where it emerges at the roadside, a stone with an old inscription is placed. As we passed this point, I drew my head in and sat down, and in the corner of the chaise was the monkey.

'For a moment I felt faint, and then quite wild with despair and horror. I called to the driver, and got out, and sat down at the road-side, and prayed to God silently for mercy. A despairing resignation supervened. My companion was with me as I re-entered the vicarage. The same persecution followed. After a short struggle I submitted, and soon I left the place.

'I told you,' he said, 'that the beast had before this become in certain ways aggressive. I will explain a little. It seemed to be actuated by intense and increasing fury, whenever I said my prayers, or even meditated prayer. It amounted at last to a dreadful interruption. You will ask, how could a silent immaterial phantom effect that? It was thus, whenever I meditated praying; it was always before me, and nearer and nearer.

'It used to spring on a table, on the back of a chair, on the chimney-piece, and slowly to swing itself from side to side, looking at me all the time. There is in its motion an indefinable power to dissipate thought, and to contract one's attention to that monotony, till the ideas shrink, as it were, to a point, and at last to nothing— and unless I had started up, and shook off the catalepsy I have felt as if my mind were on the point of losing itself. There are other ways,' he sighed heavily; 'thus, for instance, while I pray with my eyes closed, it comes closer and closer, and I see it. I know it is not to be accounted for physically, but I do actually see it, though my lids are closed, and so it rocks my mind, as it were, and overpowers me, and I am obliged to rise from my knees. If you had ever yourself known this, you would be acquainted with desperation.'

9 *The Third Stage*

'I see, Dr Hesselius, that you don't lose one word of my statement. I need not ask you to listen specially to what I am now going to tell you. They talk of the optic nerves, and of spectral illusions, as if the organ of sight was the only point assailable by the influences that have fastened upon me—I know better. For two years in my direful case that limitation prevailed. But as food is taken in softly at the lips, and then brought under the teeth, as the tip of the little finger caught in a mill crank will draw in the hand, and the arm, and the whole body, so the miserable mortal who has been once caught firmly by the end of the finest fibre of his nerve, is drawn in and in, by the enormous machinery of hell, until he is as I am. Yes, Doctor, as *I* am, for while I talk to you, and implore relief, I feel that my prayer is for the impossible, and my pleading with the inexorable.'

I endeavoured to calm his visibly increasing agitation, and told him that he must not despair.

While we talked the night had overtaken us. The filmy moonlight was wide over the scene which the window commanded, and I said:

'Perhaps you would prefer having candles. This light, you know, is odd. I should wish you, as much as possible, under your usual conditions while I make my diagnosis, shall I call it—otherwise I don't care.'

'All lights are the same to me,' he said; 'except when I read or write, I care not if night were perpetual. I am going to tell you what happened about a year ago. The thing began to speak to me.'

'Speak! How do you mean—speak as a man does, do you mean?'

'Yes; speak in words and consecutive sentences, with perfect coherence and articulation; but there is a peculiarity. It is not like the tone of a human voice. It is not by my ears it reaches me—it comes like a singing through my head.

'This faculty, the power of speaking to me, will be my undoing. It won't let me pray, it interrupts me with dreadful blasphemies. I dare not go on, I could not. Oh! Doctor, can the skill, and thought, and prayers of man avail me nothing!'

'You must promise me, my dear sir, not to trouble yourself with unnecessarily exciting thoughts; confine yourself strictly to the narrative of *facts*; and recollect, above all, that even if the thing that infests you be, you seem to suppose, a reality with an actual independent life and will, yet it can have no power to hurt you, unless it be given from above: its access to your senses depends mainly upon your physical condition—this is, under God, your comfort and reliance: we are all alike environed. It is only that in your case, the *paries,* the veil of the flesh, the screen, is a little out of repair, and sights and sounds are transmitted. We must enter on a new

course, sir—be encouraged. I'll give tonight to the careful consideration of the whole case.'

'You are very good, sir; you think it worth trying, you don't give
me quite up; but, sir, you don't know, it is gaining such an influence
over me; it orders me about, it is such a tyrant, and I'm growing so
helpless. May God deliver me!'

'It orders you about—of course you mean by speech?'

'Yes, yes; it is always urging me to crimes, to injure others, or
myself. You see, Doctor, the situation is urgent, it is indeed. When
I was in Shropshire, a few weeks ago' (Mr Jennings was speaking
rapidly and trembling now, holding my arm with one hand, and
looking in my face), 'I went out one day with a party of friends for
a walk: my persecutor, I tell you, was with me at the time. I lagged
behind the rest: the country near the Dee, you know, is beautiful.
Our path happened to lie near a coal mine, and at the verge of the
wood is a perpendicular shaft, they say, a hundred and fifty feet
deep. My niece had remained behind with me—she knows, of
course, nothing of the nature of my sufferings. She knew, however,
that I had been ill, and was low, and she remained to prevent my
being quite alone. As we loitered slowly on together, the brute that
accompanied me was urging me to throw myself down the shaft.

'I tell you now—oh, sir, think of it!—the one consideration that
saved me from that hideous death was the fear lest the shock of
witnessing the occurrence should be too much for the poor girl.
I asked her to go on and walk with her friends, saying that I could
go no further. She made excuses, and the more I urged her the
firmer she became. She looked doubtful and frightened. I suppose
there was something in my looks or manner that alarmed her; but
she would not go, and that literally saved me. You had no idea,
sir, that a living man could be made so abject a slave of Satan,'
he said, with a ghastly groan and shudder.

There was a pause here, and I said, 'You *were* preserved nevertheless. It was the act of God. You are in His hands and in the
power of no other being: be therefore confident for the future.'

10 *Home*

I made him have candles lighted, and saw the room looking cheery
and inhabited before I left him. I told him that he must regard his
illness strictly as one dependent on physical, though *subtle* physical
causes. I told him that he had evidence of God's care and love in

the deliverance which he had just described, and that I had perceived with pain that he seemed to regard its peculiar features as indicating that he had been delivered over to spiritual reprobation. Than such a conclusion nothing could be, I insisted, less warranted; and not only so, but more contrary to facts, as disclosed in his mysterious deliverance from that murderous influence during his Shropshire excursion. First, his niece had been retained by his side without his intending to keep her near him; and, secondly, there had been infused into his mind an irresistible repugnance to execute the dreadful suggestion in her presence.

As I reasoned this point with him, Mr Jennings wept. He seemed comforted. One promise I exacted, which was that should the monkey at any time return, I should be sent for immediately; and, repeating my assurance that I would give neither time nor thought to any other subject until I had thoroughly investigated his case, and that tomorrow he should hear the result, I took my leave.

Before getting into the carriage I told the servant that his master was far from well, and that he should make a point of frequently looking into his room.

My own arrangements I made with a view to being quite secure from interruption.

I merely called at my lodgings, and with a travelling-desk and carpet-bag, set off in a hackney-carriage for an inn about two miles out of town, called The Horns, a very quiet and comfortable house, with good thick walls. And there I resolved, without the possibility of intrusion or distraction, to devote some hours of the night, in my comfortable sitting-room, to Mr Jennings' case, and so much of the morning as it might require.

(There occurs here a careful note of Dr Hesselius' opinion upon the case, and of the habits, dietary, and medicines which he prescribed. It is curious—some persons would say mystical. But, on the whole, I doubt whether it would sufficiently interest a reader of the kind I am likely to meet with, to warrant its being here reprinted. The whole letter was plainly written at the inn where he had hid himself for the occasion. The next letter is dated from his town lodgings.)

I left town for the inn where I slept last night at half-past nine, and did not arrive at my room in town until one o'clock this afternoon. I found a letter in Mr Jennings' hand upon my table. It had not come by post, and, on inquiry, I learned that Mr Jennings'

C

servant had brought it, and on learning that I was not to return until today, and that no one could tell him my address, he seemed very uncomfortable, and said his orders from his master were that he was not to return without an answer.

I opened the letter and read:

DEAR DR HESSELIUS.—It is here. You had not been an hour gone when it returned. It is speaking. It knows all that has happened. It knows everything—it knows you, and is frantic and atrocious. It reviles. I send you this. It knows every word I have written—I write. This I promised, and I therefore write, but, I fear, very confused, very incoherently. I am so interrupted, disturbed.

Ever yours, sincerely yours,
ROBERT LYNDER JENNINGS.

'When did this come?' I asked.

'About eleven last night: the man was here again, and has been here three times today. The last time is about an hour since.'

Thus answered, and with the notes I had made upon his case in my pocket, I was in a few minutes driving towards Richmond, to see Mr Jennings.

I by no means, as you perceive, despaired of Mr Jennings' case. He had himself remembered and applied, though quite in a mistaken way, the principle which I lay down in my Metaphysical Medicine, and which governs all such cases. I was about to apply it in earnest. I was profoundly interested, and very anxious to see and examine him while the 'enemy' was actually present.

I drove up to the sombre house, and ran up the steps, and knocked. The door, in a little time, was opened by a tall woman in black silk. She looked ill, and as if she had been crying. She curtseyed, and heard my question, but she did not answer. She turned her face away, extending her hand towards two men who were coming downstairs; and thus having, as it were, tacitly made me over to them, she passed through a side-door hastily and shut it.

The man who was nearest the hall, I at once accosted, but being now close to him, I was shocked to see that both his hands were covered in blood.

I drew back a little, and the man, passing downstairs, merely said in a low tone, 'Here's the servant, sir.'

The servant had stopped on the stairs, confounded and dumb at seeing me. He was rubbing his hands in a handkerchief, and it was steeped in blood.

'Jones, what is it? what has happened?' I asked, while a sickening suspicion overpowered me.

The man asked me to come up to the lobby. I was beside him in a moment, and, frowning and pallid, with contracted eyes, he told me the horror which I already half guessed.

His master had made away with himself.

I went upstairs with him to the room—what I saw there I won't tell you. He had cut his throat with his razor. It was a frightful gash. The two men had laid him on the bed, and composed his limbs. It had happened, as the immense pool of blood on the floor declared, at some distance between the bed and the window. There was carpet round his bed, and a carpet under his dressing-table, but none on the rest of the floor, for the man said he did not like a carpet in his bedroom. In this sombre and now terrible room, one of the great elms that darkened the house was slowly moving the shadow of one of its great boughs upon this dreadful floor.

I beckoned to the servant, and we went downstairs together. I turned off the hall into an old-fashioned panelled room, and there standing, I heard all the servant had to tell. It was not a great deal.

'I concluded, sir, from your words, and looks, sir, as you left last night, that you thought my master was seriously ill. I thought it might be that you were afraid of a fit, or something. So I attended very close to your directions. He sat up late, till past three o'clock. He was not writing or reading. He was talking a great deal to himself, but that was nothing unusual. At about that hour I assisted him to undress, and left him in his slippers and dressing-gown. I went back softly in about half-an-hour. He was in his bed, quite undressed, and a pair of candles lighted on the table beside his bed. He was leaning on his elbow, and looking out at the other side of the bed when I came in. I asked him if he wanted anything, and he said no.

'I don't know whether it was what you said to me, sir, or something a little unusual about him, but I was uneasy, uncommon uneasy about him last night.

'In another half hour, or it might be a little more, I went up again. I did not hear him talking as before. I opened the door a little. The candles were both out, which was not usual. I had a bed-room candle, and I let the light in, a little bit, looking softly round.

'I saw him sitting in that chair beside the dressing-table with his clothes on again. He turned round and looked at me. I thought it strange he should get up and dress, and put out the candles to sit in the dark, that way. But I only asked him again if I could do anything for him. He said no, rather sharp, I thought. I asked him if I might light the candles and he said, "Do as you like, Jones". So I lighted them, and I lingered about the room, and he said, "Tell me truth, Jones; why did you come again—you did not hear anyone cursing?" "No, sir," I said, wondering what he could mean.

' "No," said he, after me, "of course, no"; and I said to him, "Wouldn't it be well, sir, you went to bed? It's just five o'clock", and he said nothing, but, "Very likely; good-night, Jones". So I went, sir, but in less than an hour I came again. The door was fast, and he heard me, and called as I thought from the bed to know what I wanted, and he desired me not to disturb him again. I lay down and slept for a little.

'It must have been between six and seven when I went up again. The door was still fast, and he made no answer, so I did not like to disturb him, and thinking he was asleep, I left him till nine. It was his custom to ring when he wished me to come, and I had no particular hour for calling him. I tapped very gently, and getting no answer, I stayed away a good while, supposing he was getting some rest then. It was not till eleven o'clock I grew really uncomfortable about him—for at the latest he was never, that I could remember, later than half-past ten. I got no answer. I knocked and called, and still no answer. So not being able to force the door, I called Thomas from the stables, and together we forced it, and found him in the shocking way you saw.'

Jones had no more to tell. Poor Mr Jennings was very gentle, and very kind. All his people were fond of him. I could see that the servant was very much moved.

So, dejected and agitated, I passed from that terrible house, and its dark canopy of elms, and I hope I shall never see it more. While I write to you I feel like a man who has but half waked from a frightful and monotonous dream. My memory rejects the picture with incredulity and horror. Yet I know it is true. It is the story of the process of a poison, a poison which excites the reciprocal action of spirit and nerve, and paralyses the tissue that separates those cognate functions of the senses, the external and the interior. Thus we find strange bed-fellows, and the mortal and immortal prematurely make acquaintance.

Conclusion: A word for those who suffer

My dear Van L—, you have suffered from an affection similar to that which I have just described. You twice complained of a return of it.

Who, under God, cured you? Your humble servant, Martin Hesselius. Let me rather adopt the more emphasised piety of a certain good old French surgeon of three hundred years ago: 'I treated, and God cured you.'

Come, my friend, you are not to be hippish. Let me tell you a fact.

I have met with, and treated, as my book shows, fifty-seven cases of this kind of vision, which I term indifferently 'sublimated', 'precocious', and 'interior'.

There is another class of affections which are truly termed—though commonly confounded with those which I describe—spectral illusions. These latter I look upon as being no less simply curable than a cold in the head or a trifling dyspepsia.

It is those which rank in the first category that test our promptitude of thought. Fifty-seven such cases have I encountered, neither more nor less. And in how many of these have I failed? In no single instance.

There is no one affliction of mortality more easily and certainly reducible, with a little patience, and a rational confidence in the physician. With these simple conditions, I look upon the cure as absolutely certain.

You are to remember that I had not even commenced to treat Mr Jennings' case. I have not any doubt that I should have cured him perfectly in eighteen months, or possibly it might have extended to two years. Some cases are very rapidly curable, others extremely tedious. Every intelligent physician who will give thought and diligence to the task, will effect a cure.

You know my tract on The Cardinal Functions of the Brain. I there, by the evidence of innumerable facts, prove, as I think, the high probability of a circulation arterial and venous in its mechanism, through the nerves. Of this system, thus considered, the brain is the heart. The fluid, which is propagated hence through one class of nerves, returns in an altered state through another, and the nature of that fluid is spiritual, though not immaterial, any more than, as I before remarked, light or electricity are so.

By various abuses, among which the habitual use of such agents as green tea is one, this fluid may be affected as to its quality, but it is more frequently disturbed as to equilibrium. This fluid being that which we have in common with spirits, a congestion found upon the masses of brain or nerve, connected with the interior sense, forms a surface unduly exposed, on which disembodied spirits may operate: communication is thus more or less effectually established. Between this brain circulation and the heart circulation there is an intimate sympathy. The seat, or rather the instrument of exterior vision, is the eye. The seat of interior vision is the nervous tissue and brain, immediately about and above the eyebrow.

You remember how effectually I dissipated your pictures by the simple application of iced eau-de-cologne. Few cases, however, can be treated exactly alike with anything like rapid success. Cold acts powerfully as a repellant of the nervous fluid. Long enough continued it will even produce that permanent insensibility which we call numbness, and a little longer, muscular as well as sensational paralysis.

I have not, I repeat, the slightest doubt that I should have first dimmed and ultimately sealed that inner eye which Mr Jennings had inadvertently opened. The same senses are opened in delirium tremens, and entirely shut up again when the overaction of the cerebral heart, and the prodigious nervous congestions that attend it, are terminated by a decided change in the state of the body. It is by acting steadily upon the body by a simple process, that this result is produced—and inevitably produced—I have never yet failed.

Poor Mr Jennings made away with himself. But that catastrophe was the result of a totally different malady, which, as it were, projected itself upon the disease which was established. His case was in the distinctive manner a complication, and the complaint under which he really succumbed, was a hereditary suicidal mania. Poor Mr Jennings I cannot call a patient of mine, for I had not even begun to treat his case, and he had not yet given me, I am convinced, his full and unreserved confidence. If the patient do not array himself on the side of the disease, his cure is certain.

The Novel of the White Powder

ARTHUR MACHEN

MY NAME IS LEICESTER; my father, Major-General Wyn Leicester, a distinguished officer of artillery, succumbed five years ago to a complicated liver complaint acquired in the deadly climate of India. A year later my only brother, Francis, came home after an exceptionally brilliant career at the University, and settled down with the resolution of a hermit to master what has been well called the great legend of the law. He was a man who seemed to live in utter indifference to everything that is called pleasure; and though he was handsomer than most men, and could talk as merrily and wittily as if he were a mere vagabond, he avoided society, and shut himself up in a large room at the top of the house to make himself a lawyer. Ten hours a day of hard reading was at first his allotted portion; from the first light in the east to the late afternoon he remained shut up with his books, taking a hasty half-hour's lunch with me as if he grudged the wasting of the moments, and going out for a short walk when it began to grow dusk. I thought that such relentless application must be injurious, and tried to cajole him from the crabbed textbooks, but his ardour seemed to grow rather than diminish, and his daily tale of hours increased. I spoke to him seriously, suggesting some occasional relaxation, if it were but an idle afternoon with a harmless novel; but he laughed, and said that he read about feudal tenures when he felt in need of amusement, and scoffed at the notions of theatres, or a month's fresh air. I confessed that he looked well, and seemed not to suffer from his labours, but I knew that such unnatural toil would take revenge at last, and I was not mistaken. A look of anxiety began to lurk about his eyes, and he seemed languid, and at last he avowed that he was no longer in perfect health; he was troubled, he said, with a sensation of dizziness, and awoke now and then of nights from fearful dreams, terrified and cold with icy sweats. 'I am taking care of myself,' he said, 'so you must not trouble; I passed the whole of yesterday afternoon in idleness, leaning back in that comfortable chair you gave me, and scribbling nonsense on a sheet of paper. No, no; I will not overdo my work; I shall be well enough in a week or two, depend upon it.'

Yet in spite of his assurances I could see that he grew no better, but rather worse; he would enter the drawing-room with a face all miserably wrinkled and despondent, and endeavour to look gaily when my eyes fell on him, and I thought such symptoms of evil omen, and was frightened sometimes at the nervous irritation of his movements, and at glances which I could not decipher. Much against his will, I prevailed on him to have medical advice, and with an ill grace he called in our old doctor.

Dr Haberden cheered me after examination of his patient.

'There is nothing really much amiss,' he said to me. 'No doubt he reads too hard and eats hastily, and then goes back again to his books in too great a hurry, and the natural sequence is some digestive trouble and a little mischief in the nervous system. But I think —I do indeed, Miss Leicester—that we shall be able to set this all right. I have written him a prescription which ought to do great things. So you have no cause for anxiety.'

My brother insisted on having the prescription made up by a chemist in the neighbourhood. It was an odd, old-fashioned shop, devoid of the studied coquetry and calculated glitter that make so gay a show on the counters and shelves of the modern apothecary; but Francis liked the old chemist, and believed in the scrupulous purity of his drugs. The medicine was sent in due course, and I saw that my brother took it regularly after lunch and dinner. It was an innocent-looking white powder, of which a little was dissolved in a glass of cold water; I stirred it in, and it seemed to disappear, leaving the water clear and colourless. At first Francis seemed to benefit greatly; the weariness vanished from his face, and he became more cheerful than he had ever been since the time when he left school; he talked gaily of reforming himself, and avowed to me that he had wasted his time.

'I have given too many hours to law,' he said, laughing; 'I think you have saved me in the nick of time. Come, I shall be Lord Chancellor yet, but I must not forget life. You and I will have a holiday together before long; we will go to Paris and enjoy ourselves, and keep away from the Bibliothèque Nationale.'

I confessed myself delighted with the prospect.

'When shall we go?' I said. 'I can start the day after tomorrow if you like.'

'Ah! that is perhaps a little too soon; after all, I do not know London yet, and I suppose a man ought to give the pleasures of his own country the first choice. But we will go off together in a week or two, so try and furbish up your French. I only know law French myself, and I am afraid that wouldn't do.'

We were just finishing dinner, and he quaffed off his medicine with a parade of carousal as if it had been wine from some choicest bin.

'Has it any particular taste?' I said.

'No; I should not know I was not drinking water,' and he got up from his chair and began to pace up and down the room as if he were undecided as to what he should do next.

'Shall we have coffee in the drawing-room?' I said; 'or would you like to smoke?'

'No, I think I will take a turn; it seems a pleasant evening. Look at the afterglow; why, it is as if a great city were burning in flames, and down there between the dark houses it is raining blood fast. Yes, I will go out; I may be in soon, but I shall take my key; so good-night, dear, if I don't see you again.'

The door slammed behind him, and I saw him walk lightly down the street, swinging his malacca cane, and I felt grateful to Dr Haberden for such an improvement.

I believe my brother came home very late that night, but he was in a merry mood the next morning.

'I walked on without thinking where I was going,' he said, 'enjoying the freshness of the air, and livened by the crowds as I reached more frequented quarters. And then I met an old college friend, Orford, in the press of the pavement, and then—well, we enjoyed ourselves. I have felt what it is to be young and a man; I find I have blood in my veins, as other men have. I made an appointment with Orford for tonight; there will be a little party of us at the restaurant. Yes; I shall enjoy myself for a week or

C*

two, and hear the chimes at midnight, and then we will go for our
little trip together.'

Such was the transmutation of my brother's character that in
a few days he became a lover of pleasure, a careless and merry
idler of western pavements, a hunter out of snug restaurants, and
a fine critic of fantastic dancing; he grew fat before my eyes, and
said no more of Paris, for he had clearly found his paradise in
London. I rejoiced, and yet wondered a little; for there was, I
thought, something in his gaiety that indefinitely displeased me,
though I could not have defined my feeling. But by degrees there
came a change; he returned still in the cold hours of the morning,
but I heard no more about his pleasures, and one morning as we
sat at breakfast together I looked suddenly into his eyes and saw
a stranger before me.

'Oh, Francis!' I cried. 'Oh, Francis, Francis, what have you
done?' and rending sobs cut the words short. I went weeping out
of the room; for though I knew nothing, yet I knew all, and by
some odd play of thought I remembered the evening when he first
went abroad, and the picture of the sunset sky glowed before me;
the clouds like a city in burning flames, and the rain of blood. Yet
I did battle with such thoughts, resolving that perhaps, after all,
no great harm had been done, and in the evening at dinner I
resolved to press him to fix a day for our holiday in Paris. We had
talked easily enough, and my brother had just taken his medicine,
which he continued all the while. I was about to begin my topic
when the words forming in my mind vanished, and I wondered
for a second what icy and intolerable weight oppressed my heart
and suffocated me as with the unutterable horror of the coffin lid
nailed down on the living.

We had dined without candles; the room had slowly grown
from twilight to gloom, and the walls and corners were indistinct
in the shadow. But from where I sat I looked out into the street;
and as I thought of what I would say to Francis, the sky began
to flush and shine, as it had done on a well-remembered evening,
and in the gap between two dark masses that were houses an awful
pageantry of flame appeared—lurid whorls of writhed cloud, and
utter depths burning, grey masses like the fume blown from a
smoking city, and an evil glory blazing far above shot with tongues
of more ardent fire, and below as if there were a deep pool of
blood. I looked down to where my brother sat facing me, and the

words were shaped on my lips, when I saw his hand resting on the table. Between the thumb and forefinger of the closed hand there was a mark, a small patch about the size of a sixpence, and somewhat of the colour of a bad bruise. Yet, by some sense I cannot define, I knew that what I saw was no bruise at all; oh! if human flesh could burn with flame, and if flame could be black as pitch, such was that before me. Without thought or fashioning of words grey horror shaped within me at the sight, and in an inner cell it was known to be a brand. For the moment the stained sky became dark as midnight, and when the light returned to me I was alone in the silent room, and soon after I heard my brother go out.

Late as it was, I put on my hat and went to Dr Haberden, and in his great consulting room, ill lighted by a candle which the doctor brought in with him, with stammering lips, and a voice that would break in spite of my resolve, I told him all, from the day on which my brother began to take the medicine down to the dreadful thing I had seen scarcely half an hour before.

When I had done, the doctor looked at me for a minute with an expression of great pity on his face.

'My dear Miss Leicester,' he said, 'you have evidently been anxious about your brother; you have been worrying about him, I am sure. Come, now, is it not so?'

'I have certainly been anxious,' I said. 'For the last week or two I have not felt at ease.'

'Quite so; you know, of course, what a queer thing the brain is?'

'I understand what you mean; but I was not deceived. I saw what I have told you with my own eyes.'

'Yes, yes, of course. But your eyes had been staring at that very curious sunset we had tonight. That is the only explanation. You will see it in the proper light tomorrow, I am sure. But, remember, I am always ready to give any help that is in my power; do not scruple to come to me, or to send for me if you are in any distress.'

I went away but little comforted, all confusion and terror and sorrow, not knowing where to turn. When my brother and I met the next day, I looked quickly at him, and noticed, with a sickening at heart, that the right hand, the hand on which I had clearly seen the patch as of a black fire, was wrapped up with a handkerchief.

'What is the matter with your hand, Francis?' I said in steady voice.

'Nothing of consequence. I cut a finger last night, and it bled rather awkwardly. So I did it up roughly to the best of my ability.'

'I will do it neatly for you, if you like.'

'No, thank you, dear; this will answer very well. Suppose we have breakfast; I am quite hungry.'

We sat down and I watched him. He scarcely ate or drank at all, but tossed his meat to the dog when he thought my eyes were turned away; there was a look in his eyes that I had never yet seen, and the thought flashed across my mind that it was a look that was scarcely human. I was firmly convinced that awful and incredible as was the thing I had seen the night before, yet it was no illusion, no glamour of bewildered sense, and in the course of the evening I went again to the doctor's house.

He shook his head with an air puzzled and incredulous, and seemed to reflect for a few minutes.

'And you say he still keeps up the medicine? But why? As I understand, all the symptoms he complained of have disappeared long ago; why should he go on taking the stuff when he is quite well? And by the by, where did he get it made up? At Sayce's? I never send any one there; the old man is getting careless. Suppose you come with me to the chemist's; I should like to have some talk with him.'

We walked together to the shop; old Sayce knew Dr Haberden, and was quite ready to give any information.

'You have been sending that in to Mr Leicester for some weeks, I think, on my prescription,' said the doctor, giving the old man a pencilled scrap of paper.

The chemist put on his great spectacles with trembling uncertainty, and held up the paper with a shaking hand.

'Oh, yes,' he said, 'I have very little of it left; it is rather an uncommon drug, and I have had it in stock some time. I must get in some more, if Mr Leicester goes on with it.'

'Kindly let me have a look at the stuff,' said Haberden, and the chemist gave him a glass bottle. He took out the stopper and smelt the contents, and looked strangely at the old man.

'Where did you get this?' he said, 'and what is it? For one thing, Mr Sayce, it is not what I prescribed. Yes, yes, I see the label is right enough, but I tell you this is not the drug.'

'I have had it a long time,' said the old man in feeble terror; 'I got it from Burbage's in the usual way. It is not prescribed often, and I have had it on the shelf for some years. You see there is very little left.'

'You had better give it to me,' said Haberden, 'I am afraid something wrong has happened.'

We went out of the shop in silence, the doctor carrying the bottle neatly wrapped in paper under his arm.

'Dr Haberden,' I said, when we had walked a little way—'Dr Haberden.'

'Yes,' he said, looking at me gloomily enough.

'I should like you to tell me what my brother has been taking twice a day for the last month or so.'

'Frankly, Miss Leicester, I don't know. We will speak of this when we get to my house.'

We walked on quickly without another word till we reached Dr Haberden's. He asked me to sit down, and began pacing up and down the room, his face clouded over, as I could see, with no common fears.

'Well,' he said at length, 'this is all very strange; it is only natural that you should feel alarmed, and I must confess that my mind is far from easy. We will put aside, if you please, what you told me last night and this morning, but the fact remains that for the last few weeks Mr Leicester has been impregnating his system with a drug which is completely unknown to me. I tell you, it is not what I ordered; and what the stuff in the bottle really is remains to be seen.'

He undid the wrapper, and cautiously tilted a few grains of the white powder on to a piece of paper, and peered curiously at it.

'Yes,' he said, 'it is like the sulphate of quinine, as you say; it is flaky. But smell it.'

He held the bottle to me, and I bent over it. It was a strange, sickly smell, vaporous and overpowering, like some strong anæsthetic.

'I shall have it analysed,' said Haberden; 'I have a friend who has devoted his whole life to chemistry as a science. Then we shall have something to go upon. No, no! say no more about that other matter; I cannot listen to that; and take my advice and think no more about it yourself.'

That evening my brother did not go out as usual after dinner.

'I have had my fling,' he said with a queer laugh, 'and I must go back to my old ways. A little law will be quite a relaxation after so sharp a dose of pleasure,' and he grinned to himself, and soon after went up to his room. His hand was still all bandaged.

Dr Haberden called a few days later.

'I have no special news to give you,' he said. 'Chambers is out of town, so I know no more about that stuff than you do. But I should like to see Mr Leicester, if he is in.'

'He is in his room,' I said; 'I will tell him you are here.'

'No, no, I will go up to him; we will have a little quiet talk together. I dare say that we have made a good deal of fuss about a very little; for, after all, whatever the powder may be, it seems to have done him good.'

The doctor went upstairs, and standing in the hall I heard his knock, and the opening and shutting of the door; and then I waited in the silent house for an hour, and the stillness grew more and more intense as the hands of the clock crept round. Then there sounded from above the noise of a door shut sharply, and the doctor was coming down the stairs. His footsteps crossed the hall, and there was a pause at the door; I drew a long, sick breath with difficulty, and saw my face white in a little mirror, and he came in and stood at the door. There was an unutterable horror shining in his eyes; he steadied himself by holding the back of a chair with one hand, his lower lip trembled like a horse's, and he gulped and stammered unintelligible sounds before he spoke.

'I have seen that man,' he began in a dry whisper. 'I have been sitting in his presence for the last hour. My God! And I am alive and in my senses! I, who have dealt with death all my life, and have dabbled with the melting ruins of the earthly tabernacle. But not this, oh! not this,' and he covered his face with his hands as if to shut out the sight of something before him.

'Do not send for me again, Miss Leicester,' he said with more composure. 'I can do nothing in this house. Goodbye.'

As I watched him totter down the steps, and along the pavement towards his house, it seemed to me that he had aged by ten years since the morning.

My brother remained in his room. He called out to me in a voice I hardly recognised that he was very busy, and would like his meals brought to his door and left there, and I gave the order to the servants. From that day it seemed as if the arbitrary conception we call time had been annihilated for me; I lived in an ever present sense of horror, going through the routine of the house mechanically, and only speaking a few necessary words to the servants. Now and then I went out and paced the streets for an hour or two and came home again; but whether I were without or within, my spirit delayed before the closed door of the upper room, and, shuddering, waited for it to open. I have said that I scarcely reckoned time; but I suppose it must have been a fortnight after Dr Haberden's visit that I came home from my stroll a little refreshed and lightened. The air was sweet and pleasant, and the hazy form of green leaves, floating cloud-like in the square, and the smell of blossoms, had charmed my senses, and I felt happier and walked more briskly. As I delayed a moment at the verge of the pavement, waiting for a van to pass by before crossing over to the house, I happened to look up at the windows, and instantly there was the rush and swirl of deep cold water in my ears, my heart leapt up and fell down, down as into a deep hollow, and I was amazed with a dread and terror without form or shape. I stretched out a hand blindly through the folds of thick darkness, from the black and shadowy valley, and held myself from falling, while the stones beneath my feet rocked and swayed and tilted, and the sense of solid things seemed to sink away from under me. I had glanced up at the window of my brother's study, and at that moment the blind was drawn aside, and something that had life stared out into the world. Nay, I cannot say I saw a face or any human likeness; a living thing, two eyes of burning flame glared at me, and they were in the midst of something as formless as my fear, the symbol and presence of all evil and all hideous corruption. I stood shuddering and quaking as with the grip of ague, sick with unspeakable agonies of fear and loathing, and for five minutes I could not summon force or motion to my limbs. When I was within the door, I ran up the stairs to my brother's room and knocked.

'Francis, Francis,' I cried, 'for Heaven's sake, answer me. What is the horrible thing in your room? Cast it out, Francis; cast it from you.'

I heard a noise as of feet shuffling slowly and awkwardly, and a choking, gurgling sound, as if someone was struggling to find utterance, and then the noise of a voice, broken and stifled, and words that I could scarcely understand.

'There is nothing here,' the voice said. 'Pray do not disturb me. I am not very well today.'

I turned away, horrified, and yet helpless. I could do nothing, and I wondered why Francis had lied to me, for I had seen the appearance beyond the glass too plainly to be deceived, though it was but the sight of a moment. And I sat still, conscious that there had been something else, something I had seen in the first flash of terror, before those burning eyes had looked at me. Suddenly I remembered; as I lifted my face the blind was being drawn back, and I had had an instant's glance of the thing that was moving it, and in my recollection I knew that a hideous image was engraved forever on my brain. It was not a hand; there were no fingers that held the blind, but a black stump pushed it aside, the mouldering outline and the clumsy movement as of a beast's paw had glowed into my senses before the darkling waves of terror had overwhelmed me as I went down quick into the pit. My mind was aghast at the thought of this, and of the awful presence that dwelt with my brother in his room; I went to his door and cried to him again, but no answer came. That night one of the servants came up to me and told me in a whisper that for three days food had been regularly placed at the door and left untouched; the maid had knocked but had received no answer; she had heard the noise of shuffling feet that I had noticed. Day after day went by, and still my brother's meals were brought to his door and left untouched; and though I knocked and called again and again, I could get no answer. The servants began to talk to me; it appeared they were as alarmed as I; the cook said that when my brother first shut himself up in his room she used to hear him come out at night and go about the house; and once, she said, the hall door had opened and closed again, but for several nights she had heard no sound. The climax came at last; it was in the dusk of the evening, and I was sitting in the darkening dreary room when a terrible shriek jarred and rang harshly out of the silence, and I heard a frightened scurry of feet dashing down the stairs. I waited, and the servant maid staggered into the room and faced me, white and trembling.

'Oh, Miss Helen!' she whispered; 'oh! for the Lord's sake, Miss Helen, what has happened? Look at my hand, miss; look at that hand?'

'I do not understand you,' I said. 'Will you explain to me?'

'I was doing your room just now,' she began. 'I was turning down the bedclothes, and all of a sudden there was something fell upon my hand, wet, and I looked up, and the ceiling was black and dripping on me.'

I looked hard at her and bit my lip.

'Come with me,' I said. 'Bring your candle with you.'

The room I slept in was beneath my brother's, and as I went in I felt I was trembling. I looked up at the ceiling, and saw a patch, all black and wet, and a dew of black drops upon it, and a pool of horrible liquor soaking into the white bedclothes.

I ran upstairs, and knocked loudly.

'Oh, Francis, Francis, my dear brother,' I cried, 'what has happened to you?'

And I listened. There was a sound of choking, and a noise like water bubbling and regurgitating, but nothing else, and I called louder, but no answer came.

In spite of what Dr Haberden had said, I went to him; with tears streaming down my cheeks I told him all that had happened, and he listened to me with a face set hard and grim.

'For your father's sake,' he said at last, 'I will go with you, though I can do nothing.'

We went out together; the streets were dark and silent, and heavy with heat and a drought of many weeks. I saw the doctor's face white under the gas-lamps, and when he reached the house his hand was shaking.

We did not hesitate, but went upstairs directly. I held the lamp, and he called out in a loud, determined voice

'Mr Leicester, do you hear me? I insist on seeing you. Answer me at once.'

There was no answer, but we both heard that choking noise I have mentioned.

'Mr Leicester, I am waiting for you. Open the door this instant, or I shall break it down.' And he called a third time in a voice that rang and echoed from the walls—

'Mr Leicester! For the last time I order you to open the door.'

'Ah!' he said, after a pause of heavy silence, 'we are wasting time here. Will you be so kind as to get me a poker, or something of the kind?'

I ran into a little room at the back where odd articles were kept, and found a heavy adze-like tool that I thought might serve the doctor's purpose.

'Very good,' he said, 'that will do, I dare say. I give you notice, Mr Leicester,' he cried loudly at the keyhole, 'that I am now about to break into your room.'

Then I heard the wrench of the adze, and the woodwork split and cracked under it; with a loud crash the door suddenly burst open, and for a moment we started back aghast at a fearful screaming cry, no human voice, but as the roar of a monster, that burst forth inarticulate and struck at us out of the darkness.

'Hold the lamp,' said the doctor, and we went in and glanced quickly round the room.

'There it is,' said Dr Haberden, drawing a quick breath; 'look, in that corner.'

I looked, and a pang of horror seized my heart as with a white-hot iron. There upon the floor was a dark and putrid mass, seething with corruption and hideous rottenness, neither liquid nor solid, but melting and changing before our eyes, and bubbling with unctuous oily bubbles like boiling pitch. And out of the midst of it shone two burning points like eyes, and I saw a writhing and stirring as of limbs, and something moved and lifted up what might have been an arm. The doctor took a step forward, raised the iron bar and struck at the burning points; he drove in the weapon, and struck again and again in the fury of loathing.

A week or two later, when I had recovered to some extent from the terrible shock, Dr Haberden came to see me.

'I have sold my practice,' he began, 'and tomorrow I am sailing on a long voyage. I do not know whether I shall ever return to England; in all probability I shall buy a little land in California, and settle there for the remainder of my life. I have brought you this packet, which you may open and read when you feel able to do so. It contains the report of Dr Chambers on what I submitted to him. Goodbye, Miss Leicester, goodbye.'

When he had gone I opened the envelope; I could not wait, and proceeded to read the papers within. Here is the manuscript, and if you will allow me, I will read you the astounding story it contains.

My dear Haberden, the letter began, *I have delayed inexcusably in answering your question as to the white substance you sent me. To tell you the truth, I have hesitated for some time as to what course I should adopt, for there is a bigotry and orthodox standard in physical science as in theology, and I knew that if I told you the truth I should offend rooted prejudices which I once held dear my-*

self. However, I have determined to be plain with you, and first I must enter into a short personal explanation.

You have known me, Haberden, for many years as a scientific man; you and I have often talked of our profession together, and discussed the hopeless gulf that opens before the feet of those who think to attain to truth by any means whatsoever except the beaten way of experiment and observation in the sphere of material things. I remember the scorn with which you have spoken to me of men of science who have dabbled a little in the unseen, and have timidly hinted that perhaps the senses are not, after all, the eternal, impenetrable bounds of all knowledge, the everlasting walls beyond which no human being has ever passed. We have laughed together heartily, and I think justly, at the 'occult' follies of the day, disguised under various names—the mesmerisms, spiritualisms, materialisations, theosophies, all the rabble rout of imposture, with their machinery of poor tricks and feeble conjuring, the true back parlour of shabby London streets. Yet, in spite of what I have said, I must confess to you that I am no materialist, taking the word of course in its usual signification. It is now many years since I have convinced myself— convinced myself, a sceptic, remember—that the old ironbound theory is utterly and entirely false. Perhaps this confession will not wound you so sharply as it would have done twenty years ago; for I think you cannot have failed to notice that for some time hypotheses have been advanced by men of pure science which are nothing less than transcendental, and I suspect that most modern chemists and biologists of repute would not hesitate to subscribe the dictum of the old Schoolman, Omnia exeunt in mysterium, which means, I take it, that every branch of human knowledge if traced up to its source and final principles vanishes into mystery. I need not trouble you now with a detailed account of the painful steps which led me to my conclusions; a few simple experiments suggested a doubt as to my then standpoint, and a train of thought that rose from circumstances comparatively trifling brought me far; my old conception of the universe has been swept away, and I stand in a world that seems as strange and awful to me as the endless waves of the ocean seen for the first time, shining, from a peak in Darien. Now I know that the walls of sense that seemed so impenetrable, that seemed to loom up above the heavens and to be founded below the depths, and to shut us in for evermore, are no such everlasting impassable barriers as we fancied, but thinnest and most airy veils that melt *away before the seeker, and dissolve as the early mist of the morning about the brooks. I know that you never adopted the extreme materialistic position; you did not go about trying to prove a universal negative, for your logical sense withheld you from that crowning absurdity; but I am sure that you will find all that I am saying strange and repellent to your habits of thought. Yet, Haberden, what I tell you is the truth, nay, to adopt our common language, the sole and scientific truth, verified by experience; and the universe is verily more splendid and more awful than we used to dream. The whole universe, my friend, is a tremendous sacrament; a mystic, ineffable force and energy, veiled by an outward form of matter; and man, and the sun and the other stars, and the flower of the grass, and the crystal in the test-tube, are each and every one as spiritual, as material, and subject to an inner working.*

You will perhaps wonder, Haberden, whence all this tends; but I think a little thought will make it clear. You will understand that from such a standpoint the whole view of things is changed, and what we thought incredible and absurd may be possible enough. In short, we must look at legend and belief with other eyes, and be prepared to accept tales that had become mere fables. Indeed this is no such great demand. After all, modern science will concede as much, in a hypocritical manner; you must not, it is true, believe in witchcraft, but you may credit hypnotism; ghosts are out of date, but there is a good deal to be said for the theory of telepathy. Give superstition a Greek name, and believe in it, should almost be a proverb.

So much for my personal explanation. You sent me, Haberden, a phial, stoppered and sealed, containing a small quantity of flaky white powder, obtained from a chemist who had been dispensing it to one of your patients. I am not surprised to hear that this powder refused to yield any results to your analysis. It is a substance which was known to a few many hundred years ago, but which I never expected to have submitted to me from the shop of a modern apothecary. There seems no reason to doubt the truth of the man's tale; he no doubt got, as he says, the rather uncommon salt you prescribed from the wholesale chemist's; and it has probably remained on his shelf for twenty years, or perhaps longer. Here what we call chance and coincidence begin to work; during all these years the salt in the bottle was exposed to certain recurring variations of temperature, variations probably ranging from 40° to 80°. And, as

*it happens, such changes, recurring year after year at irregular inter-
vals, and with varying degrees of intensity and duration, have con-
stituted a process, and a process so complicated and so delicate, that
I question whether modern scientific apparatus directed with the
utmost precision could produce the same result. The white powder
you sent me is something very different from the drug you prescribed;
it is the powder from which the wine of the Sabbath, the* Vinum
Sabbati, *was prepared. No doubt you have read of the Witches'
Sabbath, and have laughed at the tales which terrified our ancestors;
the black cat, and the broomsticks, and dooms pronounced against
some old woman's cow. Since I have known the truth I have often
reflected that it is on the whole a happy thing that such burlesque
as this is believed, for it serves to conceal much that it is better
should not be known generally. However, if you care to read the
appendix to Payne Knight's monograph, you will find that the true
Sabbath was something very different, though the writer has very
nicely refrained from printing all he knew. The secrets of the true
Sabbath were the secrets of remote times surviving into the Middle
Ages, secrets of an evil science which existed long before Aryan
man entered Europe. Men and women, seduced from their homes
on specious pretences, were met by beings well qualified to assume,
as they did assume, the part of devils, and taken by their guides to
some desolate and lonely place, known to the initiate by long tradition, and unknown to all else. Perhaps it was a cave in some bare
and windswept hill, perhaps some inmost recess of a great forest,
and there the Sabbath was held. There, in the blackest hour of night,
the* Vinum Sabbati *was prepared, and this evil graal was poured
forth and offered to the neophytes, and they partook of an infernal sacrament;* sumentes calicem principis inferorum, *as an old
author well expresses it. And suddenly, each one that had drunk
found himself attended by a companion, a shape of glamour and
unearthly allurement, beckoning him apart, to share in joys more
exquisite, more piercing than the thrill of any dream, to the con-
summation of the marriage of the Sabbath. It is hard to write of
such things as these, and chiefly because that shape that allured
with loveliness was no hallucination, but, awful as it is to express,
the man himself. By the power of that Sabbath wine, a few grains
of white powder thrown into a glass of water, the house of life
was riven asunder and the human trinity dissolved, and the worm
which never dies, that which lies sleeping within us all, was made*

tangible and an external thing, and clothed with a garment of flesh. And then, in the hour of midnight, the primal fall was repeated and re-presented, and the awful thing veiled in the mythos of the Tree in the Garden was done anew. Such was the nuptiæ Sabbati.

I prefer to say no more; you, Haberden, know as well as I do that the most trivial laws of life are not to be broken with impunity; and for so terrible an act as this, in which the very inmost place of the temple was broken open and defiled, a terrible vengeance followed. What began with corruption ended also with corruption.

Underneath is the following in Dr Haberden's writing: —

The whole of the above is unfortunately strictly and entirely true. Your brother confessed all to me on that morning when I saw him in his room. My attention was first attracted to the bandaged hand, and I forced him to show it me. What I saw made me, a medical man of many years' standing, grow sick with loathing, and the story I was forced to listen to was infinitely more frightful than I could have believed possible. It has tempted me to doubt the Eternal Goodness which can permit nature to offer such hideous possibilities; and if you had not with your own eyes seen the end, I should have said to you—disbelieve it all. I have not, I think, many more weeks to live, but you are young, and may forget all this.

Joseph Haberden, M.D.

In the course of two or three months I heard that Dr Haberden had died at sea shortly after the ship left England.

Enoch Soames

MAX BEERBOHM

WHEN A BOOK about the literature of the eighteen-nineties was given by Mr Holbrook Jackson to the world, I looked eagerly in the index for SOAMES, ENOCH. I had feared he would not be there. He was not there. But everybody else was. Many writers whom I had quite forgotten, or remembered but faintly, lived again for me, they and their work, in Mr Holbrook Jackson's pages. The book was as thorough as it was brilliantly written. And thus the omission found by me was an all the deadlier record of poor Soames' failure to impress himself on his decade.

I daresay I am the only person who noticed the omission. Soames had failed so piteously as all that! Nor is there a counterpoise in the thought that if he had had some measure of success he might have passed, like those others, out of my mind, to return only at the historian's beck. It is true that had his gifts, such as they were, been acknowledged in his lifetime, he would never have made the bargain I saw him make—that strange bargain whose results have kept him always in the foreground of my memory. But it is from those very results that the full piteousness of him glares out.

Not my compassion, however, impels me to write of him. For his sake, poor fellow, I should be inclined to keep my pen out of the ink. It is ill to deride the dead. And how can I write about Enoch Soames without making him ridiculous? Or rather, how am I to hush up the horrid fact that he *was* ridiculous? I shall not be able to do that. Yet, sooner or later, write about him I must. You will see, in due course, that I have no option. And I may as well get the thing done now.

In the Summer Term of '93 a bolt from the blue flashed down on Oxford. It drove deep, it hurtlingly embedded itself in the soil. Dons and undergraduates stood around, rather pale, discussing nothing but it. Whence came it, this meteorite? From Paris. Its name? Will Rothenstein. Its aim? To do a series of twenty-four portraits in lithograph. These were to be published from the Bodley Head, London. The matter was urgent. Already the Warden of A, and the Master of B, and the Regius Professor of C, had meekly 'sat'. Dignified and doddering old men, who had never consented to sit to any one, could not withstand this dynamic little stranger. He did not sue: he invited; he did not invite: he commanded. He was twenty-one years old. He wore spectacles that flashed more than any other pair ever seen. He was a wit. He was brimful of ideas. He knew Whistler. He knew Edmond de Goncourt. He knew everyone in Paris. He knew them all by heart. He was Paris in Oxford. It was whispered that, so soon as he had polished off his selection of dons, he was going to include a few undergraduates. It was a proud day for me when I—I—was included. I liked Rothenstein not less than I feared him; and there arose between us a friendship that has grown ever warmer, and been more and more valued by me, with every passing year.

At the end of Term he settled in—or rather, meteorically into—London. It was to him I owed my first knowledge of that forever enchanting little world-in-itself, Chelsea, and my first acquaintance with Walter Sickert and other august elders who dwelt there. It was Rothenstein that took me to see, in Cambridge Street, Pimlico, a young man whose drawings were already famous among the few —Aubrey Beardsley, by name. With Rothenstein I paid my first visit to the Bodley Head. By him I was inducted into another haunt of intellect and daring, the domino room of the Café Royal.

There, on that October evening—there, in that exuberant vista of gilding and crimson velvet set amidst all those opposing mirrors and upholding caryatids, with fumes of tobacco ever rising to the painted and pagan ceiling, and with the hum of presumably cynical conversation broken into so sharply now and again by the clatter of dominoes shuffled on marble tables, I drew a deep breath, and 'This indeed,' said I to myself, 'is life!'

It was the hour before dinner. We drank vermouth. Those who knew Rothenstein were pointing him out to those who knew him only by name. Men were constantly coming in through the swing-doors and wandering slowly up and down in search of vacant tables, or of tables occupied by friends. One of those rovers interested me because I was sure he wanted to catch Rothenstein's eye. He had twice passed our table, with a hesitating look; but Rothenstein, in the thick of a disquisition on Puvis de Chavannes, had not seen him. He was a stooping, shambling person, rather tall, very pale, with longish and brownish hair. He had a thin vague beard—or rather, he had a chin on which a large number of hairs weakly curled and clustered to cover its retreat. He was an odd-looking person; but in the 'nineties odd apparitions were more frequent, I think, than they are now. The young writers of that era—and I was sure this man was a writer—strove earnestly to be distinct in aspect. This man had striven unsuccessfully. He wore a soft black hat of clerical kind but of Bohemian intention, and a grey waterproof cape which, perhaps because it was waterproof, failed to be romantic. I decided that 'dim' was the *mot juste* for him. I had already essayed to write, and was immensely keen on the *mot juste*, that Holy Grail of the period.

The dim man was now again approaching our table, and this time he made up his mind to pause in front of it. 'You don't remember me,' he said in a toneless voice.

Rothenstein brightly focussed him. 'Yes, I do,' he replied after a moment, with pride rather than effusion—pride in a retentive memory. 'Edwin Soames.'

'Enoch Soames,' said Enoch.

'Enoch Soames,' repeated Rothenstein in a tone implying that it was enough to have hit on the surname. 'We met in Paris two or three times when you were living there. We met at the Café Groche.'

'And I came to your studio once.'

'Oh yes; I was sorry I was out.'

'But you were in. You showed me some of your paintings, you know . . . I hear you're in Chelsea now.'

'Yes.'

I almost wondered that Mr Soames did not, after this monosyllable, pass along. He stood patiently there, rather like a dumb animal, rather like a donkey looking over a gate. A sad figure, his. It occurred to me that 'hungry' was perhaps the *mot juste* for him; but—hungry for what? He looked as if he had little appetite for anything. I was sorry for him; and Rothenstein, though he had not invited him to Chelsea, did ask him to sit down and have something to drink.

Seated, he was more self-assertive. He flung back the wings of his cape with a gesture which—had not those wings been water-proof—might have seemed to hurl defiance at things in general. And he ordered an absinthe. '*Je me tiens toujours fidèle*,' he told Rothenstein, '*à la sorcière glauque*.'

'It is bad for you,' said Rothenstein drily.

'Nothing is bad for one,' answered Soames. '*Dans ce monde il n'y a ni de bien ni de mal*.'

'Nothing good and nothing bad? How do you mean?'

'I explained it all in the preface to *Negations*.'

'*Negations*?'

'Yes; I gave you a copy of it.'

'Oh yes, of course. But did you explain—for instance—that there was no such thing as bad or good grammar?'

'N-no,' said Soames. 'Of course in Art there is the good and the evil. But in Life—no.' He was rolling a cigarette. He had weak white hands, not well washed, and with finger-tips much stained by nicotine. 'In Life there are illusions of good and evil, but'—his voice trailed away to a murmur in which the words 'vieux jeu' and 'rococo' were faintly audible. I think he felt he was not doing himself justice, and feared that Rothenstein was going to point out fallacies. Anyway, he cleared his throat and said '*Parlons d'autre chose*.'

It occurs to you that he was a fool? It didn't to me. I was young, and had not the clarity of judgment that Rothenstein already had. Soames was quite five or six years older than either of us. Also, he had written a book.

It was wonderful to have written a book.

If Rothenstein had not been there, I should have revered Soames. Even as it was, I respected him. And I was very near indeed to reverence when he said he had another book coming out soon. I asked if I might ask what kind of book it was to be.

'My poems,' he answered. Rothenstein asked if this was to be the title of the book. The poet meditated on this suggestion, but said he rather thought of giving the book no title at all. 'If a book is good in itself—' he murmured, waving his cigarette.

Rothenstein objected that absence of title might be bad for the sale of a book. 'If,' he urged, 'I went into a bookseller's and said simply "Have you got?" or "Have you a copy of?" how would they know what I wanted?'

'Oh, of course I should have my name on the cover,' Soames answered earnestly. 'And I rather want,' he added, looking hard at Rothenstein, 'to have a drawing of myself as frontispiece.' Rothenstein admitted that this was a capital idea, and mentioned that he was going into the country and would be there for some time. He then looked at his watch, exclaimed at the hour, paid the waiter, and went away with me to dinner. Soames remained at his post of fidelity to the glaucous witch.

'Why were you so determined not to draw him?' I asked.

'Draw him? Him? How can one draw a man who doesn't exist?'

'He is dim,' I admitted. But my *mot juste* fell flat. Rothenstein repeated that Soames was non-existent.

Still, Soames had written a book. I asked if Rothenstein had read *Negations*. He said he had looked into it, 'but,' he added crisply, 'I don't profess to know anything about writing.' A reservation very characteristic of the period! Painters would not then allow that any one outside their own order had a right to any opinion about painting. This law (graven on the tablets brought down by Whistler from the summit of Fujiyama) imposed certain limitations. If other arts than painting were not utterly unintelligible to all but the men who practised them, the law tottered—the Monroe Doctrine, as it were, did not hold good. Therefore no painter would offer an opinion of a book without warning you at any rate that his opinion was worthless. No one is a better judge of literature than Rothenstein; but it wouldn't have done to tell him so in those days; and I knew that I must form an unaided judgment on *Negations*.

Not to buy a book of which I had met the author face to face would have been for me in those days an impossible act of self-denial. When I returned to Oxford for the Christmas Term I had duly secured *Negations*. I used to keep it lying carelessly on the table in my room, and whenever a friend took it up and asked what it was about I would say, 'Oh, it's rather a remarkable book. It's by a man whom I know.' Just 'what it was about' I never was able to say. Head or tail was just what I hadn't made of that slim green volume. I found in the preface no clue to the exiguous labyrinth of contents, and in that labyrinth nothing to explain the preface.

Lean near to life. Lean very near—nearer.
Life is web, and therein nor warp nor woof is, but web only.
It is for this I am Catholick in church and in thought, yet do let
swift Mood weave there what the shuttle of Mood wills.

These were the opening phrases of the preface, but those which
followed were less easy to understand. Then came 'Stark: A *Conte*',
about a midinette who, so far as I could gather, murdered, or was
about to murder, a mannequin. It seemed to me like a story by
Catulle Mendès in which the translator had either skipped or cut
out every alternate sentence. Next, a dialogue between Pan and St
Ursula—lacking, I rather felt, in 'snap'. Next, some aphorisms
(entitled ἀφορίσματα). Throughout, in fact, there was a great
variety of form; and the forms had evidently been wrought with
much care. It was rather the substance that eluded me. Was there,
I wondered, any substance at all? It did now occur to me: suppose
Enoch Soames was a fool! Up cropped a rival hypothesis: suppose
I was! I inclined to give Soames the benefit of the doubt. I had
read *L'Après-midi d'un Faune* without extracting a glimmer of
meaning. Yet Mallarmé—of course—was a Master. How was I to
know that Soames wasn't another? There was a sort of music in
his prose, not indeed arresting, but perhaps, I thought, haunting,
and laden perhaps with meanings as deep as Mallarmé's own. I
awaited his poems with an open mind.

And I looked forward to them with positive impatience after I
had had a second meeting with him. This was on an evening in
January. Going into the aforesaid domino room, I passed a table
at which sat a pale man with an open book before him. He looked
from his book to me, and I looked back over my shoulder with a
vague sense that I ought to have recognised him. I returned to
pay my respects. After exchanging a few words, I said with a
glance to the open book, 'I see I am interrupting you,' and was
about to pass on, but 'I prefer,' Soames replied in his toneless
voice, 'to be interrupted,' and I obeyed his gesture that I should sit
down.

I asked him if he often read here. 'Yes; things of this kind I read
here,' he answered, indicating the title of his book—*The Poems of
Shelley*.

'Anything that you really'—and I was going to say 'admire?'
But I cautiously left my sentence unfinished, and was glad that

I had done so, for he said, with unwonted emphasis, 'Anything second-rate.'

I had read little of Shelley, but 'Of course,' I murmured, 'he's very uneven.'

'I should have thought evenness was just what was wrong with him. A deadly evenness. That's why I read him here. The noise of this place breaks the rhythm. He's tolerable here.' Soames took up the book and glanced through the pages. He laughed. Soames' laugh was a short, single and mirthless sound from the throat, unaccompanied by any movement of the face or brightening of the eyes. 'What a period!' he uttered, laying the book down. And 'What a country!' he added.

I asked rather nervously if he didn't think Keats had more or less held his own against the drawbacks of time and place. He admitted that there were 'passages in Keats', but did not specify them. Of 'the older men', as he called them, he seemed to like only Milton. 'Milton,' he said, 'wasn't sentimental.' Also 'Milton had a dark insight.' And again, 'I can always read Milton in the reading-room.'

'The reading-room?'

'Of the British Museum. I go there every day.'

'You do? I've only been there once. I'm afraid I found it rather a depressing place. It—it seemed to sap one's vitality.'

'It does. That's why I go there. The lower one's vitality, the more sensitive one is to great art. I live near the Museum. I have rooms in Dyott Street.'

'And you go round to the reading-room to read Milton?'

'Usually Milton.' He looked at me. 'It was Milton,' he certificatively added, 'who converted me to Diabolism.'

'Diabolism? Oh yes? Really?' said I, with that vague discomfort and that intense desire to be polite which one feels when a man speaks of his own religion. 'You—worship the Devil?'

Soames shook his head. 'It's not exactly worship,' he qualified, sipping his absinthe. 'It's more a matter of trusting and encouraging.'

'Ah, yes . . . But I had rather gathered from the preface to *Negations* that you were a—a Catholic.'

'*Je l'étais à cette époque.* Perhaps I still am. Yes, I'm a Catholic Diabolist.'

This profession he made in an almost cursory tone. I could see that what was upmost in his mind was the fact that I had read *Negations*. His pale eyes had for the first time gleamed. I felt as one who is about to be examined, *viva voce*, on the very subject in which he is shakiest. I hastily asked him how soon his poems were to be published. 'Next week,' he told me.

'And are they to be published without a title?'

'No. I found a title, at last. But I shan't tell you what it is,' as though I had been so impertinent as to inquire. 'I am not sure that it wholly satisfies me. But it is the best I can find. It does suggest something of the quality of the poems . . . Strange growths, natural and wild; yet exquisite,' he added, 'and many-hued, and full of poisons.'

I asked him what he thought of Baudelaire. He uttered the snort that was his laugh, and 'Baudelaire,' he said, 'was a *bourgeois malgré lui.*' France had had only one poet: Villon: 'and two-thirds of Villon were sheer journalism.' Verlaine was 'an *épicier malgré lui.*' Altogether, rather to my surprise, he rated French literature lower than English. There were 'passages' in Villiers de l'Isle Adam. But, 'I,' he summed up, 'owe nothing to France.' He nodded at me. 'You'll see,' he predicted.

I did not, when the time came, quite see that. I thought the author of *Fungoids* did—unconsciously, no doubt—owe something to the young Parisian décadents, or to the young English ones who owed something to *them*. I still think so. The little book—bought by me in Oxford—lies before me as I write. Its pale grey buckram cover and silver lettering have not worn well. Nor have its contents. Through these, with a melancholy interest, I have again been looking. They are not much. But at the time of their publication I had a vague suspicion that they *might* be. I suppose it is my capacity for faith, not poor Soames' work, that is weaker than it once was . . .

To a Young Woman

Thou art, who hast not been!
 Pale tunes irresolute
 And traceries of old sounds
 Blown from a rotted flute
Mingle with noise of cymbals rouged with rust,
Nor not strange forms and epicene
 Lie bleeding in the dust,
  Being wounded with wounds.

> For this it is
> That is thy counterpart
> Of age-long mockeries
> *Thou hast not been nor art!*

There seemed to me a certain inconsistency as between the first and last lines of this. I tried, with bent brows, to resolve the discord. But I did not take my failure as wholly incompatible with a meaning in Soames' mind. Might it not rather indicate the depth of his meaning? As for the craftsmanship, 'rouged with rust' seemed to me a fine stroke, and 'nor not' instead of 'and' had a curious felicity. I wondered who the Young Woman was, and what she had made of it all. I sadly suspect that Soames could not have made more of it than she. Yet, even now, if one doesn't try to make any sense at all of the poem, and reads it just for the sound, there is a certain grace of cadence. Soames was an artist—in so far as he was anything, poor fellow!

It seemed to me, when I first read *Fungoids*, that, oddly enough, the Diabolistic side of him was the best. Diabolism seemed to be a cheerful, even a wholesome, influence in his life.

NOCTURNE

> Round and round the shutter'd Square
> I stroll'd with the Devil's arm in mine.
> No sound but the scrape of his hoofs was there
> And the ring of his laughter and mine.
>   We had drunk black wine.
>
> *I scream'd 'I will race you, Master!'*
> *'What matter,' he shriek'd, 'tonight*
> *Which of us runs the faster?*
> *There is nothing to fear tonight*
>   *In the foul moon's light!'*
>
> Then I look'd him in the eyes,
> And I laugh'd full shrill at the lie he told
> And the gnawing fear he would fain disguise.
> It was true, what I'd time and again been told:
>   He was old—old.

There was, I felt, quite a swing about that first stanza—a joyous and rollicking note of comradeship. The second was slightly hysterical perhaps. But I liked the third: it was so bracingly unorthodox, even according to the tenets of Soames' peculiar sect in the faith. Not much 'trusting and encouraging' here! Soames triumphantly exposing the Devil as a liar, and laughing 'full shrill', cut a quite heartening figure, I thought—then! Now, in the light of what befell, none of his poems depresses me so much as 'Nocturne.'

I looked out for what the metropolitan reviewers would have to say. They seemed to fall into two classes: those who had little to say and those who had nothing. The second class was the larger, and the words of the first were cold; insomuch that

Strikes a note of modernity throughout. . . These tripping numbers.—*Preston Telegraph.*

was the sole lure offered in advertisements by Soames' publisher. I had hoped that when next I met the poet I could congratulate him on having made a stir; for I fancied he was not so sure of his intrinsic greatness as he seemed. I was but able to say, rather coarsely, when next I did see him, that I hoped *Fungoids* was 'selling splendidly.' He looked at me across his glass of absinthe and asked if I had bought a copy. His publisher had told him that three had been sold. I laughed, as at a jest.

'You don't suppose I *care*, do you?' he said, with something like a snarl. I disclaimed the notion. He added that he was not a tradesman. I said mildly that I wasn't, either, and murmured that an artist who gave truly new and great things to the world had always to wait long for recognition. He said he cared not a sou for recognition. I agreed that the act of creation was its own reward.

His moroseness might have alienated me if I had regarded myself as a nobody. But ah! hadn't both John Lane and Aubrey Beardsley suggested that I should write an essay for the great new venture that was afoot—*The Yellow Book?* And hadn't Henry Harland, as editor, accepted my essay? And wasn't it to be in the very first number? At Oxford I was still *in statu pupillari.* In London I regarded myself as very much indeed a graduate now—one whom no Soames could ruffle. Partly to show off, partly in sheer goodwill, I told Soames he ought to contribute to *The Yellow Book*. He uttered from the throat a sound of scorn for that publication.

Nevertheless, I did, a day or two later, tentatively ask Harland if he knew anything of the work of a man called Enoch Soames. Harland paused in the midst of his characteristic stride around the room, threw up his hands towards the ceiling, and groaned aloud: he had often met 'that absurd creature' in Paris, and this very morning had received some poems in manuscript from him.

'Has he *no* talent?' I asked.

'He has an income. He's all right.' Harland was the most joyous of men and most generous of critics, and he hated to talk of anything about which he couldn't be enthusiastic. So I dropped the subject of Soames. The news that Soames had an income did take the edge off solicitude. I learned afterwards that he was the son of an unsuccessful and deceased bookseller in Preston, but had inherited an annuity of £500 from a married aunt, and had no surviving relatives of any kind. Materially, then, he was 'all right'. But there was still a spiritual pathos about him, sharpened for me now by the possibility that even the praises of the *Preston Telegraph* might not have been forthcoming had he not been the son of a Preston man. He had a sort of weak doggedness which I could not but admire. Neither he nor his work received the slightest encouragement; but he persisted in behaving as a personage: always he kept his dingy little flag flying. Wherever congregated the *jeunes féroces* of the arts, in whatever Soho restaurant they had just discovered, in whatever music-hall they were most frequenting, there was Soames in the midst of them, or rather on the fringe of them, a dim but inevitable figure. He never sought to propitiate his fellow-writers, never bated a jot of his arrogance about his own work or of his contempt for theirs. To the painters he was respectful, even humble; but for the poets and prosaists of *The Yellow Book,* and later of *The Savoy*, he had never a word but of scorn. He wasn't resented. It didn't occur to anybody that he or his Catholic Diabolism mattered. When, in the autumn of '96, he brought out (at his own expense, this time) a third book, his last book, nobody said a word for or against it. I meant, but forgot, to buy it. I never saw it, and am ashamed to say I don't even remember what it was called. But I did, at the time of its publication, say to Rothenstein that I thought poor old Soames was really a rather tragic figure, and that I believed he would literally die for want of recognition. Rothenstein scoffed.

D

He said I was trying to get credit for a kind heart which I didn't possess; and perhaps this was so. But at the private view of the New English Art Club, a few weeks later, I beheld a pastel portrait of 'Enoch Soames, Esq.' It was very like him, and very like Rothenstein to have done it. Soames was standing near it, in his soft hat and his waterproof cape, all through the afternoon. Anybody who knew him would have recognised the portrait at a glance, but nobody who didn't know him would have recognised the portrait from its bystander: it 'existed' so much more than he; it was bound to. Also, it had not that expression of faint happiness which on this day was discernible, yes, in Soames' countenance. Fame had breathed on him. Twice again in the course of the month I went to the New English, and on both occasions Soames himself was on view there. Looking back, I regard the close of that exhibition as having been virtually the close of his career. He had felt the breath of Fame against his cheek—so late, for such a little while; and at its withdrawal he gave in, gave up, gave out. He, who had never looked strong or well, looked ghastly now—a shadow of the shade he had once been. He still frequented the domino room, but, having lost all wish to excite curiosity, he no longer read books there. 'You read only at the Museum now?' asked I, with attempted cheerfulness. He said he never went there now. 'No absinthe there,' he muttered. It was the sort of thing that in the old days he would have said for effect; but it carried conviction now. Absinthe, erst but a point in the 'personality' he had striven so hard to build up, was solace and necessity now. He no longer called it 'la sorcière glauque.' He had shed away all his French phrases. He had become a plain, unvarnished, Preston man.

Failure, if it be a plain, unvarnished, complete failure, and even though it be a squalid failure, has always a certain dignity. I avoided Soames because he made me feel rather vulgar. John Lane had published, by this time, two little books of mine, and they had had a pleasant little success of esteem. I was a—slight but definite—'personality'. Frank Harris had engaged me to kick up my heels in *The Saturday Review*, Alfred Harmsworth was letting me do likewise in the *Daily Mail*. I was just what Soames wasn't. And he shamed my gloss. Had I known that he really and firmly believed in the greatness of what he as an artist had achieved, I might not have shunned him. No man who hasn't lost his vanity can be held to have altogether failed. Soames' dignity was an illusion of mine.

One day in the first week of June, 1897, that illusion went. But on the evening of that day Soames went too.

I had been out most of the morning, and, as it was too late to reach home in time for luncheon, I sought 'the Vingtième.' This little place—Restaurant du Vingtième Siècle, to give it its full title—had been discovered in '96 by the poets and prosaists, but had now been more or less abandoned in favour of some later find. I don't think it lived long enough to justify its name; but at that time there it still was, in Greek Street, a few doors from Soho Square, and almost opposite to that house where, in the first years of the century, a little girl, and with her a boy named De Quincey, made nightly encampment in darkness and hunger among dust and rats and old legal parchments. The Vingtième was but a small whitewashed room, leading out into the street at one end and into a kitchen at the other. The proprietor and cook was a Frenchman, known to us as Monsieur Vingtième; the waiters were his two daughters, Rose and Berthe; and the food, according to faith, was good. The tables were so narrow, and were set so close together, that there was space for twelve of them, six jutting from either wall.

Only the two nearest to the door, as I went in, were occupied. On one side sat a tall, flashy, rather Mephistophelian man whom I had seen from time to time in the domino room and elsewhere. On the other side sat Soames. They made a queer contrast in that sunlit room—Soames sitting haggard in that hat and cape which nowhere at any season had I seen him doff, and this other, this keenly vital man, at sight of whom I more than ever wondered whether he were a diamond merchant, a conjuror, or the head of a private detective agency. I was sure Soames didn't want my company; but I asked, as it would have seemed brutal not to, whether I might join him, and took the chair opposite to his. He was smoking a cigarette, with an untasted salmi of something on his plate and a half-empty bottle of Sauterne before him; and he was quite silent. I said that the preparations for the Jubilee made London impossible. (I rather liked them, really.) I professed a wish to go right away till the whole thing was over. In vain did I attune myself to his gloom. He seemed not to hear me nor even to see me. I felt that his behaviour made me ridiculous in the eyes of the other man. The gangway between the two rows of tables at the Vingtième was hardly more than two feet wide (Rose and Berthe, in their minis-

trations, had always to edge past each other, quarrelling in whispers
as they did so), and any one at the table abreast of yours was practically at yours. I thought our neighbour was amused at my failure
to interest Soames, and so, as I could not explain to him that my
insistence was merely charitable, I became silent. Without turning
my head, I had him well within my range of vision. I hoped I looked
less vulgar than he in contrast with Soames. I was sure he was not
an Englishman, but what *was* his nationality? Though his jet-black
hair was *en brosse*, I did not think he was French. To Berthe, who
waited on him, he spoke French fluently, but with a hardly native
idiom and accent. I gathered that this was his first visit to the
Vingtième; but Berthe was off-hand in her manner to him: he had
not made a good impression. His eyes were handsome, but—like
the Vingtième's tables—too narrow and set too close together. His
nose was predatory, and the points of his moustache, waxed up
beyond his nostrils, gave a fixity to his smile. Decidedly, he was
sinister. And my sense of discomfort in his presence was intensified
by the scarlet waistcoat which tightly, and so unseasonably in June,
sheathed his ample chest. This waistcoat wasn't wrong merely
because of the heat, either. It was somehow all wrong in itself. It
wouldn't have done on Christmas morning. It would have struck
a jarring note at the first night of *Hernani*. I was trying to account
for its wrongness when Soames suddenly and strangely broke silence.
'A hundred years hence!' he murmured, as in a trance.

'We shall not be here!' I briskly but fatuously added.

'We shall not be here. No,' he droned, 'but the Museum will
still be just where it is. And the reading-room, just where it is. And
people will be able to go and read there.' He inhaled sharply, and
a spasm as of actual pain contorted his features.

I wondered what train of thought poor Soames had been following. He did not enlighten me when he said, after a long pause, 'You
think I haven't minded.'

'Minded what, Soames?'

'Neglect. Failure.'

'*Failure?*' I said heartily. 'Failure?' I repeated vaguely. 'Neglect
—yes, perhaps; but that's quite another matter. Of course you haven't
been—appreciated. But what then? Any artist who—who gives—'
What I wanted to say was, 'Any artist who gives truly new and great
things to the world has always to wait long for recognition'; but
the flattery would not out: in the face of his misery, a misery

so genuine and so unmasked, my lips would not say the words. And then—he said them for me. I flushed. 'That's what you were going to say, isn't it?' he asked.

'How did you know?'

'It's what you said to me three years ago, when *Fungoids* was published.' I flushed the more. I need not have done so at all, for 'It's the only important thing I ever heard you say,' he continued. 'And I've never forgotten it. It's a true thing. It's a horrible truth. But—d'you remember what I answered? I said "I don't care a sou for recognition." And you believed me. You've gone on believing I'm above that sort of thing. You're shallow. What should *you* know of the feelings of a man like me? You imagine that a great artist's faith in himself and in the verdict of posterity is enough to keep him happy. . . . You've never guessed at the bitterness and loneliness, the'—his voice broke; but presently he resumed, speaking with a force that I had never known in him. 'Posterity! What use is it to *me*? A dead man doesn't know what people are visiting his grave—visiting his birthplace—putting up tablets to him—unveiling statues of him. A dead man can't read the books that are written about him. A hundred years hence! Think of it! If I could come back to life *then*—just for a few hours—and go to the reading-room, and *read*! Or better still: if I could be projected, now, at this moment, into the future, into that reading-room, just for this one afternoon! I'd sell myself body and soul to the devil, for that! Think of the pages and pages in the catalogue: "SOAMES, ENOCH" endlessly—endless editions, commentaries, prolegomena, biographies' —but here he was interrupted by a sudden loud creak of the chair at the next table. Our neighbour had half risen from his place. He was leaning towards us, apologetically intrusive.

'Excuse—permit me,' he said softly. 'I have been unable not to hear. Might I take a liberty? In this little restaurant-sans-façon'— he spread wide his hands—'might I, as the phrase is, "cut in"?'

I could but signify our acquiescence. Berthe had appeared at the kitchen door, thinking the stranger wanted his bill. He waved her away with his cigar, and in another moment had seated himself beside me, commanding a full view of Soames.

'Though not an Englishman,' he explained, 'I know my London well, Mr Soames. Your name and fame—Mr Beerbohm's too—are known to me. Your point is: who am *I*?' He glanced quickly over his shoulder, and in a lowered voice said 'I am the Devil.'

I couldn't help it: I laughed. I tried not to, I knew there was nothing to laugh at, my rudeness shamed me, but—I laughed with increasing volume. The Devil's quiet dignity, the surprise and disgust of his raised eyebrows, did but the more dissolve me. I rocked to and fro, I lay back aching. I behaved deplorably.

'I am a gentleman, and,' he said with intense emphasis, 'I thought I was in the company of *gentlemen.*'

'Don't!' I gasped faintly. 'Oh, don't!'

'Curious, *nicht wahr?*' I heard him say to Soames. 'There is a type of person to whom the very mention of my name is—oh-so-awfully-funny! In your theatres the dullest comédien needs only to say "The Devil!" and right away they give him "the loud laugh that speaks the vacant mind". Is it not so?'

I had now just breath enough to offer my apologies. He accepted them, but coldly, and re-addressed himself to Soames.

'I am a man of business,' he said, 'and always I would put things through "right now", as they say in the States. You are a poet. *Les affaires*—you detest them. So be it. But with me you will deal, eh? What you have said just now gives me furiously to hope.'

Soames had not moved, except to light a fresh cigarette. He sat crouched forward, with his elbows squared on the table, and his head just above the level of his hands, staring up at the Devil. 'Go on,' he nodded. I had no remnant of laughter in me now.

'It will be the more pleasant, our little deal,' the Devil went on, 'because you are—I mistake not?—a Diabolist.'

'A Catholic Diabolist,' said Soames.

The Devil accepted the reservation genially. 'You wish,' he resumed, 'to visit now—this afternoon as-ever-is—the reading-room of the British Museum, yes? but of a hundred years hence, yes? *Parfaitement.* Time—an illusion. Past and future—they are as ever-present as the present, or at any rate only what you call "just-round-the-corner". I switch you on to any date. I project you—pouf! You wish to be in the reading-room just as it will be on the afternoon of June 3rd, 1997? You wish to find yourself standing in that room, just past the swing-doors, this very minute, yes? and to stay there till closing time? Am I right?'

Soames nodded.

The Devil looked at his watch. 'Ten past two,' he said. 'Closing time in summer same then as now: seven o'clock. That will give you almost five hours. At seven o'clock—pouf!—you find yourself

again here, sitting at this table. I am dining tonight *dans le monde*
—*dans le higlif*. That concludes my present visit to your great city.
I come and fetch you here, Mr Soames, on my way home.'

'Home?' I echoed.

'Be it never so humble!' said the Devil lightly.

'All right,' said Soames.

'Soames!' I entreated. But my friend moved not a muscle.

The Devil had made as though to stretch forth his hand across
the table and touch Soames' forearm; but he paused in his gesture.

'A hundred years hence, as now,' he smiled, 'no smoking allowed
in the reading-room. You would better therefore—'

Soames removed the cigarette from his mouth and dropped it
into his glass of Sauterne.

'Soames!' again I cried. 'Can't you'—but the Devil had now
stretched forth his hand across the table. He brought it slowly down
on—the table-cloth. Soames' chair was empty. His cigarette floated
sodden in his wine-glass. There was no other trace of him.

For a few moments the Devil let his hand rest where it lay,
gazing at me out of the corners of his eyes, vulgarly triumphant.

A shudder shook me. With an effort I controlled myself and rose
from my chair. 'Very clever,' I said condescendingly. 'But—*The
Time Machine* is a delightful book, don't you think? So entirely
original!'

'You are pleased to sneer,' said the Devil, who had also risen,
'but it is one thing to write about a not possible machine; it is quite
other thing to be a Supernatural Power.' All the same, I had scored.

Berthe had come forth at the sound of our rising. I explained
to her that Mr Soames had been called away, and that both he and
I would be dining here. It was not until I was out in the open air
that I began to feel giddy. I have but the haziest recollection of
what I did, where I wandered, in the glaring sunshine of that
endless afternoon. I remember the sound of carpenters' hammers
all along Piccadilly, and the bare chaotic look of the half-erected
'stands'. Was it in the Green Park, or in Kensington Gardens, or
where was it that I sat on a chair beneath a tree, trying to read
an evening paper? There was a phrase in the leading article that
went on repeating itself in my fagged mind—'Little is hidden from
this august Lady full of the garnered wisdom of sixty years of
Sovereignty'. I remember wildly conceiving a letter (to reach
Windsor by express messenger told to await answer):

MADAM,—Well knowing that your Majesty is full of the garnered wisdom of sixty years of Sovereignty, I venture to ask your advice in the following delicate matter. Mr Enoch Soames, whose poems you may or may not know,' . . .

Was there *no* way of helping him—saving him? A bargain was a bargain, and I was the last man to aid or abet anyone in wriggling out of a reasonable obligation. I wouldn't have lifted a little finger to save Faust. But poor Soames!—doomed to pay without respite an eternal price for nothing but a fruitless search and a bitter dis-illusioning . . .

Odd and uncanny it seemed to me that he, Soames, in the flesh, in the waterproof cape, was at this moment living in the last decade of the next century, poring over books not yet written, and seeing and seen by men not yet born. Uncannier and odder still, that tonight and evermore he would be in Hell. Assuredly, truth was stranger than fiction.

Endless that afternoon was. Almost I wished I had gone with Soames—not indeed to stay in the reading-room, but to sally forth for a brisk sight-seeing walk around a new London. I wandered restlessly out of the Park I had sat in. Vainly I tried to imagine myself an ardent tourist from the eighteenth century. Intolerable was the strain of the slow-passing and empty minutes. Long before seven o'clock I was back at the Vingtième.

I sat there just where I had sat for luncheon. Air came in listlessly through the open door behind me. Now and again Rose or Berthe appeared for a moment. I had told them I would not order any dinner till Mr Soames came. A hurdy-gurdy began to play, abruptly drowning the noise of a quarrel between some Frenchmen further up the street. Whenever the tune was changed I heard the quarrel still raging. I had bought another evening paper on my way. I unfolded it. My eyes gazed ever away from it to the clock over the kitchen door . . .

Five minutes, now, to the hour! I remembered that clocks in restaurants are kept five minutes fast. I concentrated my eyes on the paper. I vowed I would not look away from it again. I held it upright, at its full width, close to my face, so that I had no view of anything but it . . . Rather a tremulous sheet? Only because of the draught, I told myself.

My arms gradually became stiff; they ached; but I could not drop them—now. I had a suspicion, I had a certainty. Well, what then? . . . What else had I come for? Yet I held tight that barrier of newspaper. Only the sound of Berthe's brisk footstep from the kitchen enabled me, forced me, to drop it, and to utter:

'What shall we have to eat, Soames?'

'*Il est souffrant, ce pauvre Monsieur Soames?*' asked Berthe.

'He's only—tired.' I asked her to get some wine—Burgundy— and whatever food might be ready. Soames sat crouched forward against the table, exactly as when last I had seen him. It was as though he had never moved—he who had moved so unimaginably far. Once or twice in the afternoon it had for an instant occurred to me that perhaps his journey was not to be fruitless—that perhaps we had all been wrong in our estimate of the works of Enoch Soames. That we had been horribly right was horribly clear from the look of him. But 'Don't be discouraged,' I falteringly said. 'Perhaps it's only that you—didn't leave enough time. Two, three centuries hence, perhaps—'

'Yes,' his voice came. 'I've thought of that.'

'And now—now for the immediate future! Where are you going to hide? How would it be if you caught the Paris express from Charing Cross? Almost an hour to spare. Don't go on to Paris. Stop at Calais. Live in Calais. He'd never think of looking for you in Calais.'

'It's like my luck,' he said, 'to spend my last hours on earth with an ass.' But I was not offended. 'And a treacherous ass,' he strangely added, tossing across to me a crumpled bit of paper which he had been holding in his hand. I glanced at the writing on it—some sort of gibberish, apparently. I laid it impatiently aside.

'Come, Soames! pull yourself together! This isn't a mere matter of life and death. It's a question of eternal torment, mind you! You don't mean to say you're going to wait limply here till the Devil comes to fetch you?'

'I can't do anything else. I've no choice.'

'Come! This is "trusting and encouraging" with a vengeance! This is Diabolism run mad!' I filled his glass with wine. 'Surely, now that you've *seen* the brute—'

'It's no good abusing him.'

'You must admit there's nothing Miltonic about him, Soames.'

'I don't say he's not rather different from what I expected.'

D*

'He's a vulgarian, he's a swell-mobsman, he's the sort of man who hangs about the corridors of trains going to the Riviera and steals ladies' jewel-cases. Imagine eternal torment presided over by *him*!'

'You don't suppose I look forward to it, do you?'

'Then why not slip quietly out of the way?'

Again and again I filled his glass, and always, mechanically, he emptied it; but the wine kindled no spark of enterprise in him. He did not eat, and I myself ate hardly at all. I did not in my heart believe that any dash for freedom could save him. The chase would be swift, the capture certain. But better anything than this passive, meek, miserable waiting. I told Soames that for the honour of the human race he ought to make some show of resistance. He asked what the human race had ever done for him. 'Besides,' he said, 'can't you understand that I'm in his power? You saw him touch me, didn't you? There's an end of it. I've no will. I'm sealed.'

I made a gesture of despair. He went on repeating the word 'sealed'. I began to realise that the wine had clouded his brain. No wonder! Foodless he had gone into futurity, foodless he still was. I urged him to eat at any rate some bread. It was maddening to think that he, who had so much to tell, might tell nothing. 'How was it all,' I asked, 'yonder? Come! Tell me your adventures.'

'They'd make first-rate "copy", wouldn't they?'

'I'm awfully sorry for you, Soames, and I make all possible allowances; but what earthly right have you to insinuate that I should make "copy", as you call it, out of you?'

The poor fellow pressed his hands to his forehead. 'I don't know, he said. 'I had some reason, I'm sure . . . I'll try to remember.'

'That's right. Try to remember everything. Eat a little more bread. What did the reading-room look like?'

'Much as usual,' he at length muttered.

'Many people there?'

'Usual sort of number.'

'What did they look like?'

Soames tried to visualise them. 'They all,' he presently remembered, 'looked very like one another.'

My mind took a fearsome leap. 'All dressed in Jaeger?'

'Yes. I think so. Greyish-yellowish stuff.'

'A sort of uniform?' He nodded. 'With a number on it, perhaps? —a number on a large disc of metal sewn to the left sleeve?

DKF 78,910—that sort of thing?' It was even so. 'And all of them —men and women alike—looking very well-cared-for? very Utopian? and smelling rather strongly of carbolic? and all of them quite hairless?' I was right every time. Soames was only not sure whether the men and women were hairless or shorn. 'I hadn't time to look at them very closely,' he explained.

'No, of course not. But—'

'They stared at *me*, I can tell you. I attracted a great deal of attention.' At last he had done that! 'I think I rather scared them. They moved away whenever I came near. They followed me about at a distance, wherever I went. The men at the round desk in the middle seemed to have a sort of panic whenever I went to make inquiries.'

'What did you do when you arrived?'

Well, he had gone straight to the catalogue, of course—to the S volumes, and had stood long before SN-SOF, unable to take this volume out of the shelf, because his heart was beating so . . . At first, he said, he wasn't disappointed—he only thought there was some new arrangement. He went to the middle desk and asked where the catalogue of *twentieth*-century books was kept. He gathered that there was still only one catalogue. Again he looked up his name, stared at the three little pasted slips he had known so well. Then he went and sat down for a long time . . .

'And then,' he droned, 'I looked up the *Dictionary of National Biography* and some encyclopædias . . . I went back to the middle desk and asked what was the best modern book on late nineteenth-century literature. They told me Mr T. K. Nupton's book was considered the best. I looked it up in the catalogue and filled in a form for it. It was brought to me. My name wasn't in the index, but— Yes!' he said with a sudden change of tone. 'That's what I'd forgotten. Where's that bit of paper? Give it me back.'

I, too, had forgotten that cryptic screed. I found it fallen on the floor, and handed it to him.

He smoothed it out, nodding and smiling at me disagreeably. 'I found myself glancing through Nupton's book,' he resumed. 'Not very easy reading. Some sort of phonetic spelling . . . All the modern books I saw were phonetic.'

'Then I don't want to hear any more, Soames, please.'

'The proper names seemed all to be spelt in the old way. But for that, I mightn't have noticed my own name.'

'Your own name? Really? Soames, I'm *very* glad.'

'And yours.'

'No!'

'I thought I should find you waiting here tonight. So I took the trouble to copy out the passage. Read it.'

I snatched the paper. Soames' handwriting was characteristically dim. It, and the noisome spelling, and my excitement, made me all the slower to grasp what T. K. Nupton was driving at.

The document lies before me at this moment. Strange that the words I here copy out for you were copied out for me by poor Soames just seventy-eight years hence . . .

From p. 234 of 'Inglish Littracher 1890–1900', bi T. K. Nupton, published bi th Stait, 1992:

'Fr. egzarmpl, a riter ov th time, naimd Max Beerbohm, hoo woz stil alive in th twentieth senchri, rote a stauri in wich e pautraid an immajnari karrakter kauld "Enoch Soames"—a thurdrait poit hoo beleevz imself a grate jeneus an maix a bargin with th Devil in auder ter no wot posterriti thinx ov im! It iz a sumwot labud sattire but not without vallu az showing hou seriusli the yung men ov th aiteen-ninetiz took themselvz. Nou that the littreri profeshn haz bin auganized az a department of publik servis, our riters hav found their levvl an hav lernt ter doo their duti without thort ov th morro. "Th laibrer is werthi ov hiz hire", an that iz aul. Thank hevvn we hav no Enoch Soameses amung us to-dai!'

I found that by murmuring the words aloud (a device which I commend to my reader) I was able to master them, little by little. The clearer they became, the greater was my bewilderment, my distress and horror. The whole thing was a nightmare. Afar, the great grisly background of what was in store for the poor dear art of letters; here, at the table, fixing on me a gaze that made me hot all over, the poor fellow whom—whom evidently . . . but no: whatever down-grade my character might take in coming years, I should never be such a brute as to—

Again I examined the screed. 'Immajnari'—but here Soames was, no more imaginary, alas! than I And 'labud'—what on earth was that? (To this day, I have never made out that word.) 'It's all very —baffling,' I at length stammered.

Soames said nothing, but cruelly did not cease to look at me.

'Are you sure,' I temporised, 'quite sure you copied the thing out correctly?'

'Quite.'

'Well, then it's this wretched Nupton who must have made— must be going to make—some idiotic mistake . . . Look here, Soames! you know me better than to suppose that I . . . After all, the name "Max Beerbohm" is not at all an uncommon one, and there must be several Enoch Soameses running around—or rather, "Enoch Soames" is a name that might occur to anyone writing a story. And I don't write stories: I'm an essayist, an observer, a recorder . . . I admit that it's an extraordinary coincidence. But you must see—'

'I see the whole thing,' said Soames quietly. And he added, with a touch of his old manner, but with more dignity than I had ever known in him, *'Parlons d'autre chose.'*

I accepted that suggestion very promptly. I returned straight to the more immediate future. I spent most of the long evening in renewed appeals to Soames to slip away and seek refuge somewhere. I remember saying at last that if indeed I was destined to write about him, the supposed 'stauri' had better have at least a happy ending. Soames repeated those last three words in a tone of intense scorn. 'In Life and in Art,' he said, 'all that matters is an *inevitable* ending.'

'But,' I urged, more hopefully than I felt, 'an ending that can be avoided *isn't* inevitable.'

'You aren't an artist,' he rasped. 'And you're so hopelessly not an artist that, so far from being able to imagine a thing and make it seem true, you're going to make even a true thing seem as if you'd made it up. You're a miserable bungler. And it's like my luck.'

I protested that the miserable bungler was not I—was not going to be I—but T. K. Nupton; and we had a rather heated argument, in the thick of which it suddenly seemed to me that Soames saw he was in the wrong; he had quite physically cowered. But I wondered why—and now I guessed with a cold throb just why—he stared so, past me. The bringer of that 'inevitable ending' filled the doorway.

I managed to turn in my chair and to say, not without a semblance of lightness, 'Aha, come in!' Dread was indeed rather blunted in me by his looking so absurdly like a villain in a melodrama. The sheen of his tilted hat and of his shirt-front, the repeated twists he was giving to his moustache, and most of all the magnificence of his sneer, gave token that he was there only to be foiled.

He was at our table in a stride. 'I am sorry,' he sneered witheringly, 'to break up your pleasant party, but—'

'You don't: you complete it,' I assured him. 'Mr Soames and I want to have a little talk with you. Won't you sit? Mr Soames got nothing—frankly nothing—by his journey this afternoon. We don't wish to say that the whole thing was a swindle—a common swindle. On the contrary, we believe you meant well. But of course the bargain, such as it was, is off.'

The Devil gave no verbal answer. He merely looked at Soames and pointed with rigid forefinger to the door. Soames was wretchedly rising from his chair when, with a desperate quick gesture, I swept together two dinner-knives that were on the table, and laid their blades across each other. The Devil stepped sharp back against the table behind him, averting his face and shuddering.

'You are not superstitious!' he hissed.

'Not at all,' I smiled.

'Soames!' he said as to an underling, but without turning his face, 'put those knives straight!'

With an inhibitive gesture to my friend, 'Mr Soames,' I said emphatically to the Devil, 'is a *Catholic* Diabolist'; but my poor friend did the Devil's bidding, not mine; and now, with his master's eyes again fixed on him, he arose, he shuffled past me. I tried to speak. It was he that spoke. 'Try,' was the prayer he threw back at me as the Devil pushed him roughly out through the door, '*try* to make them know that I did exist!'

In another instant I too was through that door. I stood staring all ways—up the street, across it, down it. There was moonlight and lamplight, but there was not Soames nor that other.

Dazed, I stood there. Dazed, I turned back, at length, into the little room; and I suppose I paid Berthe or Rose for my dinner and luncheon, and for Soames': I hope so, for I never went to the Vingtième again. Ever since that night I have avoided Greek Street altogether. And for years I did not set foot even in Soho Square, because on that same night it was there that I paced and loitered, long and long, with some such dull sense of hope as a man has in not straying far from the place where he has lost something . . . 'Round and round the shutter'd Square'—that line came back to me on my lonely beat, and with it the whole stanza, ringing in my brain and bearing in on me how tragically different from the happy scene imagined by him was the poet's actual experience of that prince in whom of all princes we should put not our trust.

But—strange how the mind of an essayist, be it never so stricken, roves and ranges!—I remember pausing before a wide doorstep and wondering if perchance it was on this one that the young De Quincey lay ill and faint while poor Ann flew as fast as her feet would carry her to Oxford Street, the 'stony-hearted stepmother' of them both, and came back bearing that 'glass of port wine and spices' but for which he might, so he thought, actually have died. Was this the very doorstep that the old De Quincey used to revisit in homage? I pondered Ann's fate, the cause of her sudden vanishing from the ken of her boy-friend; and presently I blamed myself for letting the past over-ride the present. Poor vanished Soames!

And for myself, too, I began to be troubled. What had I better do? Would there be a hue and cry—Mysterious Disappearance of an Author, and all that? He had last been seen lunching and dining in my company. Hadn't I better get a hansom and drive straight to Scotland Yard? . . . They would think I was a lunatic. After all, I reassured myself, London was a very large place, and one very dim figure might easily drop out of it unobserved—now especially, in the blinding glare of the near Jubilee. Better say nothing at all, I thought.

And I was right. Soames' disappearance made no stir at all. He was utterly forgotten before anyone, as far as I am aware, noticed that he was no longer hanging around. Now and again some poet or prosaist may have said to another, 'What has become of that man Soames?' but I never heard any such question asked. The solicitor through whom he was paid his annuity may be presumed to have made inquiries, but no echo of these resounded. There was some thing rather ghastly to me in the general unconsciousness that Soames had existed, and more than once I caught myself wondering whether Nupton, that babe unborn, were going to be right in thinking him a figment of my brain.

In the extract from Nupton's repulsive book there is one point which perhaps puzzles you. How is it that the author, though I have here mentioned him by name and have quoted the exact words he is going to write, is not going to grasp the obvious corollary that I have invented nothing? The answer can but be this: Nupton will not have read the later passages of this memoir. Such lack of thoroughness is a serious fault in anyone who undertakes to do scholar's work. And I hope these words will meet the eye of some contemporary rival to Nupton and be the undoing of Nupton.

I like to think that some time between 1992 and 1997 somebody will have looked up this memoir, and will have forced on the world his inevitable and startling conclusions. And I have reasons for believing that this will be so. You realise that the reading-room into which Soames was projected by the Devil was in all respects precisely as it will be on the afternoon of June 3rd, 1997. You realise, therefore, that on that afternoon, when it comes round, there the self-same crowd will be, and there Soames too will be, punctually, he and they doing precisely what they did before. Recall now Soames' account of the sensation he made. You may say that the mere difference of his costume was enough to make him sensational in that uniformed crowd. You wouldn't say so if you had ever seen him. I assure you that in no period could Soames be anything but dim. The fact that people are going to stare at him, and follow him around, and seem afraid of him, can be explained only on the hypothesis that they will somehow have been prepared for his ghostly visitation. They will have been awfully waiting to see whether he really would come. And when he does come the effect will of course be—awful.

An authentic, guaranteed, proven ghost, but—only a ghost, alas! Only that. In his first visit, Soames was a creature of flesh and blood, whereas the creatures into whose midst he was projected were but ghosts, I take it—solid, palpable, vocal, but unconscious and automatic ghosts, in a building that was itself an illusion. Next time, that building and those creatures will be real. It is of Soames that there will be but the semblance. I wish I could think him destined to revisit the world actually, physically, consciously. I wish he had this one brief escape, this one small treat, to look forward to. I never forget him for long. He is where he is, and forever. The more rigid moralists among you may say he has only himself to blame. For my part, I think he has been very hardly used. It is well that vanity should be chastened; and Enoch Soames' vanity was, I admit, above the average, and called for special treatment. But there was no need for vindictiveness. You say he contracted to pay the price he is paying; yes; but I maintain that he was induced to do so by fraud. Well-informed in all things, the Devil must have known that my friend would gain nothing by his visit to futurity. The whole thing was a very shabby trick. The more I think of it, the more detestable the Devil seems to me.

Of him I have caught sight several times, here and there, since that day at the Vingtième. Only once, however, have I seen him at close quarters. This was in Paris. I was walking, one afternoon, along the Rue d'Antin, when I saw him advancing from the opposite direction—over-dressed as ever, and swinging an ebony cane, and altogether behaving as though the whole pavement belonged to him. At thought of Enoch Soames and the myriads of other sufferers eternally in this brute's dominion, a great cold wrath filled me, and I drew myself up to my full height. But—well, one is so used to nodding and smiling in the street to anybody whom one knows, that the action becomes almost independent of oneself: to prevent it requires a very sharp effort and great presence of mind. I was miserably aware, as I passed the Devil, that I nodded and smiled to him. And my shame was the deeper and hotter because he, if you please, stared straight at me with the utmost haughtiness.

To be cut—deliberately cut—by *him*! I was, I still am, furious at having had that happen to me.

The Uncorked Governess

RONALD FIRBANK

ONE EVENING, as Mrs Montgomery was reading *Vanity Fair* for the fifteenth time, there came a tap at the door. It was not the first interruption since opening the cherished green-bound book, and Mrs Montgomery seemed disinclined to stir. With the Court about to return to winter quarters, and the Summer Palace upside down, the royal governess was still able to command her habitual British phlegm. It had been decided, moreover, that she should remain behind in the forsaken palace with his Naughtiness, the better to 'prepare' him for his forthcoming Eton exam.

Still, with disputes as to the precedence of trunks and dress-baskets simmering in the corridors without, it was easier to enjoy the barley-sugar stick in one's mouth than the novel in one's hand.

'Thank God I'm not touchy!' Mrs Montgomery reflected, rolling her eyes lazily about the little white-wainscoted room.

It was as if something of her native land had crept in through the doorway with her, so successful had she inculcated its tendencies, or spiritual Ideals, upon everything around.

A solitary teapot, on a bracket, above the door, two *Jubilee* plates, some peacocks' feathers, an image of a little fisher-boy in bathing-drawers with a broken hand—'a work of delicate beauty!'—a mezzotint, *The Coiffing of Maria*—these were some of the treasures which the room contained.

'A blessing to be sure when the Court has gone!' she reflected, half rising to drop a curtsey to Prince Olaf who had entered.

'Word from your country,' sententiously he broke out. 'My brother's betrothed! So need I go on with my preparation?'

'Put your tie straight! And just look at your socks all tumbling down. Such great jambons of knees! . . . What will become of you, I ask myself, when you're a lower boy at Eton.'

'How can I be a lower boy when I'm a Prince?'

'Probably the Rev Ruggles-White, when you enter his House, will be able to explain.'

'I won't be a lower boy! I will *not*!'

'Cs, Cs.'

'Damn the democracy.'

'Fie, sir.'

'Down with it.'

'For shame.'

'Revenge.'

'That will do: and now, let me hear your lessons: I should like,' Mrs Montgomery murmured, her eyes set in detachment upon the floor, 'the present-indicative tense of the Verb *To be*! Adding the words, Political h-Hostess; more for the sake of the pronunciation than for anything else.'

And after considerable persuasion, prompting, and 'bribing' with various sorts of sweets:

> 'I am a Political Hostess,
> Thou art a Political Hostess,
> He is a Political Hostess,
> We are Political Hostesses,
> Ye are Political Hostesses,
> They are Political Hostesses.'

'Very good, dear, and only one mistake. *He* is a Political h-Hostess: can you correct yourself? The error is so slight . . .'

But alas the Prince was in no mood for study; and Mrs Montgomery very soon afterwards was obliged to let him go.

Moving a little anxiously about the room, her meditations turned upon the future.

With the advent of Elsie a new régime would be established: increasing Britishers would wish to visit Pisuerga; and it seemed a propitious moment to abandon teaching, and to inaugurate in Kairoulla an English hotel.

'I have no more rooms. I am quite full up!' she smiled, addressing the silver andirons in the grate.

And what a deliverance to have done with instructing unruly

children, she reflected, going towards the glass mail-box attached to her vestibule door. Sometimes about this hour there would be a letter in it, but this evening, there was only a picture postcard of a field mouse in a bonnet, from her old friend Mrs Bedley.

'We have *Valmouth* at last,' she read, 'and was it you, my dear, who asked for *The Beard Throughout the Ages?* It is in much demand, but I am keeping it back anticipating a *reply.* Several of the plates are missing I see, among them those of the late King Edward and of Assur Bani Pal; I only mention it that you may know I shan't blame you! We are having wonderful weather, and I am keeping pretty well, although poor Mrs Barleymoon, I fear, will not see through another winter. Trusting you are benefiting by the beautiful country air : your obedient servant to command,

ANN BEDLEY.

'P.S.—*Man, and All About Him,* is rebinding. Ready I expect soon.

'Ah! Cunnie, Cunnie . . . ?' Mrs Montgomery murmured, laying the card down near a photograph of the Court-physician with a sigh. 'Ah! Arthur Amos Cuncliffe Babcock . . . ?' she invoked his name dulcetly in full : and, as though in telepathic response, there came a tap at the door, and the doctor himself looked in.

He had been attending, it seemed, the young wife of the Comptroller of the Household at the extremity of the corridor, a creature who, after two brief weeks of marriage, imagined herself to be in an interesting state. *'I believe baby's coming!'* she would cry out every few hours.

'Do I intrude?' he demanded, in his forceful, virile voice, that ladies knew and liked : 'pray say so if I do.'

'Does he intrude!' Mrs Montgomery flashed an arch glance towards the cornice.

'Well, and how are you keeping?' the doctor asked, dropping on to a rep causeuse that stood before the fire.

'I'm only semi-well, doctor, thanks!'

'Why, what's the trouble?'

'You know my organism is not a very strong one, Dr Cuncliffe . . .' Mrs Montgomery replied, drawing up a chair, and settling a cushion with a sigh of resignation at her back.

'Imagination!'

'If only it were!'

'Imagination,' he repeated, fixing a steady eye on the short train of her black brocaded robe that all but brushed his feet.

'If that's your explanation for continuous broken sleep . . .' she gently snapped.

'Try mescal.'

'I'm trying Dr Fritz Millar's treatment,' the lady stated, desiring to deal a slight *scratch* to his masculine *amour propre*.

'Millar's an Ass.'

'I don't agree at all!' she incisively returned, smiling covertly at his touch of pique.

'What is it?'

'Oh it's horrid. You first of all lie down; and then you drink cold water in the sun.'

'Cold what? I never *heard* of such a thing: it's enough to kill you.'

Mrs Montgomery took a deep-drawn breath of languor.

'And would you care, doctor, so *very* much if it did?' she asked, as a page made his appearance with an ice-bucket and champagne.

'To toast our young Princess!'

'Oh, oh, Dr Cuncliffe! What a wicked man you are.' And for a solemn moment their thoughts went out in unison to the sea-girt land of their birth—Barkers', Selfridge's, Brighton Pier, the Zoological Gardens on a Sunday afternoon.

'Here's to the good old country!' the doctor quaffed.

'The Bride, and,' Mrs Montgomery raised her glass, 'the Old Folks at h-home.'

'The Old Folks at home!' he vaguely echoed.

'Bollinger, you naughty man,' the lady murmured, amiably seating herself on the causeuse at his side.

'You'll find it dull here all alone after the Court has gone,' he observed, smiling down, a little despotically, on to her bright, abundant hair.

Mrs Montgomery sipped her wine.

'When the wind goes whistling up and down under the colonnades; oh, then!' she shivered.

'You'll wish for a fine, bold Pisuergian husband; shan't you?' he answered, his foot drawing closer to hers.

'Often of an evening I feel I need fostering,' she owned, glancing up yearningly into his face.

'Fostering, eh?' he chuckled, refilling with exuberance her glass.

'Why is it that wine always makes me feel *so good?*'

'Probably because it fills you with affection for your neighbour!'

'It's true; I feel I could be very affectionate: I'm what they call an "amoureuse" I suppose, and there it is . . .'

There fell a busy silence between them.

'It's almost too warm for a fire,' she murmured, repairing towards the window; 'but I like to hear the crackle!'

'Company, eh?' he returned, following her (a trifle unsteadily) across the room.

'The night is so clear the moon looks to be almost transparent,' she languorously observed, with a long tugging sigh.

'And so it does,' he absently agreed.

'I adore the pigeons in my wee court towards night, when they sink down like living sapphires upon the stones,' she sentimentally said, sighing languorously again.

'Ours,' he assured her; 'since the surgery looks on to it, too . . .'

'Did you ever see anything so ducky-wucky, so completely twee!' she inconsequently chirruped.

'Allow me to fill this empty glass.'

'I want to go out on all that gold floating water!' she murmured listlessly, pointing towards the lake.

'Alone?'

'Drive me towards the sweet seaside,' she begged, taking appealingly his hand.

'Aggie?'

'Arthur—Arthur, for God's sake!' she shrilled, as with something between a snarl and a roar he impulsively whipped out the light.

'H-Help! Oh, Arth—'

Thus did they celebrate the 'Royal engagement.'

Julia and the Bazooka

ANNA KAVAN

JULIA IS A LITTLE GIRL with long straight hair and big eyes. Julia loved flowers. In the cornfield she has picked an enormous untidy bunch of red poppies which she is holding up so that most of her face is hidden except the eyes. Her eyes look sad because she has just been told to throw the poppies away, not to bring them inside to make a mess dropping their petals all over the house. Some of them have shed their petals already, the front of her dress is quite red. Julia is also a quiet schoolgirl who does not make many friends. Then she is a tall student standing with other students who have passed their final examinations, whose faces are gay and excited, eager to start life in the world. Only Julia's eyes are sad. Although she smiles with the others, she does not share their enthusiasm for living. She feels cut off from people. She is afraid of the world.

Julia is also a young bride in a white dress, holding a sheaf of roses in one hand and in the other a very small flat white satin bag containing a lace-edged handkerchief scented with Arpège and a plastic syringe. Now Julia's eyes are not at all sad. She has one foot on the step of a car, its door held open by a young man with kinky brown hair and a rose in his buttonhole. She is laughing because of something he's said or because he has just squeezed her arm or because she no longer feels frightened or cut off now that she has the syringe. A group of indistinct people in the background look on approvingly as if they are glad to transfer responsibility for Julia to the young man. Julia who loves flowers waves to them with her roses as she drives off with him.

Julia is also dead without any flowers. The doctor sighs when he looks at her lying there. No one else comes to look except the official people. The ashes of the tall girl Julia barely fill the silver cup she won in the tennis tournament. To improve her game the tennis professional gives her the syringe. He is a joking kind of man and calls the syringe a bazooka. Julia calls it that too, the name sounds funny, it makes her laugh. Of course she knows all the sensational stories about drug addiction, but the word bazooka makes nonsense of them, makes the whole drug business seem not serious. Without the bazooka she might not have won the cup, which as a container will at least serve a useful purpose. It is Julia's serve that wins the decisive game. Holding two tennis balls in her left hand, she throws one high in the air while her right hand flies up over her head, brings the racket down, wham, and sends the ball skimmering over the opposite court hardly bouncing at all, a service almost impossible to return. Holding two balls in her hand Julia also lies in bed beside the young man with kinky hair. Julia is also lying in wreckage under an army blanket, and eventually Julia's ashes go into the silver cup.

The undertaker or somebody closes the lid and locks the cup in a pigeon-hole among thousands of identical pigeon-holes in a wall at the top of a cliff overlooking the sea. The winter sea is the colour of pumice, the sky cold as grey ice, the icy wind charges straight at the wall making it tremble so that the silver cup in its pigeon-hole shivers and tinkles faintly. The wind is trying to tear to pieces a few frost-bitten flowers which have not been left for Julia at the foot of the wall. Julia is also driving with her bridegroom in the high mountains through fields of flowers. They stop the car and pick armfuls of daffodils and narcissi. There are no flowers for Julia in the pigeon-hole and no bridegroom either.

'This is her syringe, her bazooka she always called it,' the doctor says with a small sad smile. 'It must be twenty years old at least. Look how the measures have been worn away by continuous use.' The battered old plastic syringe is unbreakable, unlike the glass syringes which used to be kept in boiled water in metal boxes and reasonably sterile. This discoloured old syringe has always been left lying about somewhere, accumulating germs and the assorted dirt of wars and cities. All the same, it has not done Julia any great harm. An occasional infection easily cured with penicillin, nothing serious. 'Such dangers are grossly exaggerated.'

Julia and her bazooka travel all over the world. She wants to see everything, every country. The young man with kinky hair is not there, but she is in a car and somebody sits beside her. Julia is a good driver. She drives anything, racing cars, heavy lorries. Her long hair streams out from under the crash helmet as she drives for the racing teams. Today she is lapping only a fraction of a second behind the number one driver when a red-hot bit of his clutch flies off and punctures her nearside tyre, and the car somersaults twice and tears through a wall. Julia steps out of the wreck uninjured and walks away holding her handbag with the syringe inside it. She is laughing. Julia always laughs at danger. Nothing can frighten her while she has the syringe. She has almost forgotten the time when she was afraid. Sometimes she thinks of the kinky-haired man and wonders what he is doing. Then she laughs. There are always plenty of people to bring her flowers and make her feel gay. She hardly remembers how sad and lonely she used to feel before she had the syringe.

Julia likes the doctor as soon as she meets him. He is understanding and kind like the father she has imagined but never known. He does not want to take her syringe away. He says, 'You've used it for years already and you're none the worse. In fact you'd be far worse off without it.' He trusts Julia, he knows she is not irresponsible, she does not increase the dosage too much or experiment with new drugs. It is ridiculous to say all drug addicts are alike, all liars, all vicious, all psychopaths or delinquents just out for kicks. He is sympathetic towards Julia whose personality has been damaged by no love in childhood so that she can't make contact with people or feel at home in the world. In his opinion she is quite right to use the syringe, it is as essential to her as insulin to a diabetic. Without it she could not lead a normal existence, her life would be a shambles, but with its support she is conscientious and energetic, intelligent, friendly. She is most unlike the popular notion of a drug addict. Nobody could call her vicious.

Julia who loves flowers has made a garden on a flat roof in the city, all round her are pots of scarlet geraniums. Throughout the summer she has watered them every day because the pots dry out so fast up here in the sun and wind. Now summer is over, there is frost in the air. The leaves of the plants have turned yellow. Although the flowers have survived up to now the next frost will finish them off. It is wartime, the time of flying bombs, they come over all the time, there seems to be nothing to stop them. Julia is used to them, she ignores them, she does not look. To save the flowers from the frost she picks them all quickly and takes them indoors. Then it is winter and Julia is on the roof planting bulbs to flower in the spring. The flying bombs are still coming over, quite low, just above roofs and chimneys, their chugging noise fills the sky. One after another, they keep coming over, making their monotonous mechanical noise. When the engine cuts out there is a sudden startling silence, suspense, everything suddenly goes unnaturally still. Julia does not look up when the silence comes, but all at once it seems very cold on the roof, and she plants the last bulb in a hurry.

The doctor has gone to consult a top psychiatrist about one of his patients. The psychiatrist is immensely dignified, extremely well-dressed, his voice matches his outer aspect. When the bomb silence starts, his clear grave voice says solemnly, 'I advise you to take cover under that table beside you,' as he himself glides with the utmost dignity under his impressive desk. Julia leaves the roof and steps on to the staircase, which is not there. The stairs have crumbled, the whole house is crumbling, collapsing, the world bursts and burns, while she falls through the dark. The A.R.P. men dig Julia out of the rubble. Red geraniums are spilling down the front of her dress, she has forgotten the time between, and is forgetting more and more every moment. Someone spreads a grey blanket over her, she lies underneath it in her red-stained dress, her bag, with the bazooka inside, safely hooked over one arm. How cold it is in the exploding world. The northern lights burst out in frigid brilliance across the sky. The ice roars and thunders like gunfire. The cold is glacial, a glass dome of cold covers the globe. Icebergs tower high as mountains, furious blizzards swoop at each other like white wild beasts. All things are turning to ice in the mortal cold, and the cold has a face which sparkles with frost. It seems to be a face Julia knows, though she has forgotten whose face it is.

The undertaker hurriedly shuts himself inside his car, out of the cruel wind. The parson hurries towards his house, hatless, thin grey hair blowing about wildly. The wind snatches a tattered wreath of frost-blackened flowers and rolls it over the grass, past the undertaker and the parson, who both pretend not to see. They are not going to stay out in the cold any longer, it is not their job to look after the flowers. They do not know that Julia loves flowers and they do not care. The wreath was not put there for her, anyhow.

Julia is rushing after the nameless face, running as fast as if she was playing tennis. But when she comes near she does not, after all, recognise that glittering death-mask. It has gone now, there's nothing but arctic glitter, she is a bride again beside the young man with brown hair. The lights are blazing, but she shivers a little in her thin dress because the church is so cold. The dazzling brilliance of the aurora borealis has burnt right through the roof with its frigid fire. Snow slants down between the rafters, there is ice on the altar, snowdrifts in the aisles, the holy water and the communion wine have been frozen solid. Snow is Julia's bridal white, icicles are her jewels. The diamond-sparkling coronet on her head confuses her thoughts. Where has everyone gone? The bridegroom is dead, or in bed with some girl or other, and she herself lies under a dirty blanket with red on her dress.

'Won't somebody help me?' she calls. 'I can't move.' But no one takes any notice. She is not cold any longer. Suddenly now she is burning, a fever is burning her up. Her face is on fire, her dry mouth seems to be full of ashes. She sees the kind doctor coming and tries to call him, but can only whisper, 'Please help me . . .' so faintly that he does not hear. Sighing, he takes off his hat, gazing down at his name printed inside in small gold letters under the leather band. The kinky-haired young man is not in bed with anyone. He is wounded in a sea battle. He falls on the warship's deck, an officer tries to grab him but it's too late, over and over he rolls down the steeply sloping deck to the black bottomless water. The officer looks over the side, holding a lifebelt, but does not throw it down to the injured man; instead, he puts it on himself, and runs to a boat which is being lowered. The doctor comes home from the house of the famous psychiatrist. His head bent, his eyes covered, he walks slowly because he feels tired and sad. He does not look up so he never sees Julia waving to him with a bunch of geraniums from the window.

The pigeon-hole wall stands deserted in the cold dusk. The undertaker has driven home. His feet are so cold he can't feel them, these winter funerals are the very devil. He slams the car door, goes inside stamping his feet, and shouts to his wife to bring, double quick, a good strong hot rum with plenty of lemon and sugar, in case he has caught a chill. The wife, who was just going out to a bingo session, grumbles at being delayed, and bangs about in the kitchen. At the vicarage the parson is eating a crumpet for tea, his chair pulled so close to the fire that he is practically in the grate.

It has got quite dark outside, the wall has turned black. As the wind shakes it, the faintest of tinkles comes from the pigeon-hole where all that is left of Julia has been left. Surely there were some red flowers somewhere, Julia would be thinking, if she could still think. Then she would think something amusing, she would remember the bazooka and start to laugh. But nothing is left of Julia really, she is not there. The only occupant of the pigeon-hole is the silver cup, which can't think or laugh or remember. There is no more Julia anywhere. Where she was there is only nothing.

The Fabled Nizam

JARMANI DASS

FAITHFUL ALLY OF THE British Government, Lieutenant General His Exalted Highness Asafjah Muzaffar-ul-mulk Nizam-ul-mulk, Nizam-ud-daula Sir Mir Osman Ali Khan Bahadur, Fateh Jang, GCSI, GBE, the tenth ruler of the line, was installed on the throne of Hyderabad in 1911.

H.E.H. the Nizam's Dominions covered an extensive plateau with an average elevation of about 1,250 ft. above sea level interspersed with hills rising to 2,500 ft. and in one case even 3,500 ft. high. The total area of over 80,000 square miles is larger than that of England and Scotland put together.

The house of Hyderabad was founded by Nawab Asaf Jah Bahadur, the most distinguished general of Aurangzeb.

After long service under the Delhi Emperor, distinguished alike in war and political sagacity, he was appointed Viceroy of the Deccan region in 1713, with the title of Nizam-ul-mulk which has since become the hereditary title of the family.

The Moghul Empire was on the verge of decline, owing to internal dissensions and attacks from without. Amid general confusion Nawab Asaf Jah had little difficulty in asserting his independence against the weak occupants of the throne of Delhi, but he had to repel the inroads of the Marathas who were harassing the western parts of his newly acquired territory. His independence was the cause of much jealousy in Delhi, and the court party secretly instructed Mubariz Khan, Governor of Khandesh, to oppose him by force of arms. A battle was fought at Shakarkhelda in the Buldana District of Berar in 1724, and Mubariz Khan was totally defeated and lost his life.

The battle established the independence of Nawab Asaf Jah who annexed Berar and made Hyderabad his seat.

At the time of his death in 1741 he was established as the independent sovereign of the Kingdom co-extensive with the present Dominions, including the province of Berar.

Nizam means an administrator who was the Governor of Hyderabad during the Mughal period, and after the fall of the Mughal empire the Nizam became independent and entered into a treaty with the East India Company.

Later, when the British Power became paramount in India, the Nizam like the other Maharajas and ruling princes of India came under the suzerainty of the emperor of Great Britain.

His forefathers gathered enormous wealth and piled up a huge stock of jewels unparallelled in the history of the world and Nizam Osman Ali Khan inherited all the massive gold bars and bricks, fabulous diamonds, other precious stones and jewellery. Several cellars of his palace were hoarded with jewellery, gold and silver bricks. The keys were always kept by the Nizam himself and he never trusted any officer or servant with the key of the great vaults of his fabulous wealth.

At an early age, the Nizam of Hyderabad was greatly fascinated with his wealth and he used to count the bricks of silver and gold, now and then.

From his early youth he got full satisfaction in looking at piles of these gold bricks. Having had enormous wealth, not only jewellery, gold and silver bricks and other precious articles, he had vast property in land and houses which yielded an income of millions of rupees. The Nizam possessed the famous Jacob diamond which ranked next to the Kohinoor, now set in the Crown of Queen Elizabeth of England.

With all his wealth the Nizam was a miser. He spent very little on himself. The habit of miserliness became ingrained in him more and more with advancing years. He was so steeped in this mania that whenever he invited anyone to his table, the food served to the guests was frugal and insipid. Even for tea he had barely two biscuits to offer, one for himself and the other for the guest. If the number of guests were more, the number of biscuits increased in the same proportion. At the royal table the spirit of miserliness was displayed so blatantly that any guest could easily comprehend the mentality of his host. On occasions when he entertained guests at his table, the expenses of which were not borne by his privy purse, he did not display the same trait.

He believed in getting his guests served sumptuously when the expenses were chargeable to the State Exchequer. At official banquets and receptions, the food served was sumptuous in both the European and Indian styles and even alcoholic drinks such as whisky, and he used to offer a glass of champagne to noblemen attending the banquet, sitting far away from him, and on receipt of the glass they would stand up, bow in obeisance several times to thank His Exalted Highness for the mark of Royal Honour shown to them. This meant that the Nizam publicly honoured a particular nobleman on that night and the custom was that the next morning for one cup of champagne which the noble guest had received the previous night, he had to reciprocate by sending him a present worth a hundred thousand rupees.

It became a custom for the Nizam to offer a glass of champagne to six or seven noblemen of his Kingdom at each banquet which meant that six or seven lakhs of rupees were sent to the Nizam, while the champagne was paid for by the State Exchequer. He also used to amass great wealth by sending small presents to the noblemen who in return had to offer him costly presents ten or twenty times the value of the presents sent.

Another trick the Nizam had adopted to extort money was to attend the funeral, marriages and other ceremonies of the noblemen of his State and at such functions the Nizam was presented with gold sovereigns as token of the gratitude for His Exalted Highness' gracious visit.

He devised many other ways of extracting money from his subjects, so much so that everybody in his kingdom knew what the Nizam was expecting from a particular person for the honour bestowed on him on some particular occasion.

The Nizam kept jewellery in hundreds of boxes while bricks of gold and silver were kept in large vaults. In later years of life when he had a number of children numbering about eighty to ninety he had each box of jewellery assigned to each of his sons and daughters, but these boxes were meant to be delivered to the assignee only after his death. So, none knew exactly the contents of these boxes except that it was noted down by the Nizam in his own private book kept for the purpose.

At the time of the integration of the States with the Union of the

Republic of India, the Nizam was advised by the Government of India that it would be much safer for him to keep his hoarded gold and silver bricks and other jewellery in the safe deposit vault of a bank in Bombay.

The Government of India rightly suspected that this colossal wealth might be misused by the Nizam and his advisers as it was rumoured that the Nizam had planned to get his wealth removed by secret methods to Pakistan or to some other country.

A Trust of 46 crores of rupees was created and the jewellery was removed first to the Imperial Bank of India in Bombay but afterwards to the Mercantile Bank of India, as the space for placing these numerous boxes and cartloads of gold and silver bricks was insufficient in the Imperial Bank on account of lack of accommodation. The Mercantile Bank of India had to improvise special cellars for the safe deposit of these gold and silver bricks and the jewellery of His Exalted Highness.

The Nizam, in spite of his owning such vast wealth, shed tears of sorrow when he saw them going out of the palace reserve after the 'Police Action' and the capture of Kasim Rasvi—the rebel leader of the anti-Indian movement. The Nizam was then obliged to conciliate the authorities of the Union by denouncing the suspected revolt of his own Prime Minister and declaring that he was an ally of the Indian Union and had no truck with Pakistan.

The Government of India taking the Nizam at his word appointed him as the Rajpramukh (Governor) of integrated Hyderabad. This he later relinquished and retired from public life and became a recluse. He seldom came out of King Kothi, where he resided.

His heir apparent, Prince Himayat Ali Khan (Azzam Jah) and his second son, Prince Shujaat Ali Khan (Muazzam Jah) were married to the Turkish Princesses—daughter and niece respectively of the Ex-Khalifa of Turkey—Abdul Majid.

After a few years of married life, Princess Nilofer left her husband, Muazzam Jah, the second son of the Nizam and joined her grandmother, the cousin of ex-king Abdul Majid of Turkey, one of the richest women of Turkey.

Both the Princes received huge amounts as privy purse from the Nizam with the approval of the Government of India but with the creation of the Trust, the princes were paid their privy purse from the Trust money, while the Nizam himself was paid five million rupees from his landed property as well as some extra amount from the Trust.

With all these multi-millions at his disposal, the Nizam barely spent a few thousand rupees on himself and his numerous concubines who abounded in his palace.

Though the Nizam had a large harem and several wives and eunuchs, yet the total amount he spent on his personal establishment and household was much less than anyone among the reasonably wealthy class of Bombay and Calcutta.

The dress of the Nizam was very simple. He wore an ordinary shirt and a short loose pyjama. The socks were always sagging while the pyjama was lifted so high that the legs of the Nizam—between the edges of the pyjama and the socks—were always visible. He had a fez cap for head-dress which it is reliably reported was bought by him about 35 years ago. The cap, though worn out and tattered by constant use over three decades, ever retained its royal master's favour!

The father of the Nizam of Hyderabad was a generous man. He made his subjects happy and was always anxious to effect reforms and elevate their lot and status.

Besides his many queens, the father had a liaison with a woman of ill repute who was the mistress of a Marwari banker. This woman gave birth to a boy who resembled the Marwari. It was alleged by the collaterals that this boy was brought to the Palace and declared the son of the Nizam. As the boy grew up, he had the character and resemblance of the Marwari, and likewise his habits of hoarding money.

The father, after having failed to improve the habits of the son, lodged a complaint with the Government of India that the boy was not his own son and that his two other sons from the legitimate wives, named Salabat Jah and Basabat Jah, were the rightful heirs. These princes had the character and resemblance of their father. Osman Ali, cunning as he was from the very beginning of his childhood, came to know of this plan and started praying that his father should depart from this world. Suddenly his father got seriously ill and died but the boy destined to become the Nizam did not go to see him during his illness and was not even present at his death bed.

When Osman Ali succeeded to the throne he turned out of the palace all the members of the royal family and some of them

E

actually became street beggars. Salabat Jah and Basabat Jah appealed to the British Government to restore to them the kingdom of Hyderabad as they were the legitimate sons of the Nizam and that Osman Ali was a usurper and not the son of the Nizam.

Osman Ali was lucky, as Edward VII, King of England, to whom the case was submitted and who was inclined to favour Salabat Jah and Basabat Jah as the rightful heirs, died just then. The demise of the King gave Osman Ali sufficient time to manipulate things and through the influence of gold bricks and dazzling diamonds, he got the case of his brothers brushed aside and himself became rightful and the undisputed ruler of Hyderabad.

The father of the Nizam had given the Hyderabad Palace at Bombay to Salabat Jah but Osman Ali got the house confiscated. Salabat Jah complained about the confiscation of his house to the then Resident who asked the Nizam to return the house to his brother. Tricky as Osman Ali was, he suggested to the Resident that the house should be valued and Salabat Jah should be paid the value as compensation instead of the house. Both the Resident and Salabat Jah agreed to this arrangement and Sir Cowasji Jehangir of Bombay was appointed by the Resident to evaluate the house.

Osman Ali sent his confidential private secretary to see Sir Cowasji Jehangir requesting him to undervalue the house but Sir Cowasji Jehangir being an honest man with great integrity and character turned down his request and the house was valued at Rs. 17 lakhs. Osman Ali after paying this amount from his pocket in great hurry realised that his capital was reduced by 17 lakhs. He got the house declared as Government property.

Later, Salabat Jah died in mysterious circumstances and the Nizam got all his money and property but Basabat Jah continued to get Rs. 5,000 per month as his allowance which the Government of India had fixed. This amount was paid from the Hyderabad Exchequer.

*

The Nizam was on very friendly terms with the Maharaja of Datia, a State in Central India. Osman Ali asked him to send him some tins of pure butter for which his State was well-known. The Maharaja of Datia complied with the wishes of his friend Osman Ali and sent him twelve dozen tins of the purest home-made butter from his palace stock. At the sight of so many tins of butter, Osman Ali was extremely pleased and he ordered that these tins should be preserved in a safe place in the palace godowns. There they remained untouched for two years and the contents deteriorated, emitting foul smell, and attracted the attention of the officers in charge of the godowns. No officer or subordinate dared to bring the fact to the notice of the Nizam.

However, Nawab Salar Jung, Prime Minister of Hyderabad State and a man of bold and independent character, spoke to the Nizam about the condition of the butter. Even Salar Jung was abused by the Nizam and was sent away.

Immediately afterwards, Osman Ali sent for Mr Reddy, the officer in charge of the police station of Hyderabad and asked him to go round the temples and sell the butter. The officer was abused when he remarked that the butter was unfit for human consumption and should be thrown away. Osman Ali told Mr Reddy that though the butter was not fit for human consumption it was good enough for use in temples and placing before the Hindu deities for religious ceremonies.

After seeing the attitude of the Nizam, he bowed and told him that his orders would be executed. As soon as he got out of the Palace gates, Mr Reddy threw away the tins of butter into a gutter and came back after a few hours beaming with joy and told the Nizam that the butter was sold for Rs. 201/-. The Nizam was mightily pleased with the services rendered by the officer and credited the amount of Rs. 201/- to his own bank account which already amounted to hundreds of millions of rupees. Mr Reddy was given a superior post in recognition of his services.

*

The Nizam always attended the marriages of his officials, their sons and daughters as well as the marriages of the Payagah noblemen of his kingdom. Instead of giving presents to the bride and the bridegroom he used to pick up the most valuable jewellery from the dowry and deprive the married couple of their best jewellery, in the name of kingly condescension.

Whenever the Nizam saw anyone in his Kingdom with an expensive and beautiful car, the owner was informed by the staff-officers that His Exalted Highness would like to have a drive in that car. The owner felt honoured at the gesture of His Exalted Highness and sent his car for the royal drive. The car was never returned and was driven to the palace garage to the utter dismay of the owner. Thus he collected a fleet of cars numbering three to four hundred, though they remained unused. Once after integration, the Chief Minister of Hyderabad State asked him to dispose of his two hundred and fifty cars which were rotting in his garage but the Nizam turned down the proposal and instead he spent two and a half lakhs of rupees to get them overhauled, thus displaying his utter self will.

*

The Nizam smoked heavily, but only cheap and ordinary cigarettes. He used to chain smoke, sitting on a sofa for hours. The cigarette ends and ashes of the cigarettes which he smoked accumulated on the floor which he never liked to be removed. Only when huge masses of cigarette ends and ashes were accumulated, the Controller of the Household would get them cleaned up.

Whenever the Nizam was offered a good American, British or Turkish cigarette by his friends or high Government officials, instead of picking up one cigarette he picked up four or five cigarettes at a time and put them in his cigarette box while continuing to smoke his own cheap brand.

On one occasion Mr V. P. Menon, Adviser to the Government of India in the States' Ministry, went to visit the Nizam and after a while the Nizam offered him a Hyderabad made cigarette called 'Char Minar' which the Nizam generally smoked and cost him 12 paise per packet of 10 cigarettes. But Mr Menon did not like to smoke it and respectfully declined the offer. Instead he offered his own cigarettes to the Nizam, saying that His Exalted Highness might try a new brand. The Nizam liked the cigarette and asked Mr Menon for three or four cigarettes which he kept in his own cigarette box. A few days later when Mr Menon visited the Nizam again, the Nizam instead of offering him Char Minar cigarettes, offered Mr Menon the same cigarettes which he had taken from him a few days earlier.

Fabulously rich, his personal jewellery was valued at fifty crores of rupees. The Nizam always kept a list of jewellery in his pocket whether he was awake or asleep.

He knew exactly how much he had got, in which boxes particular jewellery was kept and where any specific item of jewellery could be traced. No one was allowed to disturb the arrangements without his prior consent. If this was to be done for dusting the room, the treasurer had to explain in a most factual tone, bowing several times, that the box was only shifted temporarily to clean the place. The Nizam being suspicious by nature did not trust any of his officers with the jewellery. The treasury was opened by the officer in charge only after obtaining the special keys, which always remained in the custody of the Nizam himself.

*

The Nizam of Hyderabad possessed the world famous Jacob Diamond which weighed 282 carats. Its shape was that of a paper weight but to stave the evil eye he always kept it in a cuticura soap box and very often he used this diamond as a paper weight on his writing table.

Sir Sultan Ahmed who became the Chief Adviser to the Nizam and advised the Nizam in all constitutional affairs, pleased him a great deal by his services and flattery, in appreciation of which the Nizam allowed Sir Sultan to hold the diamond in his hands for a few minutes. The Nizam's eyes were so fixed on this stone all the time that Sultan Ahmed's hands trembled under the gaze.

*

In the great history of the Asaf Jah family to which Nizam Osman Ali belonged, there were many instances of bravery and great statesmanship. The Nizam was persuaded by Lord Curzon, the Viceroy of India, at the instructions of the King Emperor of India, to give up Berar which formed part of his domains. And the British Resident with his usual diplomatic skill was able to get a letter from the Nizam renouncing his rights on Berar. When the Prime Minister of the Nizam, Maharaja Sir Krishan Parshad was told of this letter, he went and told the Nizam that it was a great misfortune to have accepted the wishes of the British Viceroy.

The Nizam realised his mistake and told his Prime Minister that he should find out ways and means to get back the letter from the British Resident. Maharaja Sir Krishan Parshad made an appointment with the Resident and went to see him. At the interview he told the Resident that he would like to read the letter which the Nizam signed with regard to relinquishing his rights on Berar. He pretended that he would like to keep a copy of this letter for his record. As soon as the Prime Minister got the letter in his hand he put it in his mouth and swallowed it, then and there, in the presence of the British Resident and that was the end of the letter. Several years afterwards, though the Prime Minister had swallowed the letter, the British got Berar. But the Nizam hated the British ever after. And he seldom missed the opportunity for making his anti-British feelings known.

At the time of his silver jubilee, held in 1937, the British garrison consisting of twenty-four thousand troops wanted to honour the Nizam by marching past him. But after hardly one thousand troops had marched past him, the Nizam told the Commander of the British troops that he would no longer stay there. This was a mark of high discourtesy shown to the British troops and meant another black mark by the Viceroy in his Conduct Book.

On one occasion when he gave a big banquet in which the British Resident and senior officers of the Government of India and noblemen of the 'Paigahs' were present, he began to make a speech soon after the first course was served—not ordinarily done until the end of the dinner. The Nizam after making his speech in honour of the Resident left the table accompanied by most of his courtiers while the British Resident and a few other Britishers remained behind to finish the dinner. This was also a mark of high discourtesy towards the British Resident as a representative of the Crown in India.

The Heat Closing In

WILLIAM BURROUGHS

I CAN FEEL the heat closing in, feel them out there making their moves, setting up their devil doll stool pigeons, crooning over my spoon and dropper I throw away at Washington Square Station, vault a turnstile and two flights down the iron stairs, catch an uptown A train—Young, good looking, crew cut, Ivy League, advertising exec type fruit holds the door back for me. I am evidently his idea of a character. You know the type: comes on with bartenders and cab drivers, talking about right hooks and the Dodgers, calls the counterman in Nedick's by his first name. A real asshole. And right on time this narcotics dick in a white trench coat (imagine tailing somebody in a white trench coat. Trying to pass as a fag I guess) hit the platform. I can hear the way he would say it holding my outfit in his left hand, right hand on the piece: 'I think you dropped something, fella.'

But the subway is moving.

'So long flatfoot!' I yell, giving the fruit his B production. I look into the fruit's eyes, take in the white teeth, the Florida tan, the two hundred dollar sharkskin suit, the button-down Brooks Brothers shirt and carrying *The News* as a prop. 'Only thing I read is Little Abner.'

A square wants to come on hip—Talks about 'pod', and smoke it now and then, and keeps some around to offer the fast Hollywood types.

'Thanks, kid,' I say, 'I can see you're one of our own.' His face lights up like a pinball machine, with stupid, pink effect.

'Grassed on me he did,' I said morosely. (Note: Grass is English thief slang for inform.) I drew closer and laid my dirty junky fingers on his sharkskin sleeve. 'And us blood brothers in the same dirty needle. I can tell you in confidence he is due for a hot shot.' (Note: This is a cap of poison junk sold to addict for liquidation purposes. Often given to informers. Usually the hot shot is strychnine since it tastes and looks like junk.)

'Ever see a hot shot, kid? I saw the Gimp catch one in Philly. We rigged his room with a one-way whore-house mirror and charged a sawksi to watch it. He never got the needle out of his arm. They don't if the shot is right. That's the way they find them, dropper full of clotted blood hanging out of a blue arm. The look in his eyes when it hit. Kid, it was tasty.

'Recollect when I am travelling with the Vigilante, best Shake man in the industry. Out in Chi—We is working the fags in Lincoln Park. So one night the Vigilante turns up for work in cowboy boots and a black vest with a hunka tin on it and a lariat slung over his shoulder.

'So I say: "What's with you? You wig already?"

'He just looks at me and says: "Fill your hand stranger" and hauls out an old rusty six shooter and I take off across Lincoln Park, bullets cutting all around me. And he hangs three fags before the fuzz nail him. I mean the Vigilante earned his moniker.

'Ever notice how many expressions carry over from queers to con men? Like "raise", letting someone know you are in the same line?

' "Get her!"

' "Get the Paregoric Kid giving that mark the build up!"

' "Eager Beaver wooing him much too fast".

'The Shoe Store Kid (he got that moniker shaking down fetishists in shoe stores) say: "Give it to a mark with KY and he will come back moaning for more." And when the Kid spots a mark he begin to breathe heavy. His face swells and his lips turn purple like an Eskimo in heat. Then slow, slow he comes on the mark, feeling for him, palpating him with fingers of rotten ectoplasm.

'The Rube has a sincere little boy look, burns through him like blue neon. That one stepped right off a *Saturday Evening Post* cover with a string of bullheads, and preserved himself in junk. His marks never beef and the Bunko people are really carrying a needle for the Rube. One day Little Boy Blue starts to slip, and what crawls out would make an ambulance attendant puke. The Rube flips it in the end, running through empty automats and subway stations, screaming: "Come back, kid!! Come back!!" and follows his boy right into the East River, down through condoms and orange peels, mosaic of floating newspapers, down into the silent black ooze with gangsters in concrete, and pistols pounded flat to avoid the probing finger of prurient ballistic experts.'

And the fruit is thinking: 'What a character!! Wait till I tell the boys in Clark's about this one.' (He's a character collector, would stand still for Joe Gould's seagull act. So I put it on him for a sawksi and make a meet to sell him some 'pod' as he calls it, thinking 'I'll catnip the jerk.' (Note: Catnip smells like marijuana when it burns. Frequently passed on the incautious or uninstructed.)

'Well,' I said, tapping my arm, 'duty calls. As one judge said to another: "Be just and if you can't be just, be arbitrary".'

I cut into the automat and there is Bill Gains huddled in someone else's overcoat looking like a 1910 banker with paresis, and Old Bart, shabby and inconspicuous, dunking pound cake with his dirty fingers, shiny over the dirt.

I had some uptown customers Bill took care of, and Bart knew a few old relics from hop smoking times, spectral janitors, grey as ashes, phantom porters sweeping out dusty halls with a slow old man's hand, coughing and spitting in the junk-sick dawn, retired asthmatic fences in theatrical hotels. Pantopon Rose, the old madam from Peoria, stoical Chinese waiters never show sickness. Bart sought them out with his old junky walk, patient and cautious and slow, dropped into their bloodless hands a few hours of warmth.

I made the round with him once for kicks. You know how old people lose all shame about eating, and it makes you puke to watch them? Old junkies are the same about junk. They gibber and squeal at the sight of it. The spit hangs off their chin, and their stomach rumbles and all their guts grind in peristalsis while they cook up, dissolving the body's decent skin, you expect any moment a great blob of protoplasm will flop right out and surround the junk. Really disgusts you to see it.

'Well, my boys, we'll be like that one day,' I thought philosophically. 'Isn't life peculiar?'

So back downtown by the Sheridan Square Station in case the dick is lurking in a broom closet.

Like I say it couldn't last. I knew they were out there powwowing and making their evil fuzz magic, putting dolls of me in Leavenworth. 'No use sticking needles in that one, Mike.'

E*

I hear they got Chapin with a doll. This old eunuch dick just sat in the precinct basement hanging a doll of him day and night, year in year out. And when Chapin hanged in Connecticut, they find this old creep with his neck broken.

'He fell downstairs,' they say. You know the old cop bullshit.

Junk is surrounded by magic and taboos, curses and amulets. I could find my Mexico City connection by radar. 'Not this street, the next, right—now left. Now right again,' and there he is, toothless old woman face and cancelled eyes.

I know this one pusher walks around humming a tune and everybody he passes takes it up. He is so grey and spectral and anonymous they don't see him and think it is their own mind humming the tune. So the customers come in on *Smiles*, or *I'm In The Mood for Love*, or *They Say We're Too Young to Go Steady*, or whatever the song is for that day. Sometime you can see maybe fifty rattylooking junkies squealing sick, running along behind a boy with a harmonica, and there is The Man on a cane seat throwing bread to the swans, in fat queen drag walking his Afghan Hound through the East Fifties, an old wino pissing against an El post, a radical Jewish student giving out leaflets in Washington Square, a tree surgeon, an exterminator, an advertising fruit in Nedick's where he calls the counterman by his first name. The world network of junkies, tuned on a cord of rancid jissom, tying up in furnished rooms, shivering in the junk-sick morning. (Old Pete men suck the black smoke in the Chink laundry back room and Melancholy Baby dies from an overdose of time or cold turkey withdrawal of breath.) In Yemen, Paris, New Orleans, Mexico City and Istanbul —shivering under the air hammers and the steam shovels, shrieked junky curses at one another neither of us heard, and The Man leaned out of a passing steam roller and I coped in a bucket of tar. (Note: Istanbul is being torn down and rebuilt, especially shabby junky quarters. Istanbul has more heroin junkies than NYC.) The living and the dead, in sickness or on the nod, hooked or kicked or hooked again, come in on the junk beam and the Connection is eating Chop Suey on Dolores Street, Mexico DF, dunking pound cake in the automat, chased up Exchange Place by a baying pack of People. (Note: People is New Orleans slang for narcotic fuzz.)

The old Chinaman dips river water into a rusty tin can, washes down a yen pox hard and black as a cinder. (Note: Yen pox is the ash of smoked opium.)

Well, the fuzz has my spoon and dropper, and I know they are coming in on my frequency led by this blind pigeon known as Willy the Disk. Willy has a round, disk mouth lined with sensitive, erectile black hairs. He is blind from shooting in the eyeball, his nose and palate eaten away sniffing H, his body a mass of scar tissue hard and dry as wood. He can only eat the shit now with that mouth, sometimes sways out on a long tube of ectoplasm, feeling for the silent frequency of junk. He follows my trail all over the city into rooms I move out already, and the fuzz walks in on some newlyweds from Sioux Falls.

'All right, Lee!! Come out from behind that strapon! We know you' and pull the man's prick off straight-away.

Now Willy is getting hot and you can hear him always out there in darkness (he only functions at night) whimpering, and feel the terrible urgency of that blind, seeking mouth. When they move in for the bust, Willy goes all out of control, and his mouth eats a hole right through the door. If the cops weren't there to restrain him with a stock probe, he would suck the juice right out of every junky he ran down.

I knew, and everybody else knew they had the Disk on me. And if my kid customers ever hit the stand: 'He force me to commit all kinda awful sex acts in return for junk,' I could kiss the street good-bye.

So we stock up on H, buy a second-hand Studebaker, and start West.

The Vigilante coped out as a schizo possession case:

'I was standing outside myself trying to stop those hangings with ghost fingers—I am a ghost wanting what every ghost wants—a body—after the Long Time moving through odourless alleys of space where no life is only the colourless no smell of death—Nobody can breathe and smell it through pink convolutions of gristle laced with crystal snot, time shit and black blood filters of flesh.'

He stood there in elongated court room shadow, his face torn like a broken film by lusts and hungers of larval organs stirring in the tentative ectoplasmic flesh of junk kick (ten days on ice at time of the First Hearing) flesh that fades at the first silent touch of junk.

I saw it happen. Ten pounds lost in minutes standing with the syringe in one hand and holding his pants up with the other, his abdicated flesh burning in a cold yellow halo, there in the New York hotel room—night table litter of candy boxes, cigarette butts cascading out of three ashtrays, mosaic of sleepless nights and sudden food needs of the kicking addict nursing his baby flesh.

The Vigilante is prosecuted in Federal Court under a lynch bill and winds up in a Federal Nut House specially designed for the containment of ghosts: precise, prosaic impact of objects—washstand—door—toilet—bars—there they are—this is it—all lines cut—nothing beyond—Dead End—And the Dead End in every face.

The physical changes were slow at first, then jumped forward in black klunks, falling through his slack tissue, washing away the human lines—In his place of total darkness mouth and eyes are one organ that leaps forward to snap with transparent teeth—but no organ is constant as regards either function or position—sex organs sprout everywhere—rectums open, defecate and close—the entire organism changes colour and consistency in split-second adjustments.

The Rube is a social liability with his attacks as he calls them. The Mark Inside was coming up on him and that's a rumble nobody can cool; outside Philly he jumps out to con a prowl car and the fuzz takes one look at his face and busts all of us.

Seventy-two hours and five sick junkies in the cell with us. Now not wishing to break out my stash in front of these hungry coolies, it takes manoeuvering and laying of gold on the turnkey before we are in a separate cell.

Provident junkies, known as squirrels, keep stashes against a bust. Every time I take a shot I let a few drops fall into my vest pocket, the lining is stiff with stuff. I had a plastic dropper in my shoe and a safety-pin stuck in my belt. You know how this pin and dropper routine is put down: 'She seized a safety-pin caked with blood and rust, gouged a great hole in her leg which seemed to hang open like an obscene, festering mouth waiting for unspeakable congress with the dropper which she now plunged out of sight into the gaping wound. But her hideous galvanised need (hunger of insects in dry places) has broken the dropper off deep in the flesh of her ravaged thigh (looking rather like a poster on soil erosion). But what does she care? She does not even bother to remove the splintered glass, looking down at her bloody haunch with the cold blank eyes of a meat trader. What does she care for the atom bomb, the bed bugs, the cancer rent, Friendly Finance waiting to repossess her delinquent flesh—Sweet dreams, Pantapon Rose.'

The real scene you pinch up some leg flesh and make a quick stab hole with a pin. Then fit the dropper *over, not in* the hole and feed the solution slow and careful so it doesn't squirt out the sides —When I grabbed the Rube's thigh the flesh came up like wax and stayed there, and a slow drop of pus oozed out the hole. And I never touched a living body cold as the Rube there in Philly.

I decided to lop him off if it meant a smother party. (This is a rural English custom designed to eliminate aged and bedfast dependents. A family so afflicted throws a 'smother party' where the guests pile mattresses on the old liability, climb up on top of the mattresses and lush themselves out.) The Rube is a drag on the industry and should be 'led out' into the skid rows of the world. (This is an African practice. Official known as the 'Leader Out' has the function of taking old characters out in the jungle and leaving them there.)

The Rube's attacks become an habitual condition. Cops, doormen, dogs, secretaries snarl at his approach. The blond God has fallen to untouchable vileness. Con men don't change, they break, shatter —explosions of matter in cold interstellar space, drift away in cosmic dust, leave the empty body behind. Hustlers of the world, there is one Mark you cannot beat: The Mark Inside.

I left the Rube standing on a corner, red brick slums to the sky, under a steady rain of soot. 'Going to hit this croaker I know. Right back with that good pure drugstore M—No, you wait here—don't want him to rumble you.' No matter how long, Rube, wait for me right on that corner. Goodbye, Rube, goodbye kid—Where do they go when they walk out and leave the body behind?

Chicago: invisible hierarchy of decorticated wops, smell of atrophied gangsters, earthbound ghost hits you at North and Halstead, Cicero, Lincoln Park, panhandler of dreams, past invading the present, rancid magic of the slot machines and roadhouses.

Into the Interior: a vast subdivision, antennae of television to the meaningless sky. In lifeproof houses they hover over the young, sop up a little of what they shut out. Only the young bring anything in, and they are not young very long. (Through the bars of East St Louis lies the dead frontier, riverboat days.) Illinois and Missouri, miasma of mound-building peoples, grovelling worship of the Food Source, cruel and ugly festivals, dead-end horror of the

Centipede God reaches from Moundville to the lunar deserts of coastal Peru.

America is not a young land: it is old and dirty and evil before the settlers, before the Indians. The evil is there waiting.

And always cops: smooth college-trained state cops, practised, apologetic patter, electronic eyes weigh your car and luggage, clothes and face; snarling big city dicks, soft-spoken country sheriffs with something black and menacing in old eyes colour of a faded grey flannel shirt.

And always car trouble: in St Louis traded the 1942 Studebaker in (it has a built-in engineering flaw like the Rube) on an old Packard limousine heated up and barely made Kansas City, and bought a Ford turned out to be an oil burner, packed it in on a jeep we push too hard (they are no good for highway driving)— and burn something out inside, rattling around, went back to the old Ford V-8. Can't beat that engine for getting there, oil burner or no.

And the US drag closes around us like no other drag in the world, worse than the Andes, high mountain towns, cold wind down from postcard mountains, thin air like death in the throat, river towns of Ecuador, malaria grey as junk under black Stetson, muzzle loading shotguns, vultures pecking through the mud streets —and what hits you when you get off the Malmo ferry in (no juice tax on the ferry) Sweden knocks all that cheap, tax free juice right out of you and brings you all the way down: averted eyes and the cemetery in the middle of town (every town in Sweden seems to be built around a cemetery), and nothing to do in the afternoon, not a bar not a movie and I blasted my last stick of Tangier tea and I said, 'K.E. let's get right back on that ferry.'

But there is no drag like US drag. You can't see it, you don't know where it comes from. Take one of those cocktail lounges at the end of a subdivision street—every block of houses has its own bar and drugstore and market and liquorstore. You walk in and it hits you. But where does it come from?

Not the bartender, nor the customers, nor the cream-coloured plastic rounding the bar stools, nor the dim neon. Not even the TV.

And our habits build up like the drag, like cocaine will build you up staying ahead of the C bring-down. And the junk was running low. So there we are in this no-horse town strictly from cough-syrup. And vomited up the syrup and drove on and on, cold spring wind whistling through that old heap around our shivering sick sweating bodies and the cold you always come down with when the junk runs out of you—On through the peeled landscape, dead armadillos in the road and vultures over the swamp and cypress stumps. Motels and beaverboard walls, gas heater, thin pink blankets.

Itinerant short con and carny hyp men have burned down the croakers of Texas.

And no one in his right mind would hit a Louisiana croaker. State Junk Law.

Came at last to Houston where I know a druggist. I haven't been there in five years but he looks up and makes me with one quick look and just nods and says: 'Wait over at the counter—'

So I sit down and drink a cup of coffee and after a while he comes and sits beside me and says, 'What do you want?'

'A quart of PG and a hundred nembies.'

He nods, 'Come back in half an hour.'

So when I come back he hands me a package and says, 'That's fifteen dollars—Be careful.'

Shooting PG is a terrible hassle, you have to burn out the alcohol first, then freeze out the camphor and draw this brown liquid off with a dropper—have to shoot it in the vein or you get an abcess, and usually end up with an abcess no matter where you shoot it. Best deal is to drink it with goof balls—So we pour it in a Pernod bottle and start for New Orleans past iridescent lakes and orange gas flares and swamps and garbage heaps, alligators crawling around in broken bottles and tin cans, neon arabesques of motels, marooned pimps scream obscenities at passing cars from islands of rubbish.

New Orleans is a dead museum. We walk around Exchange Place, breathing PG and find The Man right away. It's a small place and the fuzz always knows who is pushing so he figures what the hell does it matter and sells to anybody. We stock up on H and backtrack for Mexico.

Back through Lake Charles and the dead slot-machine country, south end of Texas, nigger-killing sheriffs look us over and check the car papers. Something falls off you when you cross the border into Mexico, and suddenly the landscape hits you straight with nothing between you and it, desert and mountains and vultures; little wheeling specks and others so close you can hear wings cut the air (a dry husking sound), and when they spot something they pour out of the blue sky, that shattering bloody blue sky of Mexico, down in a black funnel—Drove all night, came at dawn to a warm, misty place, barking dogs and the sound of running water.

'Thomas and Charlie,' I said.

'What?'

'That's the name of this town. Sea level. We climb straight up from here ten thousand feet.' I took a fix and went to sleep in the back seat. She was a good driver. You can tell as soon as someone touches the wheel.

Mexico City where Lupita sits like an Aztec Earth Goddess doling out her little papers of lousy shit.

'Selling is more of a habit than using,' Lupita says. Non-using pushers have a contact habit, and that's one you can't kick. Agents get it too. Take Bradley the Buyer. Best narcotics agent in the industry. Anyone would make him for junk. (Note: Make in the sense of dig or size up.) I mean he can walk up to a pusher and score direct. He is so anonymous, grey and spectral the pusher don't remember him afterwards. So he twists one after the other.

Well the Buyer comes to look more and more like a junky. He can't drink. He can't get it up. His teeth fall out. (Like pregnant women lose their teeth feeding the stranger, junkies lose their yellow fangs feeding the monkey.) He is all the time sucking on a candy bar. Babe Ruths he digs special. 'It really disgusts you to see the Buyer sucking on them candy bars so nasty,' a cop says.

The Buyer takes on an ominous grey-green colour. Fact is his body is making its own junk or equivalent. The Buyer has a steady connection. A Man Within you might say. Or so he thinks. 'I'll just set in my room,' he says. 'Fuck 'em all. Squares on both sides. I am the only complete man in the industry.'

But a yen comes on him like a great black wind through the bones. So the Buyer hunts up a young junky and gives him a paper to make it.

'Oh all right,' the boy says. 'So what you want to make?'

'I just want to rub up against you and get fixed.'

'Ugh—Well all right—But why cancha just get physical like a human?'

Later the boy is sitting in a Waldorf with two colleagues dunking pound cake. 'Most distasteful thing I ever stand still for,' he says. 'Some way he make himself all soft like a blob of jelly and surround me so nasty. Then he gets wet all over like with green slime. So I guess he come to some kinda awful climax—I come near wig-ging with that green stuff all over me, and he stink like a old rotten canteloupe.'

'Well it's still an easy score.'

The boy sighed resignedly; 'Yes, I guess you can get used to anything. I've got a meet with him again tomorrow.'

The Buyer's habit keeps getting heavier. He needs a recharge every half hour. Sometimes he cruises the precincts and bribes the turnkey to let him in with a cell of junkies. It gets to where no amount of contact will fix him. At this point he receives a summons from the District Supervisor:

'Bradley, your conduct has given rise to rumours—and I hope for your sake they are no more than that—so unspeakably distasteful that—I mean Caesar's wife—hrump—that is, the Department must be above suspicion—certainly above such suspicions as you have seemingly aroused. You are lowering the entire tone of the industry. We are prepared to accept your immediate resignation.'

The Buyer throws himself on the ground and crawls over to the DS. 'No, Boss Man, no—The Department is my very lifeline.'

He kisses the DS's hand, thrusting the fingers into his mouth (the DS must feel his toothless gums) complaining he has lost his teeth 'inna thervith.' 'Please Boss Man. I'll wipe your ass, I'll wash out your dirty condoms, I'll polish your shoes with the oil of my nose—'

'Really, this is most distasteful! Have you no pride? I must tell you I feel a distinct revulsion. I mean there is something, well, rotten about you, and you smell like a compost heap.' He put a scented handkerchief in front of his face. 'I must ask you to leave this office at once.'

'I'll do anything, Boss, *anything.*' His ravaged green face splits in a horrible smile. 'I'm still young, Boss, and I'm pretty strong when I get my blood up.'

The DS retches into his handkerchief and points to the door with a limp hand. The Buyer stands up looking at the DS dreamily. His body begins to dip like a dowser's wand. He flows forward.

'No! No!' screams the DS.

'Schlup—schlup schlup.' An hour later they find the Buyer on the nod in the DS's chair. The DS has disappeared without a trace.

The Judge: 'Everything indicates that you have, in some unspeakable manner uh—assimilated the District Supervisor. Unfortunately there is no proof. I would recommend that you be confined or more accurately contained in some institution, but I know of no place suitable for a man of your calibre. I must reluctantly order your release.'

'That one should stand in an aquarium,' says the arresting officer.

The Buyer spreads terror throughout the industry. Junkies and agents disappear. Like a vampire bat he gives off a narcotic effluvium, a dank green mist that anaesthetises his victims and renders them helpless in his enveloping presence. And once he has scored he holes up for several days like a gorged boa constrictor. Finally he is caught in the act of digesting the Narcotics Commissioner and destroyed with a flame thrower—the court of inquiry ruling that such means were justified in that the Buyer had lost his human citizenship and was, in consequence, a creature without species and a menace to the narcotics industry on all levels.

In Mexico the gimmick is to find a local junky with a government scrip whereby they are allowed a certain quantity every month. Our Man was Old Ike who had spent most of his life in the States.

'I was travelling with Irene Kelly and her was a sporting woman. In Butte, state of Montana, she gets the coke horrors and run through the hotel screaming Chinese coppers chase her with meat cleavers. I knew this cop in Chicago sniff coke used to come in form of crystals, blue crystals. So he go nuts and start screaming the Federals is after him and run down this alley and stick his head in the garbage can. And I said, "What you think you are doing?" and he say, "Get away or I shoot you. I got myself hid good".'

We are getting some C on RX at this time. Shoot it in the mainline, son. You can smell it going in, clean and cold in your nose and throat then a rush of pure pleasure right through the brain lighting up those C connections. Your head shatters in white explosions. Ten minutes later you want another shot—you will walk across town for another shot. But if you can't score for C you eat, sleep and forget about it.

This is a yen of the brain alone, a need without feeling and without body, earthbound ghost need, rancid ectoplasm swept out by an old junky coughing and spitting in the sick morning.

One morning you wake up and take a speed ball, and feel bugs under your skin. 1890 cops with black moustaches block the doors and lean in through the windows snarling their lips back from blue and gold embossed badges. Junkies march through the room singing the Moslem Funeral Song, bear the body of Bill Gains, stigmata of his needle wounds glow with a soft blue flame. Purposeful schizophrenic detectives sniff at your chamber pot.

It's the coke horrors—Sit back and play it cool and shoot in plenty of that GI M.

Day of the Dead: I got the chucks and ate my little Willy's sugar skull. He cried and I had to go out for another. Walked past the cocktail lounge where they blasted Jai Lai bookie.

When they walked in on me that morning at 8 o'clock, I knew it was my last chance, my only chance. But they didn't know. How could they? Just a routine pick-up. But not quite routine.

Hauser had been eating breakfast when the Lieutenant called: 'I want you and your partner to pick up a man named Lee, William Lee, on your way downtown. He's in the Hotel Lamprey. 103 just off B way.'

'Yeah I know where it is. I remember him too.'

'Good. Room 606. Just pick him up. Don't take time to shake the place down. Except bring in all books, letters, manuscripts. *Anything* printed, typed or written, Ketch?'

'Ketch. But what's the angle—Books.'

'Just do it.' The Lieutenant hung up.

Hauser and O'Brien. They had been on the City Narcotic Squad for 20 years. Oldtimers like me. I been on the junk 16 years. They weren't bad as laws go. At least O'Brien wasn't. O'Brien was the con man, and Hauser the tough guy. A vaudeville team. Hauser had a way of hitting you before he said anything just to break the ice. Then O'Brien gives you an Old Gold—just like a cop to smoke Old Golds somehow—and starts putting down a cop con that was really bottled in bond. Not a bad guy, and I didn't want to do it. But it was my only chance.

I was just tying up for my morning shot when they walked in with a pass key. It was the special kind you can use even when the door is locked from the inside with a key in the lock. On the table in front of me was a packet of junk, spike, syringe—I got the habit of using a regular syringe in Mexico and never went back to using a dropper—alcohol, cotton and a glass of water.

'Well, well,' says O'Brien—'Long time no see eh?'

'Put on your coat, Lee,' says Hauser. He had this gun out. He always has it out when he makes a pinch for the psychological effect and to forestall a rush for toilet, sink or window.

'Can I take a bang first, boys?' I asked—'There's plenty here for evidence.'

I was wondering how I could get to my suitcase if they said no. The case wasn't locked, but Hauser had the gun in his hand.

'He wants a shot,' said Hauser.

'Now you know we can't do that, Bill,' said O'Brien in his sweet con voice, dragging out the name with an oily, insinuating familiarity, brutal and obscene.

He meant, of course, 'What can you do for *us,* Bill?' He looked at me and smiled. The smile stayed there too long, hideous and naked, the smile of an old painted pervert, gathering all the negative evil of O'Brien's ambiguous function.

'I might could set up Marty Steel for you,' I said.

I knew they wanted Marty bad. He'd been pushing for five years, and they couldn't hang one on him. Marty was an old-timer, and very careful about who he served. He had to know a man and know him well before he would pick up his money. No one can say they ever did time because of me. My rep is perfect, but still Marty wouldn't serve me because he didn't know me long enough. That's how skeptical Marty was.

'Marty!' said O'Brien. 'Can you score for him?'

'Sure I can.'

They were suspicious. A man can't be a cop all his life without developing a special set of intuitions.

'OK,' said Hauser finally. 'But you'd better deliver, Lee.'

'I'll deliver all right. Believe me I appreciate this.'

I tied up for a shot, my hands trembling with eagerness, an archetype dope fiend.

'Just an old junky, boys, a harmless old shaking wreck of a junky.' That's the way I put it down. As I had hoped, Hauser looked away when I started probing for a vein. It's a wildly unpretty spectacle.

O'Brien was sitting on the arm of a chair smoking an Old Gold, looking out the window with that dreamy what I'll do when I get my pension book.

I hit a vein right away. A column of blood shot up into the syringe for an instant sharp and solid as a red cord. I pressed the plunger down with my thumb, feeling the junk pound through my veins to feed a million junk-hungry cells, to bring strength and alertness to every nerve and muscle. They were not watching me. I filled the syringe with alcohol.

Hauser was juggling his snub-nosed detective special, a Colt, and looking around the room. He could smell danger like an animal. With his left hand he pushed the closet door open and glanced inside. My stomach contracted. I thought, 'If he looks in the suitcase now I'm done.'

Hauser turned to me abruptly. 'You through yet?' he snarled. 'You'd better not try to shit us on Marty.' The words came out so ugly he surprised and shocked himself.

I picked up the syringe full of alcohol, twisting the needle to make sure it was tight.

'Just two seconds,' I said.

I squirted a thin jet of alcohol, whipping it across his eyes with a sideways shake of the syringe. He let out a bellow of pain. I could see him pawing at his eyes with the left hand like he was tearing off an invisible bandage as I dropped to the floor on one knee, reaching for my suitcase. I pushed the suitcase open, and my left hand closed over the gun butt—I am right-handed but I shoot with my left hand. I felt the concussion of Hauser's shot before I heard it. His slug slammed into the wall behind me. Shooting from the floor, I snapped two quick shots into Hauser's belly where his vest had pulled up showing an inch of white shirt. He grunted in a way I could feel and doubled forward. Stiff with panic, O'Brien's hand was tearing at the gun in his shoulder holster. I clamped my other hand around my gun wrist to steady it for the long pull—this gun has the hammer filed off round so you can only use it double action—and shot him in the middle of his red forehead about two inches below the silver hairline. His hair had been grey the last time I saw him. That was about 15 years ago. My first arrest. His eyes went out. He fell off the chair onto his face. My hands were already reaching for what I needed, sweeping my notebooks into a briefcase with my works, junk, and a box of shells. I stuck a gun into my belt, and stepped out into the corridor putting on my coat.

I could hear the desk clerk and the bell boy pounding up the stairs. I took the self-service elevator down, walked through the empty lobby into the street.

It was a beautiful Indian Summer day. I knew I didn't have much chance, but any chance is better than none, better than being a subject for experiments with ST (6) or whatever the initials are.

I had to stock up on junk fast. Along with airports, RR stations and bus terminals, they would cover all junk areas and connections. I took a taxi to Washington Square, got out and walked along 4th Street till I spotted Nick on a corner. You can always find the pusher. Your need conjures him up like a ghost. 'Listen, Nick,' I said, 'I'm leaving town. I want to pick up a piece of H. Can you make it right now?'

We were walking along 4th Street. Nick's voice seemed to drift into my consciousness from no particular place. An eerie, disembodied voice. 'Yes, I think I can make it. I'll have to make a run uptown.'

'We can take a cab.'

'OK, but I can't take you in to the guy, you understand.'

'I understand. Let's go.'

We were in the cab heading North. Nick was talking in his flat, dead voice.

'Some funny stuff we're getting lately. It's not weak exactly— I don't know—It's different. Maybe they're putting some synthetic shit in it—Dollies or something.'

'What!!? Already?'

'Huh?—But this I'm taking you to now is OK. In fact it's about the best deal around that I know of—Stop here.'

'Please make it fast,' I said.

'It should be a matter of ten minutes unless he's out of stuff and has to make a run—Better sit down over there and have a cup of coffee—This is a hot neighbourhood.'

I sat down at a counter and ordered coffee, and pointed to a piece of Danish pastry under a plastic cover. I washed down the stale rubbery cake with coffee, praying that just this once, please God, let him make it now, and not come back to say the man is out and has to make a run to East Orange or Greenpoint.

Well here he was back, standing behind me. I looked at him, afraid to ask. Funny, I thought, here I sit with perhaps one chance in a hundred to live out the next 24 hours—I had made up my mind not to surrender and spend the next three or four months in death's waiting room. And here I was worrying about a junk score. But I only had about five shots left, and without junk I would be immobilised—Nick nodded his head.

'Don't give it to me here,' I said. 'Let's take a cab.'

We took a cab and started downtown. I held out my hand and

copped the package. I slipped a fifty-dollar bill into Nick's palm. He glanced at it and showed his gums in a toothless smile: 'Thanks a lot—This will put me in the clear.'

I sat back letting my mind work without pushing it. Push your mind too hard, and it will fuck up like an overloaded switchboard, or turn on you with sabotage—And I had no margin for error. Americans have a special horror of giving up control, of letting things happen in their own way without interference. They would like to jump down into their stomachs and digest the food and shovel the shit out.

Your mind will answer most questions if you learn to relax and wait for the answer. Like one of those thinking machines, you feed in your question, sit back, and wait.

I was looking for a name. My mind was sorting through names, discarding at once FL—Fuzz Lover, BW—Born Wrong, NCBC—Nice Cat But Chicken; putting aside to reconsider, narrowing, sifting, feeling for the name, the answer.

'Sometimes, you know, he'll keep me waiting three hours. Sometimes I make it right away like this.' Nick had a deprecating little laugh that he used for punctuation. Sort of an apology for talking at all in the telepathising world of the addict where only the quantity factor—How much $? How much junk?—requires verbal expression. He knew and I knew all about waiting. At all levels the drug trade operates without schedule. Nobody delivers on time except by accident. The addict runs on junk time. His body is his clock, and junk runs through it like an hour-glass. Time has meaning for him only with reference to his need. Then he makes his abrupt intrusion into the time of others, and, like all Outsiders, all Petitioners, he must wait, unless he happens to mesh with non-junk time.

'What can I say to him? He knows I'll wait,' Nick laughed.

I spent the night in the Ever Hard Baths—(homosexuality is the best all-round cover story an agent can use)—where a snarling Italian attendant creates such an unnerving atmosphere sweeping the dormitory with infra red see in the dark fieldglasses.

('All right in the North East corner! I see you!') switching on the floodlights, sticking his head through trapdoors in the floor and walls of the private rooms, that many a queer has been carried out in a straitjacket.

I lay there in my open top cubicle room looking at the ceiling—

listened to the grunts and squeals and snarls in the nightmare half-light of random, broken lust.

'Fuck off you!'

'Put on two pairs of glasses and maybe you can see something!'

Walked out in the precise morning and bought a paper—Nothing—I called from a drugstore phone booth—and asked for Narcotics:

'Lieutenant Gonzales—who's calling?'

'I want to speak to O'Brien.' A moment of static, dangling wires, broken connections.

'Nobody of that name in this department—Who are *you?*'

'Well let me speak to Hauser.'

'Look, Mister, no O'Brien no Hauser in this bureau. Now what do you want?'

'Look, this is important—I've got info on a big shipment of H coming in—I want to talk to Hauser or O'Brien—I don't do business with anybody else.'

'Hold on—I'll connect you with Alcibiades.'

I began to wonder if there was an Anglo-Saxon name left in the Department.

'I want to speak to Hauser or O'Brien.'

'How many times I have to tell you no Hauser no O'Brien in this department—Now who is this calling?'

I hung up and took a taxi out of the area—In the cab I realised what had happened—I had been occluded from space-time like an eel's ass occludes when he stops eating on the way to Sargasso—Locked out—Never again would I have a Key, a Point of Inter-section—The Heat was off me from here on out—relegated with Hauser and O'Brien to a land-locked junk past where heroin is always twenty-eight dollars an ounce and you can score for yen pox in the Chink Laundry of Sioux Falls—Far side of the world's mirror, moving into the past with Hauser and O'Brien.

The Blood of a Wig

TERRY SOUTHERN

My MOST OUTLANDISH DRUG experience, now that I think about it, didn't occur with beat Village or Harlem weirdos, but during a brief run with the ten-to-four Mad Ave crowd.

How it happened, this friend of mine who was working at *Lance* ('The Mag for Men') phoned me one morning—he knew I was strapped.

'One of the fiction editors is out with syph or something,' he said. 'You want to take his place for a while?'

I was still mostly asleep, so I tried to cool it by shooting a few incisive queries as to the nature of the gig—which he couldn't seem to follow.

'Well,' he said finally, 'you won't have to *do* anything, if that's what you mean.' He had a sort of blunt and sullen way about him—John Fox his name was, an ex-Yalie and would-be writer who was constantly having to 'put it back on the shelf,' as he expressed it (blunt, sullen), and take one of these hot-shot Mad Ave jobs, and always for some odd reason—like at present paying for his mom's analysis.

Anyway, I accepted the post, and now I had been working there about three weeks. It wasn't true, of course, what he'd said about not having to do anything—I mean the way he had talked I wouldn't even have to get out of bed—but after three weeks my routine was fairly smooth: up at ten, wash face, brush teeth, fresh shirt, dex, and make it. I had this transistor-shaver I'd copped for five off a junky-booster, so I would shave with it in the cab, and walk into the office at ten-thirty or so, as Dan and hip as Harry. Then into my own small office, lock the door, and start stashing the return-postage from the unsolicited mss. We would get an incredible amount of mss—about two hundred a day—and these were divided into two categories: (1) those from agents, and (2) those that came in cold, straight from the author. The ratio was about 30 to 1 in favour of the latter—which formed a gigantic heap called 'the shit-pile', or (by the girl readers) 'the garbage dump'. These always contained a lot of return-postage—so right away I was able to supplement my weekly wage by seven or eight dollars a day in postage stamps. Everyone else considered the 'shit-pile' as something heinously repugnant, especially the sensitive girl ('garbage') readers, so it was a source of irritation and chagrin to my secretary when I first told her I wished to read '*all* unsolicited manuscripts and *no* manuscripts from agents'.

John Fox found it incomprehensible.

'You must be out of your nut!' he said. 'Ha! Wait until you try to read some of that crap in the shit-pile!'

I explained however (and it was actually true in the beginning) that I had this theory about the existence of a *pure, primitive, folk-like* literature—which, if it did exist, could only turn up among the unsolicited mss. Or *weird*, something really *weird*, even insane, might turn up there—whereas I knew the stuff from the agents would be the same old predictably competent tripe. So, aside from stashing the stamps, I would read each of these shit-pile mss very carefully—reading subtleties, insinuations, multi-level entendre into what was actually just a sort of flat, straightforward simple-mindedness. I would think each was a put-on—a fresh and curious parody of some kind, and I would read on, and on, all the way to the end, waiting for the pay-off . . . but, of course, that never happened, and I gradually began to revise my theory and to refine my method. By the second week, I was able to reject an ms after reading the opening sentence, and by the third I could often reject on the basis of *title* alone—the principle being if an author would allow a blatantly dumbbell title, he was incapable of writing a story worth reading. (This was thoroughly tested and proved before adopting.) Then, instead of actually *reading* mss, I would spend hours, days really, just thinking, trying to refine and extend my method of blitz-rejection. I was able to take it a little farther, but not much. For example, any woman author who used 'Mrs' in her name could be rejected out of hand—*unless* it was used with only one name, like 'by Mrs Carter', then it might be a weirdie. And again, any author using a middle initial or a 'Jr' in his name, shoot it right back to him! I knew I was taking a chance with that one (because of Connell and Selby), but I figured what the hell, I could hardly afford to gear the sort of fast-moving synchro-mesh operation I had in mind to a couple of exceptions—which, after all, only went to prove the consarn rule, so to speak. Anyway, there it was, the end of the third week and the old job going smoothly enough, except that I had developed quite a little dexie habit by then—not actually a habit, of course, but a sort of very real dependence . . . having by nature a nocturnal metabolism whereby my day (pre-*Lance*) would ordinarily begin at three or four in the afternoon and finish at eight or nine in the morning. As a top-staffer at *Lance,* however, I had to make other arrangements. Early on I had actually asked John Fox if it would be possible for me to come in at four and work until midnight.

'Are you out of your *nut?*' (That was his standard comeback). 'Don't you know what's happening here? This is a *social* scene, man—these guys want to *see* you, they want to get to *know* you?'

'What are they, faggots?'

'No, they're not *faggots,*' he said stoutly, but then seemed hard pressed to explain, and shrugged it off. 'It's just that they don't have very much, you know, *to do.*'

It was true in a way that no one seemed to actually *do* anything —except for the typists, of course, always typing away. But the guys just sort of hung out, or around, buzzing each other, sounding the chicks, that sort of thing.

The point is though that I had to make it in by ten, or thereabouts. One reason for this was the 'pre-lunch confab' which Hacker, or the 'Old Man' (as, sure enough, the publisher was called) might decide to have on any given day. And so it came to pass that on this particular—Monday it was—morning, up promptly at nine-three-oh, wash face, brush teeth, fresh shirt, all as per usual, and reach for the dex . . . no dex, out of dex. This was especially inopportune because it was on top of two straight white and active nights, and it was somewhat as though an eight-hundred-pound bag of loosely packed sand began to settle slowly on the head. No panic, just immediate death from fatigue.

At Sheridan Square, where I usually got the taxi, I went into the drug store. The first-shift pharmacist, naturally a guy I had never seen before, was on duty. He looked like an aging efficiency expert.

'Uh, I'd like to get some dexamyl, please.'

The pharmacist didn't say anything, just raised one hand to adjust his steel-rimmed glasses, and put the other out for the prescription.

'It's on file here,' I said, nodding toward the back.

'What name?' he wanted to know, then disappeared behind the glass partition, but very briefly indeed.

'Nope,' he said, coming back, and was already looking over my shoulder to the next customer.

'Could you call Mr Robbins?' I asked. 'He can tell you about it.' Of course this was simply whistling in the dark, since I was pretty sure Robbins, the night-shift man, didn't know me by name, but I had to keep the ball rolling.

'I'm not gonna wake Robbins at this hour—he'd blow his stack. Who's next?'

'Well, listen, can't you just *give* me a couple—I've, uh, got a long drive ahead.'

'You can't get dexies without a scrip,' he said, rather reproachfully, wrapping a box of Tampax for a teenie-bopper nifty behind me, '*you* know that.'

'Okay, how about if I get the doctor to phone you?'

'Phone's up front,' he said, and to the nifty: 'That's seventy-nine.'

The phone was under siege—one person using it, and about five waiting—all, for some weird reason, spade fags and prancing gay. Not that I give a damn about who uses the phone, it was just one of those absurd incongruities that seem so often to conspire to undo sanity in times of crisis. What the hell was going on? They were obviously together, very excited, chattering like magpies. Was it the Katherine Dunham contingent of male dancers? Stranded? Lost? Why out so early? One guy had a list of numbers in his hand the size of a small flag. I stood there for a moment, confused in pointless speculation, then left abruptly and hurried down West 4th to the dinette. This was doubly to purpose, since not only is there a phone, but the place is frequented by all manner of heads, and a casual score might well be in order—though it *was* a bit early for the latter, granted.

And this did, in fact, prove to be the case. There was no one there whom I knew—and, worse still, halfway to the phone, I suddenly remembered my so-called doctor (Dr Friedman, his name was) had gone to California on vacation a few days ago. Christ almighty! I sat down at the counter. This called for a quick think-through.

Should I actually call him in California? Have him phone the drug-store from there? Quite a production for a couple of dex. I looked at my watch, it was just after seven in Los Angeles—Friedman would blow his stack. I decided to hell with it and ordered a cup of coffee. Then a remarkable thing happened. I had sat down next to a young man who now quite casually removed a small transparent silo-shaped vial from his pocket, and without so much as a glance in any direction, calmly tapped a couple of the beloved familiar green-hearted darlings into his cupped hand, and tossed them off like two salted peanuts.

Deus ex machina!

'Uh, excuse me,' I said, in the friendliest sort of way, 'I just happened to notice you taking a couple of ha, ha, dexamyl.' And I proceeded to lay my story on him—while he, after one brief look of appraisal, sat listening, his eyes straight ahead, hands still on the counter, one of them half covering the magic vial. Finally he just nodded and shook out two more on the counter. 'Have a ball,' he said.

I reached the office about five minutes late for the big pre-lunch confab. John Fox made a face of mild disgust when I came in the conference room. He always seemed to consider my flaws as his responsibility since it was he had recommended me for the post. Now he glanced uneasily at old Hacker, who was the publisher, editor-in-chief, etc., etc. A man of about fifty-five, he bore a striking resemblance to Edward G. Robinson—an image to which he gave further credence by frequently sitting in a squat-like manner, chew-ing an unlit cigar butt, and mouthing coarse expressions. He liked to characterise himself as a 'tough old bastard', one of his favourite prefaces being: 'I know most of you guys think I'm a *tough old bastard*, right? Well, maybe I am. In the quality-Lit game you *gotta* be tough!' And bla-bla-bla.

Anyway as I took my usual seat between Fox and Bert Katz, the feature-editor, old Hack looked at his watch, then back at me.

'Sorry,' I mumbled.

'We're running a *magazine* here, young man, not a *whorehouse*.'

'Right and double right,' I parried crisply. Somehow old Hack always brought out the schoolboy in me.

'If you want to be *late*,' he continued, 'be late at the *whorehouse* —and do it on your own time!'

Part of his design in remarks of this sort was to get a reaction from the two girls present—Maxine, his cutie pie private sec, and Miss Rogers, assistant to the Art Director—both of whom managed, as usual, a polite blush and half-lowered eyes for his benefit.

The next ten minutes were spent talking about whether to send our own exclusive third-rate photographer to Vietnam or to use the rejects of a second-rate one who had just come back.

'Even with the rejects we could still run our *E.L. trade*,' said Katz, referring to an italicised phrase 'Exclusively Lance' which appeared under photographs and meant they were not being published elsewhere—though less through exclusivity, in my view, than general crappiness.

Without really resolving this, we went on to the subject of Twiggy, the British fashion-model who had just arrived in New York and about whose boyish hair and bust-line raged a storm of controversy. What did it mean philosophically? Aesthetically? Did it signal a new trend? Should we adjust our centre-spread requirements (traditionally 42-24-38) to meet current taste? Or was it simply a flash fad?

'Come next issue,' said Hack, 'we don't want to find ourselves holding the wrong end of the shit-stick, now do we?'

Everyone was quick to agree.

'Well, *I* think she's absolutely *delightful*,' exclaimed Ronnie Rondell, the art director (prancing gay and proud of it), 'she's so much more . . . sensitive-looking and . . . *delicate* than those awful . . . *milk factories!*' He gave a little shiver of revulsion and looked around excitedly for corroboration.

Hack, who had a deep-rooted anti-fag streak stared at him for a moment like he was some kind of weird lizard, and he seemed about to say something cruel and uncalled for to Ron, but then he suddenly turned on me instead.

'Well, Mister Whorehouse man, isn't it about time we heard from you? Got any ideas that might conceivably keep this operation out of the shit-house for another issue or two?'

'Yeah, well I've been thinking,' I said, winging it completely, 'I mean, Fox here and I had an idea for a series of interviews with unusual persons . . .'

'Unusual *persons*?' he growled, 'what the hell does that mean?'

'Well, you know, a whole new department, like a regular feature. Maybe call it, uh, "Lance Visits . . ." '

He was scowling, but he was also nodding vigorously. ' "Lance Visits . . ." Yeh, yeh, you wantta gimme a fer instance?'

'Well, you know, like uh . . . "Lance Visits a Typical Teeny-Bopper"—cute teenny-bopper tells about cute teen-use of Saran Wrap as a contraceptive, et cetera . . . and uh, let's see . . . "Lance Visits A Giant Spade Commie Bull Dike" . . . "Lance Visits the Author of *Masturbation now!*", a really fun-guy.'

Now that I was getting really warmed up, I was aware that Fox, on my left, had raised a hand to his face and was slowly massaging it, mouth open, eyes closed. I didn't look at Hack, but I knew he had stopped nodding. I pressed on . . . 'you see, it could become a sort of regular department, we could do a *"E.L."* on it . . . *"Another Exclusive Lance Visit."* How about this one: "Lance Visits A Cute Junkie Hooker" . . . "Lance Visits A Zany Ex-Nun Nympho" . . . "Lance Visits the Fabulous Rose Chan, beautiful research and development technician for the so-called French Tickler" . . .'

'Okay,' said Hack, 'how about *this* one: "Lance Visits Lance"—know where? Up shit-creek without a paddle! Because that's where we'd be if we tried any of that stuff.' He shook his head in a lament of disgust and pity. 'Jez, that's some sense of humour you got boy.' Then he turned to Fox. 'What rock you say you found him under? Jez.'

Fox, as per usual, made no discernible effort to defend me, simply pretended to suppress a yawn, eyes averted, continuing to doodle on his 'Think Pad,' one of which lay by each of our ashtrays.

'Okay,' said Hack, lighting a new cigar, 'suppose *I* come up with an idea? I mean, I don't wantta *surprise* you guys, cause any *heart-attacks* . . . by *me* coming up with an *idea*,' he saying this with a benign serpent smile, then adding in grim significance, '*after twenty-seven years in this goddam game!*' He took a sip of water, as though trying to cool his irritation at being (as per usual) 'the only slob around here who delivers.' 'Now let's just stroke this one for a while,' he said, 'and see if it gets stiff. Okay, lemme ask you a question: what's the hottest thing in mags at this time? What's raising all the stink and hullabaloo? The *Manchester* book, right? The suppressed passages, right?' He was referring, of course, to a highly publicised account of the assassination of President Kennedy —certain passages of which had allegedly been deleted. 'Okay, now all this stink and hullabaloo—*I* don't like it, *you* don't like it. In the first place, it's infringement on freedom of the press. In the second, they've exaggerated it all out of proportion. I mean, what the hell was *in* those passages? See what I mean? All right, suppose we do a *take-off* on those same passages?'

He gave me a slow look, eyes narrowed—ostensibly to protect them from his cigar smoke, but with a Mephistophelean effect. *He* knew that *I* knew that his 'idea' was actually an idea I had gotten from Paul Krassner, editor of *The Realist,* a few evenings earlier, and had mentioned, *en passant* so to speak, at the last pre-lunch confab. He seemed to be wondering if I would crack. A test, like. I avoided his eyes, doodled on the 'Think Pad.' He exhaled in my direction, and continued:

'Know what I mean? Something *light,* something *zany,* kid the pants off the guys who suppressed it in the first place. A satire like. Get the slant?'

No one at the table seemed to. Except for Hack we were all in our thirties or early forties, and each had been hurt in some way by the President's death. It was not easy to imagine any particular 'zaniness' in that regard.

Fox was the first to speak, somewhat painfully it seemed. 'I'm, uh, not quite sure I follow,' he said. 'You mean it would be done in the style of the book?'

'Right,' said Hack, 'but get this, we don't say it *is* the real thing, we say it *purports* to be the real thing. And editorially we *challenge* the *authenticity* of it! Am I getting through to you?'

'Well, uh, yeah,' said Fox, 'but I'm not sure it can be, you know, uh, *funny.*'

Hack shrugged. 'So? *You're* not sure, *I'm* not sure. Nobody's sure it can be funny. We all take a crack at it—just stroke it a while and see if we get any jissom—right?'

Right.

After work that evening I picked up a new dexamyl prescription and stopped off at Sheridan Square to get it filled. Coming out of the drug store, I paused momentarily to take in the scene. It was a fantastic evening—late spring evening, warm breeze promise of great summer evenings imminent—and teenies in minis floating by like ballerinas, young thighs flashing. Summer, I thought, will be the acid test for minis when it gets too warm for tights, body-stockings, that sort of thing. It should be quite an interesting phenomenon. On a surge of sex-dope impulse I decided to fall by the dinette and see if anything of special interest was shaking, so to speak.

Curious that the first person I should see there, hunched over his coffee, frozen saintlike, black shades around his head as though a hippie crown of thorns, should be the young man who had given me the dex that very morning. I had the feeling he hadn't moved all day. But this wasn't true because he now had on a white linen suit and was sitting in a booth. He nodded in that brief formal way it is possible to nod and mean more than just hello. I sat down opposite him.

'I see you got yourself all straightened out,' he said with a wan smile, nodding again, this time at my little paper bag with the pharmacy label on it.

I took out the vial of dex and popped a quick one, thinking to do a bit of the old creative Lit later on. Then I shook out four or five and gave them to the young man. 'Here's some interest.'

'Anytime,' he said, dropping them in his top pocket, and after a pause, 'You ever in the mood for something beside dexies?'

'Like what?'

He shrugged, 'Oh, you know,' he said, raising a vague limp hand, then added with a smile, 'I mean you know your moods better than I do.'

During the next five minutes he proved to be the most acquisitive pusher, despite his tender years, I have ever encountered. His range was extensive—beginning with New Jersey pot, and ending with something called a 'Frisco Speedball', a concoction of heroin and cocaine, with a touch of acid ('gives it a little colour'). While we were sitting there, a veritable parade of his far flung connections commenced, sauntering over, or past the booth, pausing just long enough to inquire if he wanted to score—for sleepers, leapers, creepers . . . acid in cubes, vials, capsules, tablets, powder . . . 'hash, baby, it's black as O' . . . mushrooms, mescalin, buttons . . . cosanyl, codeine, coke . . . coke in crystals, coke in powder, coke that looked like karo syrup . . . red birds, yellow jackets, purple hearts . . . 'liquid—*O*, man, it comes straight from Indo-China, stamped right on the can' . . . and from time to time the young man ('Trick' he was called) would turn to me and say: 'Got eyes?'

After committing to a modest (thirty dollars) score for crystals, and again for two ounces of what was purported to be 'Panamanian Green' ('It's "one-poke pot", baby.') I declined further inducement. At one point an extremely down-and-out type, a guy I had known before whose actual name was Rattman, but who was known with

F

simple familiarity as 'Rat', and even more familiarly, though some-how obscurely, as 'The Rat-Prick Man', half staggered past the booth, clocked the acquisitive Trick, paused, moved uncertainly to-wards the booth, took a crumpled brown paper bag out of his coat pocket, and opened it to show.

'Trick,' he muttered, almost without moving his lips, '. . . Trick, can you use any Lights? Two-bits for the bunch.' We both looked in, on some commodity quite unrecognisable—tiny, dark cylinder-shaped capsules, brown-black with sticky guk, flat on each end, and apparently made of plastic. There was about a handful of them. The young man made a weary face of distaste and annoyance.

'Man,' he asked softly, plaintively, looking up at Rattman, *'when are you going to get buried?'*

But the latter, impervious, gave a soundless guffaw, and shuffled out.

'What,' I wanted to know, 'were those things?' asking this of the young man half in genuine interest, half in annoyance at not know-ing. He shrugged, raised a vague wave of dismissal. 'Lights they're called . . . they're used nicotine filters. You know, those nicotine filters you put in a certain kind of cigarette holder.'

'*Used* nicotine filters? What do you do with them?'

'Well, you know, drop two or three in a cup of coffee—gives you a little buzz.'

'A little *buzz?*' I said, 'are you kidding? How about a little *cancer?* That's all tar and nicotine in there, isn't it?'

'Yeah, well, you know . . .' he chuckled dryly, 'anything for kicks. Right?'

Right, right, right.

And it was just about then he sprung it—first giving me his look of odd appraisal, then the sign, the tired smile, the halting defer-ence: 'Listen, man . . . you ever made Red-Split?'

'I beg your pardon?'

'Yeah, you know—*the blood of a wig.*'

'No,' I said, not really understanding, 'I don't believe I have.'

'Well, it's something else, baby, I can tell you that.'

'Uh, well, *what* did you call it—I'm not sure I understood . . .'

' "Red-Split", man, it's called "Red-Split"—it's schizo-juice . . . *blood* . . . the blood of a wig.'

'Oh, I see.' I had, in fact, read about it in a recent article in the *Times*—how they had shot up a bunch of volunteer prisoners (very normal, healthy guys, of course) with the blood of schizophrenia patients—and the effect had been quite pronounced . . . in some cases, manic; in other cases, depressive—about 50/50 as I recalled.

'But that can be a big bring-down, can't it?'

He shook his head sombrely. 'Not with *this* juice it can't. You know who this is out of?' Then he revealed the source—Chin Lee, it was, a famous East Village resident, a Chinese symbolist poet, who was presently residing at Bellevue in a strait jacket. 'Nobody,' he said, 'and I mean *nobody,* baby, has gone anywhere but *up, up, up* on *this* taste!'

I thought that it might be an interesting experience, but using caution as my watchword (the *Times* article had been very sketchy) I had to know more about this so-called Red-Split, Blood of a Wig. 'Well, how long does it, uh, you know, *last?*'

He seemed a little vague about that—almost to the point of resenting the question. 'It's a *trip,* man—four hours, six if you're lucky. It all depends. It's a question of *combination*—how your blood makes it with his, you dig?' He paused and gave me a very straight look. 'I'll tell you this much, baby, it *cuts acid and STP* . . .' He nodded vigorously. 'That's right, cuts them both. *Back, down,* and *sideways.*'

'Really?'

He must have felt he was getting a bit too loquacious, a bit too much on the old hard-sell side, because then he just cooled it, and nodded. 'That's right,' he said, so soft and serious that it wasn't really audible.

'How much?' I asked, finally, uncertain of any other approach.

'I'll level with you,' he said, 'I've got this connection—a ward-attendant . . . you know, a male-nurse . . . has what you might call access to the hospital pharmacy . . . does a little trading with the guards on the fifth floor—that's where the *monstro*-wigs are— "High Five" it's called. That's where Chin Lee's at. Anyway, he's operating at cost right now—I mean, he'll cop as much M, or whatever other hard-shit he can, from the pharmacy, then he'll go up to High Five and trade for the juice—you know, just fresh, straight, uncut wig-juice—90 cc, that's the regular hit, about an ounce, I guess . . . I mean, that's what they hit the wigs for, a 90 cc syringe-full, then they cap the spike and put the whole outfit in an insulated wrapper. Like it's supposed to stay at body-temperature, you dig? They're very strict about that—about how much they tap the wig for, and about keeping it fresh and warm, that sort of thing. Which

is okay, because that's the trip—90 cc, "piping hot", as they say.
He gave a tired little laugh at the curious image. 'Anyway the point
is, he never knows in front what the *price* will be, my friend doesn't,
because he never knows what kind of M score he'll make. I mean
like if he scores for half-a-bill of M, then that's what he charges for
the Split, you dig?'

To me with my Mad Ave savvy, this seemed fairly illogical.

'Can't he hold out on the High Five guys?' I asked, '. . . you
know, tell them he only got half what he really got, and save it for
later.'

He shrugged, almost unhappily. 'He's a very ethical guy,' he said,
'I mean like he's pretty weird. He's not really interested in narcotics,
just *changes*. I mean, like he lets *them* do the count on the M—they
tell him how much it's worth and that's what he charges for the
Split.'

'That *is* weird,' I agreed.

'Yeah, well it's like a new market, you know. I mean there's no
established price yet, he's trying to develop a clientele—can you
make half-a-bill?'

While I pondered, he smiled his grave tired smile, and said:
'There's one thing about the cat, being so ethical and all—he'll
never burn you.'

So in the end it was agreed, and he went off to complete the
arrangements.

The effect of Red-Split was 'as advertised' so to speak—in this case,
quite gleeful. Sense-derangement-wise it was unlike acid in that it
was not a question of the *'Essential I'* having new insights, but of
becoming a different person entirely. So that in a way there was
nothing very scary about it, just extremely weird, and, as it turned
out, somewhat mischievous (Chin Lee, incidentally, was not merely
a great wig, but also a great wag). At about six in the morning I
started to work on the alleged "Manchester passages." Krassner
might be cross, I thought, but what the hell, you can't copyright an
idea. Also I intended to give him full and ample credit. 'Darn good
exposure for Paul,' I mused benignly, taking up the old magic quill.

The first few passages were fairly innocuous, the emphasis being
in a style identical to that of the work in question. Towards the end
of Chapter Six, however, I really started cooking: ' . . . wan, and
wholly bereft, she steals away from the others, moving trance-like

towards the darkened rear-compartment where the casket rests. She enters, and a whispery circle of lights shrouds her bowed head as she closes the door behind her and leans against it. Slowly she raises her eyes and takes a solemn step forward. She gasps, and is literally slammed back against the door by the sheer impact of the outrageous horror confronting her: i.e., the hulking Texan silhouette at the casket, its lid half raised, and he hunching bestially, his coarse animal member thrusting into the casket, and indeed into the neck-wound itself.

'"*Great God*," she cries, "how heinous! It must be a case of . . . of . . . *NECK*-ROPHELIA!"'

I finished at about ten, dexed, and made it to the office. I went directly into Fox's cubicle (the 'Lair' it was called).

'You know,' I began, lending the inflection a child-like candour, 'I could be wrong but I think I've *got* it,' and I handed him the ms.

'Got what?' he countered dryly, 'the clap?'

'You know, that Manchester thing we discussed at the last pre-lunch confab.' While he read, I paced about, flapped my arms in a gesture of uncertainty and humble doubt. 'Oh, it may need a little tightening up, brightening up, granted, but I hope you'll agree that the *essence* is there.'

For a while he didn't speak, just sat with his head resting on one hand staring down at the last page. Finally he raised his eyes; his eyes were always somehow sad.

'You really *are* out of your nut, aren't you?'

'Sorry, John,' I said, 'don't follow.'

He looked back at the ms, moved his hands a little away from it as though it were a poisonous thing. Then he spoke with great seriousness:

'I think you ought to have your head examined.'

'My *head* is swell,' I said, and wished to elaborate, 'my *head* . . .' but suddenly I felt very weary. I had evidently hit on a cow sacred even to the cynical Fox.

'Look,' he said, 'I'm not a *prude* or anything like that, but this . . .' he touched the ms with a cough which seemed to stifle a retch, ' . . . I mean, *this* is the most . . . *grotesque* . . . *obscene* . . . well, I'd rather not even discuss it. Frankly, I think you're in very real need of psychiatric attention.'

'Do you think Hack will go for it?' I asked in perfect candour.

Fox averted his eyes and began to drum his fingers on the desk.

'Look, uh, I've got quite a bit of work to do this morning, so, you know, if you don't mind . . .'

'Gone too far, have I, Fox? Is that it? Maybe you're missing the point of the thing—ever consider that?'

'Listen,' said Fox stoutly, lips tightened, one finger raised in accusation, 'you show this . . . *this thing* to anybody else, you're liable to get a *big smack in the kisser!*' There was an unmistakable heat and resentment in his tone—a sort of controlled hysteria.

'How do you know I'm not from the CIA?' I asked quietly. 'How do *you* know this isn't a *test*?' I gave him a shrewd narrow look of appraisal. 'Isn't it just possible, Fox, that this quasi-indignation of yours is, in point of fact, simply an *act*? A *farce*? A *charade*? An *act,* in short *to save your own skin*!?!'

He had succeeded in putting me on the defensive. But now, steeped in Chink poet cunning, I had decided that an offence was the best defence, and so plunged ahead. 'Isn't it true, Fox, that in this parable you see certain underlying homosexual tendencies which you unhappily recognise in yourself? Tendencies, I say, which to confront would bring you to the very brink of, uh, "fear and trembling", so to speak.' I was counting on the Kierkegaard allusion to bring him to his senses.

'You crazy son of a bitch,' he said flatly, rising behind his desk, hands clenching and unclenching. He actually seemed to be moving towards me in some weird menacing way. It was then I changed my tack. 'Well listen,' I said, 'what would you say if I told you that it wasn't actually *me* who did that, but a Chinese poet? Probably a Commie . . . an insane Commie-fag-spade-Chinese drug fiend. Then we could view it objectively, right?'

Fox, now crazed with his own righteous adrenalin, and somewhat encouraged by my lolling helplessly in the chair, played his indignation to the hilt.

'Okay, Buster,' he said, towering above me, 'keep talking, but make it good.'

'Well, uh, let's see now . . .' So I begin to tell him about my experience with the Red-Split. And speaking in a slow, deliberate, very serious way, I managed to cool him. And then I told him about an insight I had gained into Vietnam, Cassius Clay, Chessman, the Rosenbergs, and all sorts of interesting things. He couldn't believe it. But, of course, no one ever really does—do they?

Cable Street

LEE HARWOOD

blood
dripping slowly
from your throat.

how can I watch you anymore.

Certain individuals frequently suggest that I should write
about Brick Lane and Cable Street, two areas that I know
intimately, having lived in the same these last six years.
The two streets are situated on the western extreme of the
Borough of Stepney, now renamed Tower Hamlets under the
Greater London Scheme. (memo: are we really expected to live
up to this pastoral name retrieved from the archives. Captain
Jack is dead.)

    mid-afternoon
    in some top floor room
    sunny day outside.

Perhaps, or rather, the reason why these individuals make such
a request is that they are romantics, *nostalgie de la boue*.
Wilde's opium dens still doing good trade in their heads. X
street (ref. Dorian Gray) now renamed Y street, the haunt of
'low lascars and chinamen'. The romance of the slums. all very
romantic.

County of London (Grace's Alley, Stepney)
Compulsory Purchase Order, 1963
No. 37 Wellclose Square

    I am writing with reference to
your letter dated 12 January last and
would confirm that 37 Wellclose Square
is included within the above-named Compulsory Purchase Order, which will
shortly be submitted for confirmation
to the Minister of Housing and Local
Government.
    Subject to the Minister's con-
firmation of the Compulsory Purchase
Order, general rehousing by the Council
would be undertaken at the appropriate
time of those eligible residential
occupiers who would qualify for rehousing at that time. I would mention,
however, that it might be some twelve
to eighteen months or more before the
Council would be in a position to begin
rehousing.

                Yours faithfully,

The square at night — all wind scudding and black cobbles.
sound of fights in Cable Street, and another drunk or cursing
woman staggers round the square. one more lap. and sometimes
this scene is so clichéd, it could be out of some Brecht opera
or Zola. It's too absurd. people dying, and crowded, and
hungry.

Walk down nearby alley Sunday afternoon with spade guys and
hardcase men in blue suits and white shirts. Ford Zephyrs and
Zodiacs round the corner, all standing round in the sun, outside
jukebox cafés. smell of stuff hits you one end and by the time

you're half way down you're high too. No fuzz would dare come
down here for fear of getting high themselves.

And anyway Cable Street — half pulled down, only its
shadow left. All the melodramas that might and have happened.
the whole scene like some stage set for social protest 'movies'
the crumbling buildings and boarded shop fronts.

'Well, well,' said pussy twinkletoes, 'isn't that a surprise!'
And it was a surprise too. Everyone in woodland was talking
about it for weeks after.
'Fancy Wendel coming back after such a time. He must have had
some rare adventures.' And wherever you went the only talk was
that of Wendel.

a hundred night cafés, jukeboxes, the whole street vibrating.
Algerians twisting in the arab café. cafés filled with everybody.
what's the difference at night. Mod kids keep calling me Dennis.
Why? Do I have some other side that I don't know about? Am
I king pusher of Cable Street? Dennis the walking pleasure
dome. Have I commandeered a colour machine. roses growing
green.

And summer mornings children singing and hand in hand as they
ring-a-roses in the asphalt playground. fat women teachers somehow
on their wave length.

the moon so clear in the sky
above these city trees
your lips and eyes
so tender filled with love.

Hunger marchers. mid '30s. columns of grim pale men silent.
just a drum beat as the column moves by.
A coffin from Jarrow.
Or, May 1926. General Strike. armed food convoy moving up East
India Dock Road and Commercial Road. Pickets silent beneath

F*

navy machine gun positions. armoured cars and Coldstream Guards
in each truck.
Small meeting of strikers outside Seaman's Institute, East India
Dock Road, when covered lorry drives up. stops just past them.
then tail board goes down. and out pour the police. and from
other direction the mounted police. both charge into the crowd.
Father Grosser running out arms extended to stop them. his
fingers smashed by police batons. Thank you. Everyone running
in all directions. for safety.

what humiliations and pain. the fat men laughing in their
clubs. Churchill wanting to slaughter every striker. Odessa
Steps. Thank you.   Thank you.

the hum of factories. lorries unloading at the warehouses.
people going in all directions. carrying and moving crates
and boxes and barrels. hooters wailing. horns blowing. The
cranes grinding, ships moving into the quays.

According to Lenin part of the reason previous revolutions
failed was due to poor organisation, as he explains in the
case of street fighting and barricades. The former revolut-
ionaries, mobility often being hampered by their own
barricades. This was also the case with the 1871 Paris
Commune. In fact Lenin published in *Vyperyod* the memoirs
of General Cluseret of the Paris Commune on the tactics of
street fighting — 'considering it extremely important to
spread knowledge and understanding of military tactics and
war technique among the working class', if a revolution
was to be successful.
(MEMO: How was it Verlaine survived the Commune, passing
daily to and from his office? In fact — Why did he? N.B.
this is an even more relevant question.)
The raising of barricades and street fighting were also a
frequent occurrence in London during the anti-fascist riots
of 1936, especially in East London in the Stepney and Bethnal
Green areas.
A witness I know, then aged 16, can remember seeing whole
gangs of men prising cobbles from the street to throw at the

mounted police detachments at Gardeners Corner. The police
were trying to clear a way for the fascist march. This was
just one incident in the Battle of Cable Street, 5th October
1936.*

I turn on and then re-read your poems. a fly buzzing round
the wall and room centre. the mystery stains at the bottom
of a glass. eye slowly swivelling round. yet so soon I'm lost
in your world as I read. the room is gone and all your words

*The Battle of Cable Street was caused by the British Union
of Fascists, led by Sir Oswald Mosley, aided by the police,
attempting a propaganda march through the 'East End'. This
was opposed, naturally enough, by the Jews, Socialists and
Communists. There were three main battle points — Old Mint
Street, Cable Street and Gardeners Corner, though numerous
skirmishes took place in the many side streets in the vicinity.
On the one hand the police were trying all ways to get the
march through, first along Mile End Road via Gardeners Corner,
and alternatively along Cable Street. This, on the other hand,
was opposed by the anti-fascist forces. The dockers turned
over lorries to form barricades across Gardeners Corner and
elsewhere, and crowds erected barricades across Cable Street
'ripping doors and furniture from houses and pulling up paving
stones'. An ingenious device were planks with nails knocked
through which successfully stopped all charges by police horses
and motor-cyclists. (MEMO: marbles rolled under the horses'
hooves proved equally effective. Also the waving of sheets of
paper in front of a horse's eyes would invariably cause the horse
to rear and so throw the rider. One such unfortunate police
officer when dismounted was chased by the crowd which pelted him
with his horse's own dung. The reason for their anger was that the
said officer, issued with rum by his superiors previous to the riot,
was striking with his baton any person within reach — old women
and children included. In fact, he went berserk.) And if police tried
to penetrate a side street a group would rush to defend it, and form
a human if not physical barricade.
The fascists, who assembled 3,000 strong in full uniform at Old Mint
Street, were unable to move — the police having totally failed to
make any passage whatsoever, despite numerous baton charges. By
early afternoon the police retreated and Mosley was ordered to dis-
perse. End of battle. (NOTE: It is interesting that the Communists
rallied their supporters using the Spanish Republican motto —
'They shall not pass'.)

and pictures fill my head. and look out the window — children
playing games in the school yard. the factory girls sunning
themselves. their hair and breast obscured by white overalls.
man eternally repairing his car — just the sound of his hammer
striking the metal, so loud and important. pigeons swaying in
the tree tops.

floating through space. velvet black. my rocket ship slides to
distant white stars.
the light over my navigation table warms the charts and instru-
ments I've left there.
now smoking in the break and watching planets slowly turn. the
beauty of this clear plastic slab in the port-hole.

> sea noises outside
> and you in my arms
> among the cool milk sheets
> distant car lights sliding across the room
> high tide and the moon boats
> swaying in the night
> wind
> sea wind
> such peace
> the strength of your loins
> pressed to mine
> our seed mingled

CHECK: Is the chemistry right? Are all the factors taken into
consideration before we take further action.

> the silence of the ship at night
> the coast fading
> and black smoke from the funnels
> sweeping into the dark night sky
> our topless towers burnt
> in orange flames
> in the distance

The atom is split in order to find its exact nature, and in
turn the fundamental nature of all matter. The main research
technique is the observation of the interaction of matter and
energy, for instance the effects of radiation on the atom.
Bohr, Planck and Schrodinger (Quantum Theory, etc.) explained
the behaviour of electrons, and this, in the 1930s, answered
many of the questions related to the atom (nucleus and electrons).
But it has only been in recent years that the nucleus itself has
been seen to break up.
EXAMPLE: A piece of radium placed on a photo-sensitive plate
gives off particles — the tracks of which can be traced on the
plate. These particles are not all electrons. What is being
witnessed is the decay of the radium nucleus.
Up to 1962 thirty-two different and distinct tracks (distinct
in length, curvature, etc.) had been recorded. So the nucleus,
far from being unique, is in fact an elaborate mechanism made
up of at least 32 particles. And every day more particles are
discovered. Early in 1964 at the Brookhaven Laboratories, USA,
the omega-minus particle was discovered. But this more than
any earlier discoveries, marked a major break-through. Whereas
previous particles discovered were unplanned and unexpected,
this was a predicted particle. A theoretical chart had been made
which could tabulate the whole scheme of the particles of the
nucleus. Obviously there would be gaps in this classification,
but these could be found as was proved by omega-minus,
the discovery of which verifies the possibility of a chart, and
so is a step nearer to an understanding of the nucleus.

sometimes lying on my bed at night ships hooting on the river.

On the Sunday of May 9th, 1926, Cardinal Bourne, Roman Catholic
archbishop of Westminster, said at the high mass in Westminster
Cathedral — 'There is no moral justification for a General Strike
of this character. It is therefore a sin against the obedience which we
owe to God . . . All are bound to uphold and assist the Government,
which is the lawfully-constituted authority of the country and
represents therefore in its own appointed sphere the authority
of God Himself'.

At the East India Docks a mass of strikers outside the gates were
intimidated by the sight of bluejackets manning a machine gun
that was directly pointed at   them.

wondrous dream hashish visions of the quiet and beauty of just
every minute article and detail that surrounds me

and what can you do. every noise going through the whole house.
and cat crap and dustbins on every landing. and the stink of people
and decay. one toilet for the whole house. 15 people in 6 rooms.
all the kids reeking of piss and black with dirt.
This is an all-white house.
'Sorry. No coloureds.'

wailing indian music coming from the cafés below. Brick Lane.
and standing grey faced at the window — no flowers, no blue
skies. peeling off my overalls after the night-shift of cleaning out
office blocks. The sky is grey. the rooftops are grey. the roads
are black. Red neon signs blink.

       the river slides smoothly
       under many bridges

THE CATS   are here again

in molecular biology. . . . . .   let us be basic
        a big fat rocket is taking off
        from the launching pad.
        testes. balls. cock of great
        space galaxies.

        Do the presidents know what they're doing?

    space virgin conquests.

smoke and the sound of my own chest lungs breathing. the decision
to turn my eyes to look at another corner of the room. the ginger
of my ginger cat assassin ten times brighter.

     O I am of noble birth
     noble family
     we are poor.

this chaos, total and illogical. put all the plans and patterns back
in the box for they're quite irrelevant.
                               cat saxophones.

sitting in the dark on this summer night. turned on. window
open and cars passing. people walking by below. the slow rise
and fall of my chest. you reading me Blake in the half-light.
man in house opposite kicks a ball round his yard.

an ark is moored somewhere in South London.

     O   Prince your days are done
     The Revolution's come.

A Night on the Town... Confrontation at the Desert Inn... Drug Frenzy at the Circus-Circus

HUNTER S. THOMPSON

SATURDAY MIDNIGHT . . . Memories of this night are extremely hazy. All I have, for guide-pegs, is a pocketful of keno cards and cocktail napkins, all covered with scribbled notes. Here is one: 'Get the Ford man, demand a Bronco for race-observation purposes . . . photos? . . . Lacerda/call . . . why not a helicopter? . . . Get on the phone, *lean* on the fuckers . . . heavy yelling.'

Another says: 'Sign on Paradise Boulevard—"Stopless and Topless" . . . bush-league sex compared to LA; *pasties* here—total naked public humping in LA . . . Las Vegas is a society of armed masturbators/gambling is the kicker here/sex is extra/weird trip for high rollers . . . house-whores for winners, hand jobs for the bad luck crowd.'

A long time ago when I lived in Big Sur down the road from Lionel Olay I had a friend who liked to go to Reno for the crap-shooting. He owned a sporting-goods store in Carmel. And one month he drove his Mercedes highway-cruiser to Reno on three consecutive weekends—winning heavily each time. After three trips he was something like $15,000 ahead, so he decided to skip the fourth weekend and take some friends to dinner at Nepenthe. 'Always quit winners,' he explained. 'And besides, it's a long drive.'

On Monday morning he got a phone call from Reno—from the general manager of the casino he'd been working out on. 'We missed you this weekend,' said the GM. 'The pit-men were bored.'

'Shucks,' said my friend.

So the next weekend he flew up to Reno in a private plane, with a friend and two girls—all 'special guests' of the GM. Nothing too good for high rollers . . .

And on Monday morning the same plane—the casino's plane—flew him back to the Monterey airport. The pilot lent him a dime to call a friend for a ride to Carmel. He was $30,000 in debt, and two months later he was looking down the barrel of one of the world's heaviest collection agencies.

So he sold his store, but that didn't make the nut. They could wait for the rest, he said—but then he got stomped which convinced him that maybe he'd be better off borrowing enough money to pay the whole wad.

Mainline gambling is a very heavy business—and Las Vegas makes Reno seem like your friendly neighbourhood grocery store. For a loser, Vegas is the meanest town on earth. Until about a year ago, there was a giant billboard on the outskirts of Las Vegas, saying:

DON'T GAMBLE WITH MARIJUANA!
IN NEVADA: POSSESSION – 20 YEARS
SALE – LIFE!

So I was not entirely at ease drifting around the casinos on this Saturday night with a car full of marijuana and head full of acid. We had several narrow escapes: at one point I tried to drive the Great Red Shark into the laundry room of the Landmark Hotel—but the door was too narrow, and the people inside seemed dangerously excited.

We drove over to the Desert Inn, to catch the Debbie Reynolds/Harry James show. 'I don't know about you,' I told my attorney, 'but in my line of business it's important to be Hep.'

'Mine too,' he said. 'But as your attorney I advise you to drive over to the Tropicana and pick up on Guy Lombardo. He's in the Blue Room with his Royal Canadians.'

'Why?' I asked.

'Why *what*?'

'Why should I pay out my hard-earned dollars to watch a fucking corpse?'

'Look,' he said. 'Why are we out here? To entertain ourselves, or to *do the job*?'

'The job, of course,' I replied. We were driving around in circles, weaving through the parking lot of a place I thought was the Dunes, but it turned out to be the Thunderbird . . . or maybe it was the Hacienda . . .

My attorney was scanning *The Vegas Visitor*, looking for hints of action. 'How about "Nickel Nick's Slot Arcade?" ' he said. ' "Hot Shots", that sounds heavy . . . Twenty-nine cent hot-dogs . . .'

Suddenly people were screaming at us. We were in trouble. Two thugs wearing red-gold military overcoats were looming over the hood: 'What the hell are you doing?' one screamed. 'You can't park *here*!'

'Why not?' I said. It seemed like a reasonable place to park, plenty of space. I'd been looking for a parking spot for what seemed like a very long time. Too long. I was about ready to abandon the car and call a taxi . . . but then, yes, we found this *space*.

Which turned out to be the sidewalk in front of the main entrance to the Desert Inn. I had run over so many curbs by this time, that I hadn't even noticed this last one. But now we found ourselves in a position that was hard to explain . . . blocking the entrance, thugs yelling at us, bad confusion . . .

My attorney was out of the car in a flash, waving a five-dollar bill. 'We want this car parked! I'm an old friend of Debbie's. I used to *romp* with her.'

For a moment I thought he had blown it . . . then one of the doormen reached out for the bill, saying: 'OK, OK. I'll take care of it, sir.' And he tore off a parking stub.

'Holy shit!' I said, as we hurried through the lobby. 'They almost had us there. That was quick thinking.'

'What do you expect?' he said. 'I'm your *attorney* . . . and you owe me five bucks. I want it now.'

I shrugged and gave him a bill. This garish, deep-orlon carpeted lobby of the Desert Inn seemed an inappropriate place to be haggling about nickel/dime bribes for the parking lot attendant. This was Bob Hope's turf. Frank Sinatra's. Spiro Agnew's. The lobby fairly reeked of high-grade formica and plastic palm trees—it was clearly a high-class refuge for Big Spenders.

We approached the grand ballroom full of confidence, but they refused to let us in. We were too late, said a man in a wine-coloured tuxedo; the house was already full—no seats left, at *any* price.

'Fuck seats,' said my attorney. 'We're old friends of Debbie's. We drove all the way from LA for this show, and we're goddam well going in.'

The tux-man began jabbering about 'fire-regulations', but my attorney refused to listen. Finally, after a lot of bad noise, he let us in for nothing—provided we would stand quietly in the back and not smoke.

We promised, but the moment we got inside we lost control. The tension had been too great. Debbie Reynolds was yukking across the stage in a silver Afro wig . . . to the tune of 'Sergeant Pepper', from the golden trumpet of Harry James.

'Jesus creeping shit!' said my attorney. 'We've wandered into a time capsule!'

Heavy hands grabbed our shoulders. I jammed the hash pipe back into my pocket just in time. We were dragged across the lobby and held against the front door by goons until our car was fetched up. 'OK, get lost,' said the wine-tux-man. 'We're giving you a break. If Debbie has friends like you guys, she's in worse trouble than I thought.'

'We'll see about this!' my attorney shouted as we drove away. 'You paranoid scum!'

I drove around to the Circus-Circus Casino and parked near the back door. 'This is the place,' I said. 'They'll never fuck with us here.'

'Where's the ether?' said my attorney. 'This mescaline isn't working.'

I gave him the key to the trunk while I lit up the hash pipe. He came back with the ether-bottle, uncapped it, then poured some into a kleenex and mashed it under his nose, breathing heavily. I soaked another kleenex and fouled my own nose. The smell was overwhelming, even with the top down. Soon we were staggering up the stairs towards the entrance, laughing stupidly and dragging each other along, like drunks.

This is the main advantage of ether: it makes you behave like the village drunkard in some early Irish novel . . . total loss of all basic motor skills: blurred vision, no balance, numb tongue— severance of all connection between the body and the brain. Which is interesting, because the brain continues to function more or less normally . . . you can actually *watch* yourself behaving in this terrible way, but you can't control it.

You approach the turnstiles leading into the Circus-Circus and you know that when you get there, you have to give the man two dollars or he won't let you inside . . . but when you get there, everything goes wrong: you misjudge the distance to the turnstile and slam against it, bounce off and grab hold of an old woman to keep from falling, some angry Rotarian shoves you and you think: What's happening here? What's going on? Then you hear yourself mumbling: 'Dog's fucked the Pope, no fault of mine. Watch out! . . . Why money? My name is Brinks; I was born . . . born? Get sheep over side . . . women and children in armoured cars . . . orders from Captain Zeep.'

Ah, devil ether—a total body drug. The mind recoils in horror, unable to communicate with the spinal column. The hands flap crazily, unable to get money out of the pocket . . . garbled laughter and hissing from the mouth . . . always smiling.

Ether is the perfect drug for Las Vegas. In this town they love a drunk. Fresh meat. So they put us through the turnstiles and turned us loose inside.

The Circus-Circus is what the whole hep world would be doing on Saturday night if the Nazis had won the war. This is the Sixth Reich. The ground floor is full of gambling tables, like all the other casinos . . . but the place is about four stories high, in the style of a circus tent, and all manner of strange Country-Fair/Polish Carnival madness is going on up in this space. Right above the gambling tables the Forty Flying Carazito Brothers are doing a high-wire trapeze act, along with four muzzled Wolverines and the Six Nymphet Sisters from San Diego . . . so you're down on the main floor playing black jack, and the stakes are getting high when suddenly you chance to look up, and there, right smack above your head is a half-naked fourteen-year-old girl being chased through the air by a snarling wolverine, which is suddenly locked in a death battle with two silver-painted Polacks who come swinging down from opposite balconies and meet in mid-air on the wolverine's neck . . . both Polacks seize the animal as they fall straight down towards the crap tables—but they bounce off the net; they separate and spring back up towards the roof in three different directions, and just as they're about to fall again they are grabbed out of the air by three Korean Kittens and trapezed off to one of the balconies.

This madness goes on and on, but nobody seems to notice. The gambling action runs twenty-four hours a day on the main floor, and the circus never ends. Meanwhile, on all the upstairs balconies, the customers are being hustled by every conceivable kind of bizarre shuck. All kinds of funhouse-type booths. Shoot the pasties off the nipples of a ten-foot bull-dyke and win a cotton-candy goat. Stand in front of this fantastic machine, my friend, and for just 99c your likeness will appear, two hundred feet tall, on a screen above downtown Las Vegas. Ninety-nine cents more for a voice message. 'Say whatever you want, fella. They'll hear you, don't worry about that. Remember you'll be two hundred feet tall.'

Jesus Christ. I could see myself lying in bed in the Mint Hotel, half-asleep and staring idly out the window, when suddenly a vicious nazi drunkard appears two hundred feet tall in the midnight sky, screaming gibberish at the world: *'Woodstock Uber Alles!'*

We will close the drapes tonight. A thing like that could send a drug person careening around the room like a ping-pong ball. Hallucinations are bad enough. But after a while you learn to cope with things like seeing your dead grandmother crawling up your leg with a knife in her teeth. Most acid fanciers can handle this sort of thing.

But *nobody* can handle that other trip—the possibility that any freak with $1.98 can walk into the Circus-Circus and suddenly appear in the sky over downtown Las Vegas twelve times the size of God, howling anything that comes into his head. No, this is not a good town for psychedelic drugs. Reality itself is too twisted.

Good mescaline comes on slow. The first hour is all waiting, then about halfway through the second hour you start cursing the creep who burned you, because nothing is happening . . . and then Z A N G ! Fiendish intensity, strange glow and vibrations . . . a very heavy gig in a place like the Circus-Circus.

'I hate to say this,' said my attorney as we sat down at the Merry-Go-Round Bar on the second balcony, 'but this place is getting *to* me. I think I'm getting the Fear.'

'Nonsense,' I said. 'We came out here to find the American Dream, and now that we're right in the vortex you want to quit.' I grabbed his bicep and squeezed. 'You must *realise,*' I said, 'that we've found the main nerve.'

'I know,' he said. 'That's what gives me the Fear.'

The ether was wearing off, the acid was long gone, but the mescaline was running strong. We were sitting at a small round gold formica table, moving in orbit around the bartender.

'Look over there,' I said. 'Two women fucking a polar bear.'

'Please,' he said. 'Don't *tell* me those things. Not now.' He signalled the waitress for two more Wild Turkeys. 'This is my last drink,' he said. 'How much money can you lend me?'

'Not much,' I said. 'Why?'

'I have to go,' he said.

'Go?'

'Yes. Leave the country. Tonight.'

'Calm down,' I said. 'You'll be straight in a few hours.'

'No,' he said. 'This is serious.'

'George Metesky was serious,' I said. 'And you see what they did to him.'

'Don't fuck around!' he shouted. 'One more hour in this town and I'll kill somebody!'

I could see he was on the edge. That fearful intensity that comes at the peak of a mescaline seizure. 'OK,' I said. 'I'll lend you some money. Let's go outside and see how much we have left.'

'Can we make it?' he said.

'Well . . . that depends on how many people we fuck with between here and the door. You want to leave quietly?'

'I want to leave *fast*,' he said.

'OK. Let's pay this bill and get up very slowly. We're both out of our heads. This is going to be a long walk.' I shouted at the waitress for a bill. She came over, looking bored, and my attorney stood up.

'Do they *pay* you to screw that bear?' he asked her.

'What?'

'He's just kidding,' I said, stepping between them. 'Come on, Doc—let's go downstairs and gamble.' I got him as far as the edge of the bar, the rim of the merry-go-round, but he refused to get off until it stopped turning.

'It won't stop,' I said. 'It's not *ever* going to stop.' I stepped off and turned around to wait for him, but he wouldn't move . . . and before I could reach out and pull him off, he was carried away. 'Don't move,' I shouted. 'You'll come around!' His eyes were staring blindly ahead, squinting with fear and confusion. But he didn't move a muscle until he'd made the whole circle.

I waited until he was almost in front of me, then I reached out to grab him—but he jumped back and went around the circle again. This made me very nervous. I felt on the verge of a freakout. The bartender seemed to be watching us.

Carson City, I thought. Twenty years.

I stepped on the merry-go-round and hurried around the bar, approaching my attorney on his blind side—and when we came to the right spot I pushed him off. He staggered into the aisle and uttered a hellish scream as he lost his balance and went down, thrashing into the crowd . . . rolling like a log, then up again in a flash, fists clenched, looking for somebody to hit.

I approached him with my hands in the air, trying to smile. 'You fell,' I said. 'Let's go.'

By this time people *were* watching us. But the fool wouldn't move, and I knew what would happen if I grabbed him. 'OK,' I said. 'You stay here and go to jail. I'm leaving.' I started walking fast towards the stairs, ignoring him.

This moved him.

'Did you see that?' he said as he caught up with me. 'Some sonofabitch kicked me in the back!'

'Probably the bartender,' I said. 'He wanted to stomp you for what you said to the waitress.'

'Good *god*! Let's get out of here. Where's the elevator?'

'Don't go *near* that elevator,' I said. 'That's just what they *want* us to do . . . trap us in a steel box and take us down to the basement.' I looked over my shoulder, but nobody was following.

'Don't run,' I said. 'They'd like an excuse to shoot us.' He nodded, seeming to understand. We walked fast along the big indoor midway—shooting galleries, tattoo parlours, money-changers and cotton-candy booths—then out through a bank of glass doors and across the grass downhill to a parking lot where the Red Shark waited.

'You drive,' he said. 'I think there's something wrong with me.'

The Canebrake

MOHAMMED MRABET

KACEM AND STITO met every afternoon at a café. They were old friends. Kacem drank, and he had a wife whom he never allowed to go out of the house. No matter how much she entreated him and argued with him, he would not even let her go to the hammam to bathe. Stito had no troubles because he was a bachelor, and only smoked kif.

Kacem would come into the café with a bottle in his shopping bag, and soon both of them would go on to Kacem's house. On the way they would stop at the market to buy food, since Kacem would not permit his wife to go to market, either. Stito had no one to cook for him, and so he ate each night at Kacem's house, and always paid his share.

They would carry the food to Kacem's wife so she could prepare it. First, however, she would make tapas for Kacem's drinks, and tea for Stito's kif. Later when the food was cooking she would go in and sit with the two men.

Once when they were all sitting there together, Stito turned to Kacem and said: Sometimes I wonder how you can drink so much. Where do you store it all?

Kacem laughed. And you? You don't get anything but smoke out of your pipe. I get the alcohol right inside me, and it feels wonderful.

That's an empty idea you have, said Stito. Kif gives me more pleasure than alcohol could ever give anybody. And it makes me think straighter and talk better.

Kacem's wife decided that this was a good moment to say to her husband: Your friend's right. You drink too much.

Kacem was annoyed. Go and look at the food, he told her. It ought to be ready. We want to eat.

She brought the dinner in, and they set to work eating it. After they had finished, they talked for a half hour or so, and then Stito stood up. Until tomorrow, he told Kacem.

Yes, yes. Until tomorrow, said Kacem, who was drunk.

If Allah wills, Stito added.

Kacem's wife got up and opened the door for him.

Good night.

She shut the door, and then she and Kacem went to bed. Feeling full of love, she began to kiss her husband. But he only lay there, too drunk to notice her.

Soon she sat up and began to complain. From the day of our wedding you've never loved me, she said. You never pay me any attention at all unless you want to eat.

Go to sleep, woman, he told her.

She had started to cry, and it was a long time before she slept.

The next afternoon when he finished work, Kacem went to the café to meet Stito. They did the marketing and carried the food back to Kacem's house. The evening passed the same as always. Kacem was very drunk by the time Stito was ready to go home.

Kacem's wife opened the door for Stito and stepped outside. As he went through the doorway she whispered: Try and come alone tomorrow. Let him come by himself.

What do you mean? he said.

She pointed at the canebrake behind the garden. Hide there, she said.

Stito understood. But he'll be here, he whispered.

That's all right. Don't worry, she told him. Good night.

Good night.

The woman shut the door. Kacem was still sitting there drinking. She left him there and went to bed.

Again the following afternoon the two friends met in the café. Stito put away his pipe. How are you? he said.

Let's go, said Kacem. He was eager to get home and open his bottle.

I can't go right now, Stito told him. I've got to wait here and see somebody. I'll come later. Here's the money for the food.

Yes, said Kacem. I'll go on to the market, then.

Sit down with me a minute, said Stito.

No, no. I'll be going.

I'll see you later, Stito said.

Stito sat there in the café until dusk, and then he got up and went to the street where Kacem's house was. He waited until no one was passing by before he began to make his way through the cane-brake. He was invisible in here. He peered between the canes and saw Kacem sitting in his room with a bottle on the table beside him, and a glass in his hand. And he saw the woman bring in the taifor.

Then she came outside carrying a large basin, and walked straight to the edge of the canebrake. She set the basin down and bent over it as if she were working. She was facing her husband and talking with him, and her garments reached to the ground in front of her. In the back, however, she was completely uncovered, and Stito saw everything he wanted to see. While she pretended to be washing something in the basin, she pushed her bare haunches back against the canes, and he pressed forward and began to enjoy himself with her.

When you're ready, she whispered, pull it out and let me catch it all in my hand.

That's no way, he said. How can I do that?

The woman moved forward suddenly and made it slip out, so that Stito understood that if he were to have anything at all with her, he would have to do as she wanted.

You can do it again afterwards and finish inside, if you like, she whispered.

She backed against the canes again, and he started once more. When he was almost ready he warned her, and she reached back with her hand, and got what she wanted. Keeping her fist shut, she waited so he could do it again the way he enjoyed it. He finished and went out of the canebrake into the street. No one saw him.

The woman walked into the house. She stood by the chair where Kacem sat, looking down at him. Can I go to the hammam tomorrow? she said.

Are you starting that all over again? cried Kacem. I've told you no a thousand times. No! You can't leave this house.

She reached out her hand, opened it, and let what she had been holding drip on to the taifor beside Kacem's glass.

Kacem stared. He had been drunk a moment before, and now he was no longer drunk. He did not even ask her from whom she had got it, or how. He stood up, leaving the bottle and glass, and went to bed without his dinner.

In the morning when he went out to work, Kacem left the door of his house wide open. All day he thought about his wife. When he had finished work, he went to the café to meet Stito.

His face was sad as he sat down. Fill me a pipe, he said.

What? Stito cried.

Yes.

Stito gave him his pipe. What's happened? It's the first time you've ever asked for kif.

I'm through with drinking, Kacem told him. I'm going to start smoking kif.

But why?

Kacem did not reply, and Stito did not ask again.

That evening the two friends arrived at Kacem's house laughing and joking, with their heads full of kif. Kacem was in a fine humour all evening. After Stito had gone, he said to his wife: You went to the hammam?

Yes, she said. Thank you for leaving the door open. I thought you'd forgotten to shut it when you went out.

I'm not going to lock it any more, he told her.

She kissed him and they went to bed. It was the first time in many nights that Kacem was not too drunk to play games with his wife. They made one another very happy, and finally they fell into a perfect sleep.

The Doctor from the Chemel

MOHAMMED MRABET

AT THE ENTRANCE to the Khalifa's palace there was a garden full of fountains and flowers. It was here that a certain Nchaioui used to come each day to sit under a fig tree. He would set his basket down and take from it a sheepskin which he always carried with

him. Then he would spread out the sheepskin and sit on it. In the
basket he also had charcoal, a teapot, and a bowl of majoun. He
would place three stones in such a way that there was room between
them to make a fire, set the teapot on top, and wait for the water
to boil. Any day you could see him sitting there in the garden on
the sheepskin. He had no work, but he had many friends who kept
him alive with small sums of money which they gave him from
time to time.

It became known that the Khalifa was suffering from an abscess
in a private part of his body, and that as a result he could not sit
down. The best doctors had been called, but they were not able
to help him. The reason for this was that the Khalifa, being
ashamed, would not let them examine the abscess. He called in holy
men and tolba who chanted the Koran for him, but the pain went
on.

The Nchaioui heard about the Khalifa's difficulties, and straight-
way he went to the garden and began to eat majoun. He ate more
than usual that day, and smoked a great deal of kif as well. All
the while he was thinking about the Khalifa. When he was feeling
happy, he lay back in the shade of the fig tree and said to himself:
I think I can cure him.

Soon he rose, folded his sheepskin, put his pipe and teapot and
bowl of majoun into the basket, and went to knock at the Khalifa's
gate. A Sudanese opened it and asked him what he wanted.

I'm a doctor, he said.

Where are you from? said the black man, looking at his ragged
robes. We've had all the doctors in the country.

I'm from the Chemel, he told him. I've got medicines that will
make anybody feel better, no matter how sick he is.

Wait, said the black man. I'll be back in a while.

The Sudanese went into his master's chamber and told him that
a toubib had arrived from the Chemel.

The Khalifa was lying on his belly. He raised his head a little
and sighed. Bring him in, he said.

The servant went to the gate. Come with me, he told the
Nchaioui.

In the chamber the Nchaioui saw the Khalifa lying face down
on the bed. Bring plenty of honey and hot tea, he told the black
man, and he sat down on the bed beside the Khalifa.

When the servant returned with the tea and honey, the Nchaioui took out his bowl and scooped up a large ball of majoun, which he handed to the Khalifa. First eat this, he told him. And drink this tea afterwards.

The Khalifa did as he was told, and the Nchaioui kept giving him more tea to drink. When an hour had passed, and the Nchaioui saw that the majoun had taken effect, he sent the servant out of the room and stood up.

This is the moment for the medicine, he said. He reached down and pulled off the Khalifa's tchamir, leaving his buttocks uncovered. The Khalifa did not even notice.

Then the Nchaioui anointed his sex with honey and thrust it with great force into the Khalifa.

The Khalifa uttered a scream, and tried to throw the Nchaioui off, but he did not have the strength. After that he was quiet while the Nchaioui worked.

The operation is almost over, your Excellency, said the Nchaioui. He finished and withdrew his sex, very much pleased. The abscess had burst, and he summoned the black man and told him to bring towels and clean his master.

Meanwhile the Khalifa, who had been in pain for a long time, was so relieved by the bursting of the abscess that he fell asleep. Seeing this, the Nchaioui unrolled his sheepskin and lay down on it at the foot of the bed. In the morning when he awoke, he found the Khalifa still sleeping.

The Khalifa awoke shortly afterward, and the Nchaioui helped him out of bed.

I have no more pain, said the Khalifa.

Hamdoul'lah! said the Nchaioui.

Together they went into the Khalifa's bathing chambers. After the servants had poured water over them and gone out, the Khalifa said: Last night, when you operated on me, what did you use? A pole of some kind?

Your Excellency, I used this. He pointed at his sex.

What? cried the Khalifa. But that means you assaulted me. You assaulted your Khalifa!

No, your Excellency, I operated on you, nothing more.

Good, said the Khalifa, remembering that the Nchaioui had indeed cured him.

They came out of the hammam, and the Khalifa ordered a great festival to be given immediately. There were musicians and dancers, and the guests ate and drank tea for many hours. In the middle of the party the Nchaioui took out his bowl of majoun and gave a spoonful to the Khalifa. Soon the Khalifa began to talk and laugh and sing, and the Nchaioui knew that he was happy. He put everything into his basket and stood up.

I must leave, your Excellency, he said.

How much do I owe you? the Khalifa asked him.

Sidi, whatever you give me will be more than enough, because it comes from you.

He is a great doctor, thought the Khalifa. He sent a servant for a pouch full of dinars, and gave it to him.

The Nchaioui thanked him and left. Then he went across the street and sat under the fig tree to smoke kif.

Randel

MARK HYATT

BEING A FIXING JUNKY, I've bought this exposed castle. It's unflowered and I live here alone except for a pet cat. The building is high and windy, and rained on every hour since the last battle. I have just moved in, and it's all new or old to me depending where the sunlight falls; silence guards the place. I will get used to the emptiness. I say my name is Randel. I've got the fire going and the wind is sucking the warmth away into a raining sky. To touch the walls is like putting a hand in soft soil only to realise I am in some grave; the dust on the floor is whipped in pools.

Soon I will find courage to go round the place, step by step, step into emptiness; it's kind of strange being away from crowds, even stranger than seeing the courtyard littered with dying birds. My hands have turned into water, my hair is sticking up like a crop of barley and my eyes feel stretched for anything. I've drawn up a bed in front of the fire, I must sleep if I can get my eyes closed. The cat lies dead to the world; time is another place altogether; the heart of the fire crumbles; the architecture is full of arches. Someone is talking about me.

I suppose it's easy to live the past, to claw as a falcon at the ruins, bearing fear in the throat, dangerous creepy sleep desperately putting gloom to dream; 'Squire of the night' I quote to myself, 'Bastard!' thinking 'Shaggy head! What is mercy?' My marrow-bone chills like dark-coloured beer with thoughts of Odin's ancestors drinking blood of war. Frenzy is a stone's throw; a body of military individuals dressed for death, standing on a wet moor, watching the castle early in the afternoon; men running along the walls flag-

ging orders with their weapons singing 'War is what we live for'.
The rhymes flicker through the head. The horses stand like virgins,
the air is filled with masturbation in masculine fashion, a battle
almost in the eyes; wild grass marches to the water's edge, then
a fool cries out to the raging wind 'Victory or death! Coin and
country!' and the shouting sprouting names fly, an arrow strikes
a man's chest and he falls with a drop from inside the family castle
wall, hits the ground, gets up and dances as if he were a child, and
dies, eyes closed lifeless. Bodies knotted with heavy steel fight
enemy forms, men straight as a trumpet crying in their own blood.

A man with a sword sees another man cut out his own heart
with a little dagger engraved 'Loverboy's Here!' Another man is
sick on to his defensive gun, torn hands lie gouging the soil. 'I
trust the men know what they are doing, fighting for my views.'
An axe cuts the other cheek off. 'By all the saints erected! Where
are my black insults? Wandering over a matey scattered love on
the wet ashes of tomorrow.' The prisoner lies slain in his defeat,
the army captured in a coffin; a horse goes mad to the wall. I see
death acting in other men, the young education of a virgin lost in
a sweat, brothers uglying up a few faces in a bloody mood, men
crying at silences, blacktimes, wearing razor suits. The horror of
bodies clenched double in pain! The fountain water covered by
the birth of death! A leaf lies in fresh agony, the animals are wild,
life falls expressionless of age, wounded bones shiver with holy
prayers, a bronze axe comes through the walls of the mind, recalling
action to the law of the tide. I wash in guilt and my soul remains
a lightly-written poem; the dead are blessed in new surprises. Pain
is a slow mover. Men shine up their swords like penises for love,
a man with his guts hanging out rolls in the sun, another rips the
eyes out of conflict; a ghost of a man displays his despair, the weak
go conquering fading rainbows, two men bite at each other's neck,
kingly looks can kill a man. This battle could burn itself out in
swear words; age should slay any man, eyes of others dart at all
movement, the politics of fairground Sunday, the grave tale of
history gossiping infernal death of gloomy wonder.

Men breathe for battle over meat, a horseback rider flees in
loud-voiced helplessness, the priests claw a ruined man for holiness's
sake, an invisible man dies in the clearing, the arts of a killer run
out leaving a painful mind. The hunt for human horror must close.
I move about my castle. Men with branded faces and broken spirits

look on bloody sights, war music is sharp with the enemy's defeated cries. Some men ride away with wives, others find small reason to die at their own hand. The head is crowned in attacks, a friend dies with a mirror embracing his face, the wolf groans the hour with words trembling in disguises. Women sing exhausted in a church where the traitors home, and children trance for a feeble truth, angels oozing curdled with pain. Unskilful intellectuals call war glory, I find no forceful language, although I could if I tried, explain it. A warrior wants a paid love, a dead thought flashing frustration in a festival of evil banners, sons of armless deeds. The eldest boy is not always a man; a healthy lad does not kill a dog slowly in front of a table full of wine and roasted apples.

On the moor a heart perishing by a fallen shield, some wind echoing a rude whistling song of life. I am Randel, lost on space called time in life, not sure if the battle is mine; I think I frighten my cat, jumping around the castle, for there is a man in here raving his head off, to a stand-still about how men can't kill idiots; I frighten the cat. It feeds on sleep. I am the wind inside the cat echoing. I am Randel, the Cat, safe in my castle, waiting for my eyes to open and greet a warm coloured sun, to look upon grass singing with blowing winds around the battlements, waiting for my dreams to die where they become life once more. My body will wake up for food, and time comes whispering the date of my day, when the body needs dressing to look my awful best.

Rome

PETER RIVIERA

IT HAPPENED one warm afternoon in June. It happened to the sound of romantic church music pouring through arches. It was very beautiful. It began here: 4 pm, the Caffé Greco.

'That was a very hep thing you did to that Knight of Malta at Babington's.' (The Community of the Knights of Malta is Rome's lesser-known sovereign state).

'Hep? What do you mean hep?'

'Just hep.'

'Boogaloo bunny and all that whatever. It's meaningless anyway.'

'It's a perfectly useful—'

'OK OK, Ebb, but I still don't know what you're getting at.'

'Well, don't be ridiculous . . .'

'All right, don't go on. This time it's only a word.'

'Look, I'll tell you—'

The matter is getting through to him fast. When he says it is a jangling timewarp biofeedback amphetamine nightmare, you have to believe it. The evidence is all around. Ack-ack. Whistles. The bullet slowly sinks into the stomach.

'Who are you kidding now? I can't see anything out there,' which is what the Titanic said to the Iceberg, the mouth glued on the car bumper.

(samizdat)

(wormwood kingdoms gone blind—switched off: burned out with lasers)

(banshees are screaming throughout)

(Pushing up her nose a pair of TV sunglasses, 'Miami Glitter-green/styled', and one haemorrhage of a foot scarcely across the step of the Pantheon, a woman of Scarsdale, whose astonishing cargo of flesh must have been built up from separated milk solids over quite a period of time, was amplified by circular space booming the heavy-breasted low-down off her chest—'Christ, another goddam tomb. Ain't Europe got nothing else?' Her kid is gross too and dragged round it anyway. He makes an impress on Borromini stone creeping like flesh in comic opera antique dormitory town under load of old culture fade-out and scurrilous sniper-fire and flaking scabies).

'Schmucked-up wuzzbox?'

'Sciamachy, heah. Eyes very sanpaku. It's beginning to tell.'

'The world's ritziest stew of has-bins.'

'Something like that. Someone should fumigate this place with euthanasia. It's full of detritus.'

'And cardiac-arrested development.'

'Oh, damn your art deco coffee cups!'

'Now what've I said? No, don't—I'm not guilty, I'm not.'

'Sometimes, Ebb, you make me feel I've got my foot in something ugly and complicated.'

'You can't appreciate the nuances of that kind of torture.'

'I don't give a damn.'

'Have you ever had to handle a rabbi? In a duplex? No.'

'Oh, don't be so bloody silly.'

'So don't be so smart.'

'Seems it was that rabbi and your mother drove you to drink in the first place anyway so whatsit matter.'

'Mother? No. But that hook-nose Holy Jo with his lisp and desert talk—you see, she and Dad split up quite early, she thought I needed a backbone, she was scared I guess. That's why we vacationed in graveyards like this once or twice. Ruined me. Would you say I was an alcoholic really?'

'And what do you want me to say?'

'An alcoholic's someone who's got a complex about his drinking problem.'

'It doesn't appear to worry you at all.'

'I came to that definition in a play I once wrote. Someone of Zena's translated it into Italian. We managed 6 weeks at Palermo before the Mafia closed it—said we were freaking their infrastructure. They were very nice about it though.'

— viz: A gentle item pays Ebb a visit to his room at Des Palmes.

He doesn't look at all like James Cagney—it shakes Ebb for a second that does. He gives the man a drink—looks like a dark John F. Kennedy in fact—

'*Mama mia.* I had a mother once—she was how you say? *garrotted.*'

'Oh dear, I'm sorry to hear that.'

'Long time ago now, before the war. An eediot, he do it, from Cefalu. He say he driven crazy out of his head by the Golden Dawn—I hate your language ever since and don't talk to me about translations—how you say? *troppa gassata.* Do you know what it is to be so close to death at three years old?'

'No, I don't, er no—but I guess it's not a cool thing to have hanging out in your head at any age. Have another drink.'

The man swallows off his drink hard, brushes a speck from his black mohair knee and says 'So I hope it won't inconvenience your plans when you take it away.'

The Neapolitan producer, when Ebb told him about it, grasped the nature of the problem immediately.

'I mean, I thought he would be terrifically upset and throw fits every place, you know how they can froth on for days "every time I theenka of eet", and those Neapolitan theatrical types they're unhinged, at the sight of them hardened epileptics just jerk up and rush for cover—did I tell you about Aurelio? our male lead for two weeks. His innnerds gave out if you so much as breathed at anyone else. Many's the time I've come back to find him a total stinking mess excrement all over soaking his hands in a bowl of hot frangipane—acutely bloodshot eyes. It's rotten having to be periscopic, having to check out the situation before putting in an appearance—with friends anyhow. '

'Guano goes that way sometimes. *Violenza,* he says, *per divertimento, cattzo piu grande,* changes colour, no warning, springs it on you soaked in formaldehyde.'

'Yes, but we were banking very well that month. It had meant a liver machine for the producer's eldest daughter among other things. Altogether a very emotional subject for him to start blow-lamping on. But he just stood there, focussed his eyes—one of those rare occasions when I'd swear he was registering something close to external reality, normally his mind's never NEVER alfresco— he says to me "So what-a bambina south of Anzio should have a leever machine? Anyhow it go to her head. She theenka now she much too good to talk to her fellow leever failures, she wanna marry a German dottore, she wanna join the MSI, she gotta surprise coming". And he picks up the 'phone and we never open again.'

So it's the sickness then—it returns—anxious into the deepest crevices like dry ice and sticks there, forming an itchy deposit. Veins network the gilded body, cables and thongs and electric flex knotted up into the skull where they tangle and crackle in clouds, Mission Control was the idea. They are young and on racks of course, their fists bouquets of thumbscrews, certainly they are. A group of spivs belch farinaceous gas into the static, sweaty under a hot brown moon. They don't know. They can't begin to explain it.

Guano had four scars on his body and a few deep purple bruises across the shoulders—staring into an alien atlas and out the other side . . . there are long intervals between pulsations. He reaches for the durophet to shatter a mood. It is replaced on the window-sill in front of plane trees. Then he smokes a packet of duty-free Rothmans straight off, waiting on the winter—a phantom prospect of pigeon grey vapours and chills and droppings beyond desire.

. . . body floats headlong, electrical carcass floats face upward trailing warm translucent underwater flesh (yes, exactly that), bubble of gas held in roof of mouth steers system into weedy melancholy. Now he begins to force the elements and batten down lids on a perverse panic. All extraneous objects are vulgar after a while. One is sufficient. 'Mrs Plasm was peeling potatoes with a blunt knife when the doorbell rang . . .' it usually begins, the regular awfulness blancmange contemplated laconically in diving wobbles. 'Mrs Plasm was peeling . . .'—no, the pamphleteers never refer to Our Lady of Hiroshima.

'Don't worry, doesn't mean anything, nothing at all, beyond a carbonade flatulence of the psyche which is strictly relative, only so-so. Have we discussed trepanation? We might well, you know.'

They had reached the room painted white, large, little furniture, mattresses placed together on the floor, and a light blanket—a high feminine table has fluted legs and a gramophone on it. Mono futuristic rock record finished half an hour ago and is still revolving on the turntable with a sluggish clicketty click (danced round the room in pink leather trousers and green high-heeled boots with all the *passé urbs* to pitch from coming down the Spanish Steps like an overwhelming cream dream with a coin in his back and chintzy gigolos stare hard and silk fans freeze).

A girl called Marilyn walks into the room, screams and tries to get out again. Being a large room with several doors and she now in a non-rational frame of mind, Marilyn makes berserk grabs up at the walls. It takes her perhaps 40 seconds—a long long time— of pure terror before finding the right door AWAY FROM ALL THIS God help her—YOU BERLOODY . . . bastard. Funnily enough the crazy nymphe, she did it again in London six months later, suddenly walked into the flat, gave out a strangled grunt and sped off down the corridor at the end of which she did find the girl in her bedroom, the one she had actually come to visit.

'Does he *live* here?' said Marilyn.

'More or less, mmmm. Anything wrong?'

'I walked in on him in Rome by accident, he tried to—very funny friends. Odd hours. God, how freaky—and twice—and in two different capitals, God. I'll damn kill him, the bastard.'

'For heaven's sake, Marilyn, calm down. I mean, you know, some men like all the tricks.'

'Now don't you start, not you too.'

— and a straightback chair with a black waistcoat on it. Shelves made up from bricks and planks in provincial art student good taste. On them: a bright pink candle, two dirty glasses dried-off lemon flecs down them and greasy thumbmarks, 2,400 lire and assorted coins of three currencies, a group of keys on a leather thong worn round the neck for going out phased on drugs. A pair of green-rimmed sun glasses, the cause of severe headaches at one point (crockery crashing across tumours in throb—really loud it was). An address book is there with an incomprehensible mix of new entries, English newspaper under sticky bottles—shampoo leaked— cologne/dripped, liqueurs congealed—there's a wireless which has to be covered with cold towels to keep it going, some chewing gum, postage stamps. Door handle of a pre-functional era is impossible to repair: 5 or 6 interlocking components and a few vagrant screws and a floor-to-ceiling bar constitute this very fanciful impediment to the opening or closing of doors. A poem by Emily Dickinson about being stoned on life, cut out of a magazine and presented by Dick Baugh. He was a San Francisco sauna cowboy with a handlebar moustache in chrome yellow Californian bristle, wears sawn-off jeans, sneaks his Bullworker out from under the bed when he thinks no one's in the kitchen—Dick lives behind the kitchen and is ostensibly doing a crash course in Parliamo Italiano at Rome University (about the largest faculty they've got at that viscous establishment). At night he counts baroque churches to sleep. Then around 4 am the chest springs are ringing out with that peculiar jangle, he's worried his hard grapefruit pectorals are being infected by European Decay which is said to be very widespread in his neck of the *umwelt*. Three empty packets of cigarettes, one nearly full (Muratti Ambassador? What the hell, he's dead now anyway), some books, an exorbitant bottle of Gordon's Export which is too big to fit in the fridge, for instance.

The best thing about the flat—apart from the floor it's got—is the balcony sunstroked all day until now when an entablature creeps across and clumps of plant life on the skyline rather incinerated this time of year naturally: traffic trampolines up from the Via Nazionale because something akin to Stockhausen is down there with a whole new delinquent angle on percussion orchestra and a putsch of government-sponsored epileptics backing him up with their pathology. In the course of ten weeks no less than six major road accidents were observed from the balcony where Quattro Fontane breaks into it, high above one of those solid cool bars arcaded on to the pavement with stainless steel, green marble and beautiful rustication overhead. The waiter is in a long white apron, very narrow maroon bow-tie, open all hours for espresso, ice-cream, Fernet Branca—good for hangovers because Fernet Branca drains off the blood from vague complaints like aftosa, boheara, mollanders, dead-end jelly, waterbrash, hard-boiled kidneys and brain-plankton. Eyeballs twisted up, recalling that Argentine aeronautical ploy used for bringing cattle to their knees, are untwisted in a shot by the FB, ie by a violent encounter with internal physical reality exploding out through the teeth into sunshine. Ebb and a black cocaine friend of his he was once involved with, Otis Zoton who had one foot in the gun-running business (started off small timing it on behalf of the Kurdistan Revolution, but these things escalate—

'*Was* there a Kurdistan Revolution?'

'Well, there should've been. It was a fairly widespread intention among the Kurds around that time. They were kinda relying on me for beginners. Me and this violin player from Amon Düül, you know, that was in a Kraut rock band once. Then we blow a tyre taking the unadopted route over the border—mean country it was, no place to be found with crates like we got. So we roll the lot off a mountainside and head back to the city. Good thing the Kurds don't much socialise. If the word got round on the fanbelt my international credibility would've needed a lot more explaining than I had time for—never have carried it in Ethiopia which is the place, I fancy, my career really grew wings.') and Otis later managed to corner the banned book market in Italy, first by outmarrying his rivals— the daughter of Puzzo Piatolli is a gilt-edge running flush in the banned book world (she say 'How you say? you flip my buttons, Monsignor Maggiordomo dei Sacri Palazzi, you hear me'). And secondly by the elevation of Pope Umpa I from an overrun mission stational in Zaïre, a prodigy in itself. Umpa's education among the faithful of Lubumbashi had since borne vexatious fruit in the Metempirical Doctrine which had given infallibility for more scope than anyone originally envisaged, so much scope in fact that maybe half the Curia were seriously thinking of tossing in their tassels and taking up guerilla warfare in the hills.

'Dat sorta monkey business don't reflect well on de Tiara—Otis don't need no more trade putting his way anyhow. For these gentlemen a spell down Our Holy copper mines improve de deference no end. You see to it, Kitty, an you be incurring Our Holy Thanks an a reserved table on de right hand ob God later on.'

And after Umpa promulgated *Nihil Scribans*, Otis never looked back. He took the opportunity to avail himself of a parcel of copper mines in the region of Lubumbashi and was ready and waiting for the inevitable influx of cheap ex-communicated labour whose lack of youth and vigour was easily counter-balanced by their cult of mortification:—anyway, these two, Ebb Schutz and Otis Zoton, used to have evisceration contests with a bottle of FB on the steps of San Spirito in Sassia, a church founded in 728 by the King of Wessex. The idea was straightforward enough:—it was during one of the watersheds in their messy relationship:—whoever managed the longest reach per bout could make a selection from the joint contents of their flat. If one actually managed to strike the church doors he was entitled to demand all manner of concessions from the other one. This usually happened after dinner at Ranieri's, after dark. Ebb claimed 100% success with a lot of FB on top of a couple of plates of *trippa al sugo*, so long as the diaphragm was clenched and everything held down until the word go, which was the most difficult part of it. Ebb was asked about a demo but said 'We graduated from Trastevere quite a while back—moved on, you could say.'

So one day he was sitting out on this solid cool pavement with Ebb and Otis taking light refreshment, and after many sleepless nights feeling slightly hysterico, lampooning the passers-by giving themselves the eye-down in shop window reflections (Hey, there, fatty, pack it in! Cut it out! Howzabouta light, spastico! Fuck me, that nun's going to blow right out to Sardinia if doesn't discipline her habit, what ho, sister! and similar undergraduate cavalry lout insults) when there is the most tremendous CRASH at the crossroads. A sudden splash of red hits his triple-scoop ice-cream. It's quite alarming the way one minute everything's rowdy and normal and the next—flip! a spurt of blood lands on his little tower of vanilla ices. At once *everything* freezes. Then all hell explodes. Cars screech: women claw up shopfronts in frenzy of back-breaking convulsions: hundreds of uniforms rush amok waving steel weapons: whistles criss-cross berserk attempts at spatial communication: civilians panic and blurt hogwash at anything at all. In the middle of it a young girl (pretty flowered dress, yellow plastic handbag) is staring at a dismembered arm in the road, totally frozen she was by this detached pale limb skudded under her nose, ript away at the shoulder and the end of it frayed blue-purple muscle streaked with white nerve tissue. Sliced by collapsing metal the victim had been resting an arm on the wound-down window sunny afternoon driving back from Ostia with a couple of girlfriends when he'd accelerated into a transverse mail van slumped out of a side street while one of the girls is biting his ear.

An event in the sargasso of neutrons attracts crowds, sirens—wail ripples through—rainbow clothes—neckscarf tucked into the proper angle while frigging on grief—religious swung chains and crosses low, heads bowed, mouthing off the pit-a-patter with sideways glances. And a curious effect of fluttering hands and hankies like a pervasion of doves, everybody violently crossing themselves over and over. Couldn't stop it, fluttering uncontrollable reflexes that now had clearly become—very clearly (far-gone retinal detachment)—mass hysteria. The police and ambulance workers kept breaking out too. They simply couldn't get any rescue operation together. If they weren't locked into frantic crossing of themselves they were spitting and snarling at each other over priorities. So at the centre of this vast aggregation of thunderstruck animus, the victims bled to death, bloodslip in thick droll lines off the camber, bubbles on the hot surface, steam rising off it and from the pile

G*

of dented metal at the centre. On one side it steamed and clotted
over letters and small parcels, thousands ruptured out of bags being
sly looted by onlookers under police horse feet, whites rolling madness, muzzle froth in flying strings. The beasts empty their bowels
in panic, trample blood, letters, faint women, shit, M-1 carbines
throwing shots from bucky mounts the bullets fly at arbitrary angles
in random directions—zzzzzzzzzzzip off the bulletproof windscreen
of a grey Phantom VII that wanted to find out what the disturbance
was and how it could be turned to advantage. The car had scrunched
to a halt in a sliding mound of letters and a cardinal was dumping
them in the back seat by the armful. Umpa had stuck his tiara in
the rear window which he assumed (correctly) would be a guarantee
against assault. The cardinal is very fat. His desperate exertions
induce such sweating that the mascara runs out of his eyes in black
runnels along the crow's feet, giving him a look that is both savage
and pathetic. His hands are smeared with blood and horse dung.
Umpa dribbles in wild concentration and slits open envelopes, the
important-looking white ones, with a stiletto he always carries under
his skirt in the top of his left stocking. When the back seat is filled
up he presses a button, the door flies shut, he says to Babu 'Back
to the palace! We got some reading to do—no, no, no, not the
town—to Castelgandolfo, ya screwy niggah! . . . the cardinal→
saw → the car skidding → off → through → the crowd and the
cardinal went out of his mind. He was immediately set upon and
torn to pieces by a gang of male prostitutes up from Naples for the
tourist season.

'Nice to see a black brother getting on,' said Otis.

'Holy Cow!'—this is Ebb—'Bet my manuscript somewhere among
that lot—would have to be—oh, holy shit! it was going to
Rio where an impresario says he's interested in my *tone* . . .
aaarrrgh!'

'I want to go back to the balcony for a more objective view of
things,' said the third, finished off his ice-cream, tossed the spoon
into the steel cup with a clink, wiped a red saucedrop from his chin.
They went round into the courtyard, took an old cage lift upstairs
to the top floor where *Capriccio Espagnol* crackled on the wireless
under cold towels as they entered: lizards zip into corners: labourers
renovating the building opposite shout across ra ra ra ra randy
hallooo high above the riot. Increasingly rowdy, the two sides start
throwing off their, clothes over their respective parapets and do a

prehensile pagan dance on the rooftops to an ancient command. One or two projectile egos dip like seagulls, back and forth, sliding back and forth in erratic rapport of undulant lust a hundred feet over soft red tarmac, gaudy spongy tarmac—bunched fingers— swaying sticky skin through black curls, rigid purple skin—swollen blood, choked with blood, abstract rutty violence in the horning heat, ra ra ra ra ra ra

The Divan Dosser interrupted on the telephone—'Hullo, darling, is that you?' she said far off down a slippery tunnel.

'Ugh . . .'

'Darling?'

'Yes, most of me, yes, er . . .'

'God, I wish you'd keep off those bloody pills—look, can you come to dinner tomorrow?'

'. . . all over the floor. I actually ate it—'

'But can you?'

'When I think of that bloody man too . . .'

'Oh Jesus. Listen to me, darling, you're not listening to me, it's important.'

'I think I'll take a picnic out to the Villa Adriana tomorrow. Got to get away for a moment.'

'Well, you won't stay there all night. Or perhaps you will. I can't tell with you these days. About nine it will be.'

'You know what it's like, wine, hot afternoon, warm earth, very quiet in the groves, warm turf pressing in the back, on the belly, the farm, the swans, the wine—'

'Are you all right? Look, what's that funny noise in the background?'

'Mm? I don't hear a funny noise. It makes perfect sense from where I'm standing. Anyway, who's coming?'

'Puzzo's coming.'

'Aha! And he's put you up to it.'

'Don't be silly, darling. It's just that he's a bit worried about Otis getting on so well with the Pope.'

'Why can't he ask Otis himself?'

'His son-in-law? They couldn't discuss something like that.'

'I think it's too hot for this sort of thing.'

'You're always making excuses recently. I haven't seen you for weeks.'

'You saw me at Icon's demonstration last week.'

'That doesn't count. I was too riveted to appreciate you properly. Darling, do come, do. I'll be helpless if you don't.'

'Of course I'm coming.'

'Oh!'

'But I might be a bit late.'

'Icon's coming too. We'll be marvellous. Haven't seen my new barman, have you—arrived two days ago. He used to be Jimmy's.'

'Then I have seen him. Yes, he was rather exceptional. God, you're disgusting.'

'Don't be mean. I don't find it so easy to get by any more.'

'Zena, it's not particularly easy for anyone—look, I must go, there's a strange noise, I—'

'OK? I won't keep you. Try not to be too late. See you nine-ish. It will be divine. And don't throw any peaches at the swans tomorrow.'

'Good Lord, you have got a memory. No, I promise.'

'Well, you can be as ghastly as anyone sometimes. Oh, and don't mention Puzzo to Otis. No counter-conspiracy.'

'No, no, stop worrying. Zena, I really must go. It's important. See you tomorrow night then.'

'Oh and darling—' but the 'phone crashes down.

Fantastic remarks cruised in from the balcony and also—'Who dat?' DRUNK OBVIOUSLY, SOTTO VOCE.

'The Divan Dosser—I'm dining there tomorrow.'

'Oh St Boniface, you getting in with those types still—man, that's no improvement. Anyway we've got to get out of town for a day. At least a day.'

'The way they ripped those fingers off.'

'No other way to get the rings. Fat grown up all round them.'

'Icon Torpor's going to be there as well—gets worse.'

'Between you an me an Ebb that Icon character is on Umpa's personal list, bin earmarked for quarantine when the time comes. Limbo? Purgatory? Whatsit called? Be careful, blossom, Umpa don't know bout you yet. An Otis can only do so much.'

'Never been modest before, Otis,' said Ebb and poured a glass of Vesuvio, cherry red smelling of lilies.

Otis lifted his head half up from the mattress and a flannel fell off his forehead: 'Things moving too fast now for promises.'

(NB. Icon Torpor was an expatriate Russian philosopher/electro-physicist/geomancer, once considered the world's expert on Odic

Force, but his confidence had been shaken by his wife's suicide on the steps of the Pantheon—cut her throat with a bread knife, clumsily, while a party of American ladies looked on: one of them said later 'Sure it's a pity. But what could we do? Thought she was a sword-swallower, something European like that, a gypsy entertainer doing her thing.' After this Icon became dependent on morphine and cocaine and phenobarbital and elephant tranquillisers, all prescribed by himself in gluttonous quantities. He soaked his tobacco in dimethyltrytamine and then, on top of it all, started collecting cats. Odic Force, which he might well have made respectable according to a secret file at UNESCO, other things being equal, withered on a desk strewn with small polythene packets of white and off-white powder. Old colleagues were embarrassed to bump into him hanging round fountains all times of the day or night picking his fingernails. 'So you ze moonshiner too!' he blabbed at them out of self-disgust. They would walk away down side alleys and at a later date ask him to dinner because he never fed himself and could always amaze:— a few low-brow miracles which anybody ignorant of the properties and application of Odic Force would be quite staggered by, and that was most people. To intimates he pooh-poohed the show, referring to it as 'ze chicken feed, rudimentary liquefacts, anyone could do it.' But the Pope considered him dangerous and *in pectore* was extremely put out by these phenomena so close to home. (During the papal blessing one Easter the Pope's robes had been caught by an unnatural wind obscuring him from the multitude throughout, despite the efforts of his chamberlains to unravel him.) Five months after Zena's activist dinner party, Icon Torpor was torn to pieces and eaten in public by a gang of neo-fascist car workers down from Milan for a football match. He was shopping on the Via Condotti in a crash helmet. There was much speculation at the time:

1) The Fiat Connection was only a cover for one of the Pope's vigilante gangs (the Jelly Babies) whose tendency to remove atrocious evidence by devouring their victims had just about become a trademark at this stage of the game. The Pope quietly got it across to them via the Metempirical Doctrine that he did transubstantiate the bodies from afar and therefore these esoteric murders were sanctified by eating of the Lamb of God. An age which had made an Inquisition politically unworkable could hardly be surprised by the alternatives. The recent democratic drift had obliged the contingency

nets of practical power to operate outside the public eye. The possibility of an alliance between Odic Force and Icon's Communist Past had finally incited the Pope's responsibility to the rest of human kind.

2) Getting wind of what were nonetheless slanders upon His Most Holy Translucence, the Vatican agents explained—look at totalitarian egalitarianism, Russia's contribution to the Creation of Apedom!—the Apotheosis of Naive Dogma! Since Man is not by nature an Ape, such a system can only make headway by depriving him of all contact with the Angels, ie. by the ruthless extermination of Men of Power. Since such men are by definition attractive this must always be done in secret. Mr Torpor had certainly been eliminated by the notorious Robotniks because Moscow had succumbed to the fear that the combination of Odic Force and Icon's Anti-Communist case history might one day produce a combustion even more unfavourable to the spread of Marxist Mud than had the events which caused his exile (these amounted to persistent practical jokes of an embarrassing and inexplicable nature upon members of the Politburo). The Pope fuelled this interpretation during private audiences: 'What else can you expect from a tribe of paranoid oriental serfs? Everyone knows dem Ruskies even shit scared ob de moon.' Apparently the Robotniks have their eating habits permanently warped by being trained on a protein starvation diet almost anywhere in Russia to heighten their sense of injustice—it was feasible.

3) Zena said the murderers were spontaneous and acting under the influence of urban sprawl, high-rise slums, the economic collapse of their society. She had never had reason before to question the irrationality of the pitifully underbred. Factory workers were as a caste irresponsible. Everyone knew that car workers particularly were unfortunate mental-handicaps who could always be relied upon to go astray in a crisis. No army ever won a war without generals, etc.

4) Ebb Schutz and Signor Tivoli believed that a perverse alliance between the Copper Pope and Moscow had been developing for some time. Both men ended up in an unpleasant way—it will be described later.

Regardless of what ultimately lay behind the murder, the police did not behave like honourable men and pursue their investigations beyond a very certain point, not even when one of Icon's arms mysteriously turned up in the Pincio three weeks later covered in greenfly. All they did was identify it from the fingerprints, tie on a number tag, and throw it in the deep freeze with all the other weird stuff. Each year the cold store was minced down to provide a charity Christmas dinner for the Foundling Hospital, nick-named the Nursery because it was a major source of police recruits)—

No good, he must leave, otherwise claustrophobia settles round the internal organs like slowly drying glue, pressing them gently.

'I envy your chemistry, boy.' Which is to say that hands shiver as they go out from holy statues and solidify on contact with relics.

'You the only person I know can make me cry—what happen to me now?'

There's a special bitter taste in the mouth from excruciating sex anticipation and a cherub smell breezy in skewed sheets: all the old Mantovani moonscream.

Zena Zenda tried to supply a few bonus vitamins. Only her obtuseness saved her from being destroyed by cynics. Il Spazio Zero —inflatables and contact sculptures everywhere and an atmosphere of mucking about in boats—Zena often took along a hamper and chisel on Sundays. Beat 99—a place for experimental drama and usually closed. Maybe this was one of the experiments. Zena pledged security when one of the assistants was arrested receiving a sack of Jamaican grass. Gasolino Gasolini did a heart transplant on the Commedia dell' Arte after Zena had introduced him to the (*in tempore*) Minister of Finance. Painters: her favourite was found hanging in his Via Margutta flatlet. She didn't cultivate them much after that. Writers: graduates of Alberto Moravia like to hold court to their apprentice sycophants round her place, but she preferred the moderns. Always bumping into jetsy friends at spots like the Golden Gate or Harry's Bar and freely mixed them up. Playwrights: Ebb Schutz runs a cute line in sardonic self-deprecation wherever he can find a tablecloth. Music: Vittorio Tivoli processes sounds from water with electronic aids, a beautiful if somewhat perilous extension of Rome's famous aqua fetish. Zena had pinched him from Natalie Le Vine. Dance: Kitty knows how to move in an overheated dungeon near the Station. She comes on after the Italian rock operetta, after the strippers, but before the blue film (lady vampires in bright yellow hair infiltrate the nunnery, conduct lesbian orgies, and humiliate the local bishop with satanic afterbirth). Zena: 'She's got salt. Salt kills those yins. And she married

Jimmy de Goldstein'—the popular Jewish boy blowing profits from grandpa's sock factory outside Birmingham.

The marriage had been approved by everyone (except the families of the two people involved) because of the way it helped Jimmy with his problem, which was Reality, and Kitty with hers, which was Pregnancy. An American cousin of his had been attacked by epilepsy-in-the-architecture one morning trying to rustle up a cup of coffee in the kitchen—when she opened the drawer for a spoon, strobe and laser lights flashed down on her, rock music erupted when she switched on the percolator, as the fridge clicked shut the room turned through a right angle into the morning heat, tap water turned red, the walls went from white to a horrible green, damp and flaccid like the belly of toads, slippery under hand. She grabbed on to a draining board for support and at once a wall collapsed outwards shooting her on to a large balcony with see-through polythene floor over a terrifying drop which was where the ambulance men found her twenty minutes later—'Oh God, Millicent, I'm sorry, I must have forgotten to switch it off last night.'

But Millicent was full of ideas. She asked Jimmy to be Design Consultant to a chain of banks she'd married into and which hadn't done very well out of the —

'Wobbery Boom—Jimmy, it's just what Walt needs for his insomnia.'

'Millicent, how can you say things like that at a time like this? I'm so embarrassed I want to kill myself.'

'You're vewy sweet, Jimmy. Don't get sick. It was only a *little* turn, can happen to anybody, do say you'll think about it.'

'Millicent, you Americans are tremendous—everyone else I know would have demanded money—and I am fond of my environmental system, actually. When you are better I'll show you its computer— I've got thousands of cards, you stick them into a hole and press about five hundred buttons. It is housed in a secret room behind the Titian. Keeps the burglars away, you know. Oh, Millicent, they'll let you out tomorrow, won't they?'

'I expect so, but I'll have to keep the bandages on for a *little* while. The worst is my tongue. I half chewed it off.'

'Millicent, you can't imagine how awful it is to be me.'

'You should get married.'

Not to mention transient girlfriends, pious marchesas—so severe always, wild-eyed whores of whom Kitty was the pick, and of course the gigolos, endless young men oiling round for perks, swaggering on a collective mother hang-up in private Playboylands where all must one day be Hugh Hefners, must, must, must, but Zena wouldn't hear a word against them.

'The Government just doesn't appreciate what these boys are doing to attract foreign capital into this country. Angelino, be a dear and pass round the pistachios. Last week the Marchesa di Bossa-Nova-Piatollo-Negro-Malatesta was saying how awful it was the way everyone thinks of the Italians. How all her family were saints, these days anyway. Guano's the son of course—I had to chuckle. But how she was having to sell the villa at Arsoli. Couldn't stand the jokes any longer and what's the world coming to, they'd been there for five hundred years with no problem until now. Anyway she's transferring everything by mule train to their other one at Carsoli. It's too dumb—and there she is on my best divan looking miserable as sin with all these ropes of pearls twisted round her white knuckles. Angelino, be a sweet, my drink needs fixing— no martini this time—you'll learn. He hasn't been here long, Icon. But he's very loyal. Left Jimmy straightaway, the very moment the dear boy married Kitty. Which shows extraordinary strength of character for a Latin, I think.'

'Zey full of ze surprises,' said Icon who constantly made remarks *à propos* the future. He sniffed some pale brown powder off the end of his nail file then offered it, along with a small screwtop bottle, to Puzzo who went into an elaborately executed gesture of Latin refusal: gently inclines head, smiles, passes a huge brown hand in front of starched linen and black silk herringbone tailor- worship (fan sequence of moon manicures, magnificent detail on his fingertips) to finish under the lamp with an explosion of diamonds, Puzzo's legendary cuff-links—'Thankyou very much, Signor Torpor, I never do. Most kind, but my heart.'

At the last junction before the real crossfire heat begins on the wobbly drift south, these macaws have come to a halt in the city and sink slowly into its stonework gripping their Kincross Special life-rafts, all legs crossed on (cinquecento reconditioned) divans smoking cigarettes, exhaling the expatriate fug. 'I bet Signor Piatolli would love another, Angelo.'

'I can't stand it, can't handle it, she left an hour ago. Had a funny look in her eyes. No sort of look—I thought maybe it was a reflection from the ceiling. She'd been looking at the ceiling a lot.

You know how she does. Comes from lying on her back so much.
I'd been pacing around leaving oily fingermarks all over the walls.
And the damn radio on, Engelbert Humperdinck singing "It Might
As Well Rain Until September". Really diseased it sounded. And my
Italian's so bad. There's always a misunderstanding at some point.
Every time a breakdown. You feel it slipping, you know, and it's
painful. Moves out of control. And the more you try to do the right
thing the crazier it gets. Look at these teeth marks in my shoulder.
It's like the pay-off. And she left me her hat.'

'Here, take these. Yes, you'll feel better. Ebb, I'm not trying to
kill you. Don't be daft.'

'I must go to Brazil. Can't afford it. And you can't borrow money
in order to disappear.'

'Maybe Jimmy will give you some. He's very thoughtful.'

'Don't talk shit. He's married to her after all.'

'That's what I mean. Maybe he'll feel more settled with you in
South America.'

'People don't relate to demands like that. Not even jerks like
him. So choked on all this can't even cry no more. Drunk four bottles
of wine today. So far. What kind of diet's that? Look at me. Fat.
Disgusting. Yes I am. Don't humour me. I can do without crap like
that right now. Got to get out of this place somehow—Christ, feel
so sick it deranges me . . .'

Living in this room is like living in a drawing by Escher—
Mazzano was the same with Lenny from Marylebone pretending
to be asleep while fucking went on in the next bed, stars shooting
across a tiny window twice, the coincidence was frightening—and
if the Escher reference seems over the top or abstruse then it's the
right reference because this feeling is abstruse, the books underneath
the gramophone are abstruse, the room is abstruse. For a start the
tiles on the floor interlock in an Escher manner:—shift around in
eyeshot. The perspectives are creepy: that is, there seems to be no
perspective in the solid sense of the word. And yet there is
undoubtedly an off-beat logic in the way the angles of the room fit
together. There has to be, in the final analysis, because the place
does not collapse. For example, the ceiling—from here it should
appear to slope, but it doesn't appear to do that. The building
opposite tilts relative to the line of the balcony, quite a lot, but
really it cannot be doing that, otherwise one or the other would
have fallen down by now (although one of the workmen fell off

opposite a few days ago). The wardrobe retreats backwards at roughly half a mile an hour, a subtle phenomenon which less-attuned moments would miss, and a doppler effect is created in the indoor daylight. Red haze—crushed cardinal—an overpowering premonition of crazy flutes and hysterical violin music, overtures to chaos which is the product of implosions. And a powerful impression of necks. Necks fit to burst. Necks twisted this way and that, with veins engorged and standing out in relief like cords of choking creeper. Necks choked with blood, choked with torrents of words boiling back on themselves, cataracts of words imploding in a centreless mania, lost to themselves breaking each from each into senselessness, into dumb noise, into the entropy which is inconsequence and the opposite of death, into the inexorable sucking of a great yawn, into the uncoloured chaos which subsumes all squit of hurricanes and volcanic storms in an unimaginable upheaval beyond the eardrum and the wildest thought. For in their spluttering the necks are soundless, echoeless and blank, as if somebody had switched off the sound-track altogether, altogether—herein is the premonition of possession, the sharp oblivion of passion and other-directed acts, of an immense lifting-off of the gravitational personality like a hard turtle shell, and let the body burn in spiral elevations of air. 'I'm going out, I'm going out dancing.'

' . . . sh, sh, the bloody cannibals again. Be quiet, don't move, freeze, they might go away, they might . . .'

He fumbled in the pocket dictionary, scrambling up the tissues, then threw it angrily the length of the long corridor. It scudded along the long path of tiles and hit the bedroom door at the far end with a thump and he freely burst out laughing.

It is 4.45 in the afternoon. The heat is strong and still. The glare has withdrawn from it. Outside the air is an even yellow, and limpid inside. One of the balcony doors is banging because the handle has come to pieces—an occasional motor car can be heard very far away down in the soporific street, the buzz of a fly drowsy between the window and shutter, and the faint drone of afternoon summer aeroplanes in the remotest atmosphere. These are reverberations not so much of sounds as of clear casual pictures under the lids, spores in the lungs and breath in the genitals, unemphatic, desultory and untenable reminders of space, but housed in the rhythm of the abdomen which is at eye-level now and getting closer . . . .

Some consequences: —

a) London—shabbiness and power, the sensation of being in a real city where momentous things can happen; the originality of the population, the independence reflected in domestic architecture.

b) The Colosseum, the world's most eye-catching traffic island, started to fall down.

c) Michael Anglo went over there and wrote: the Deputy Secretary of the Communist Party turns up at fancy dress parties in drag as La Marchesa Capitalisma; everybody's flocking to a film called *Salon Kitty* about SS atrocities; two carabinieri were caught under the bridge on the lungotevere near the Ministero de Grazie e Justizia carbine-fucking a girl (cf. *Funeral Rites*); Guano's mother was detained at Kennedy Airport and is being sent to Milan for trial; the Copper Pope and the Zaïre Connection are becoming a scandal; caused a major traffic jam the other day en route to a fancy dress party dressed as a cardinal and traffic had to be diverted by local radio—wasn't presented with a bill all night, must do it again.

d) The day the report on Rome was published Guano turned up in London, dropping a pebble through a void and making uncomfortable coruscations. Remember the cave at Mazzano. It was raining. At the back of the cave a human skeleton was found in bits, a few rags stuck on to bone, teeth scattered, dead hair clung on a rock. He picks up a thigh bone, looks down at the ground. They begin to unbuckle their trousers.

The village was built high on a bluff protected by battlements. The priests used to bury the dead by throwing them out of the church window in winding sheets, corpses cartwheeling down to the river trail dirty ribbons, arms flung wide, bouncing from rock to rock leaving a small cake of flesh on each. With uncharacteristic irony the Fascists blew the church down the cliff too before they left. Guano's back was stained with squashed blackberries, yes, he remembers.

e) At a Corsini soirée last night not far from the city, the musical world suffered a tragic loss when Signor Vittorio Tivoli was electrocuted while performing his controversial new work Traumdeutung Dago! *The work, which is a setting of Horace's* O Fons Bandusiae *for six ring modulators, six phasers, six potentiometers, Hammond organ, garrotted epiglottis, fourteen prepared secular fountains, and a lot of magnetic tape, had already been the cause of last month's demonstration outside the City Waterboard by the Amici di Fontane di Roma who said this morning that 'they knew something like this would happen'.*

Trouble began when the laser guns along the roof were switched on to illuminate the second movement, Drip Two. This fused the great Borromini fountain, celebrated centrepiece of the Corsini Water Gardens, and it was as Signor Tivoli swam to reconnect its middle stone tower that a goat chewed through one of the cables and shorted him straight out of the water. The generator then broke down completely, setting off an automatic device which triple locks the photoelectric gates to the estate. For almost an hour the ambulance was prevented from reaching Signor Tivoli who—several witnesses testify—was still breathing when he landed in another part of the garden. The Princess Corsini was not available for comment because she suddenly locked herself away four months ago as a protest against the laws banning abortion and contraceptives. The Prince however, visibly shaken, told our reporter 'It was a delightful evening. Then something like this happens. I don't know how we can repair it—the carvings alone were a miracle of concentration.' Ms Zena Zenda, leading American socialite and cultural whatnot, who lives behind the Via Veneto, said 'Vittorio was a wonderful wonderful man. He will be missed by all sorts of people everywhere.'

Vittorio Tivoli received the Montreux Award in 1974 when his Trailer to World War 5.6.7.8.9 *exploded the lake there and covered the shoreline with dead fish to a depth of ten miles. It was the first work of 'legitimate environmental art' to be proclaimed a disaster area. The festival director in presenting the award said 'Today is a great day for environmental political art.'* This notice appeared in the *Daily American*.

f) The other tragedy was Ebb Schutz. He never did make it to Brazil—he was eaten to death by athlete's foot while on board the QE2 stowing down to Rio in a sports locker. A stinking heap of drek when they scraped him out. Only his gold Solomon's Seal survived biodestruction which was how his mother identified him at the dockside. She'd been flown through in a special jumbo and took back his remains in a jar for a quiet family burial. But life in Scarsdale has been very difficult for her, for her friends, and for their dead relations, because nothing will grow within 500 yards of Ebb's grave. His last recorded words were: 'Hep? Still on that ol' subject? No, no, nothing to do with hepatitis. Crone slang. Means what I'm about to make you: wised-up.'

Notes on the Authors

Sir Max Beerbohm (1872–1956), when approached in 1921 by Bohun Lynch with the proposal of a biography, said: 'My gifts are small. I've used them very well and discreetly, never straining them: and the result is that I've made a charming little reputation.' As recounted in the introductory pages of 'Enoch Soames', this reputation began at Oxford in the early Nineties and Beerbohm, though circumspect himself, will always be associated with that drug-addled decade. His literary career began in the eddy of the *Yellow Book*, contributing to its 'scandalous' pages such essays as 'The Pervasion of Rouge'. In 'Diminuendo' he wrote at the age of 23 (in a droll and languorous way that was typical): 'I shall write no more. Already I feel myself a trifle outmoded. I belong to the Beardsley period'— a period which ended rather abruptly in 1895 with the trial of Oscar Wilde. Many of these essays were collected in *The Works of Max Beerbohm* (1896). His famous cartoons have long been established; so too his only novel *Zuleika Dobson* (1911), a grotesque and accurate portrait of Oxford. But much of his other writing has survived less well. Its fastidiousness now seems mincing and the content thin. 'Enoch Soames' however, an ingenious encapsulation of the Nineties, is among the exceptions. It was published in *Seven Men* (1919) and written when Beerbohm had freed himself from the grind of being a drama critic: 'I went on for twelve whole years. On and on I went, doggedly, from the age of twenty-five to the age of thirty-seven.' It seems incredible; but it is a fact. In 1910 he had married an actress, Florence Kahn from Memphis, Tennessee (they did not have children), and went immediately to live in Rapallo, Italy. Apart from the interruptions of the Great War and the Second World War (during which he delivered a lecture on Lytton Strachey at Cambridge) Beerbohm lived at Rapallo in aloof and meticulous contentment until his death.

William Burroughs (b.1914, St Louis) had a grandfather who invented the adding machine. It is said that the Depression scotched what should have been a great family fortune. Burroughs himself has written: 'As a young child I wanted to be a writer because writers were rich and famous. They lounged around Singapore and Rangoon smoking opium in a yellow pongee silk suit. They sniffed cocaine in Mayfair and they penetrated forbidden swamps with a faithful native boy and lived in the native quarter of Tangier smoking hashish and languidly caressing a pet gazelle.' After Harvard he travelled. At one point Burroughs was studying Pre-Columbian civilisations on a GI grant in Mexico City (where he accidentally killed his wife with a revolver). Since then he has lived in New York, Tangier, Paris, and London where he was cured of heroin addiction by Dr Dent's apomorphine treatment in the Cromwell Road. Apomorphine, which acts on the hypothalamus, is a drug which William Burroughs recommends for various anxiety predicaments. Keith Richard of the Rolling Stones pop group has also tried this cure; he says 'It's a pretty mediaeval cure. You just vomit all the time.' 'The Heat Closing In' opens *Dead Fingers Talk*. A shorter version opens *The Naked Lunch*. Burroughs is often accused of paranoia; but his definition of a paranoiac is 'a man in possession of all the facts.' His writing combines manic iconoclasm with strenuous mental gymnastics and formal devices of an arbitrary, abstract kind: the screaming queen collides with the prophet of doom in bursts of outrageous comedy, gruesome mixes and probes.

Jarmani Dass was minister to the rulers of the states of Patiala and Kapurthala before 1948, the year when the Indian Princes lost their autonomy to the new Republic of India. Up to that time, unless there were unscrupulous breaches of political conduct, the British had permitted many of the maharajahs to retain self-governing powers inside their own domains. These so-called Native States, covering approximately one third of India proper and protected from without by the paramount power of the King-Emperor, were completely subject within to the temperament of their rulers. Perhaps for the first time on earth, an entire community of petty kings was in a position to pursue caprice at the expense of that expediency which in a more warlike age would have provided a natural check on their behaviour. Therefore it is not surprising that many unbridled eccentricities, like hot-house plants protected from the weather, should have assumed fabulous and in some cases ludicrous forms. 'The Fabled Nizam' comes from Mr Dass's book *Maharaja,* a record in sixty-seven vivid chapters of this unique twentieth century world, published in 1969 and still unpublished outside India. The author's style of deadpan Anglo-Indian reportage persuades one of the authenticity of what he has to say. At the same time, his objective presentation—of events that are in themselves quite extraordinary—causes the book to take on the prodigious characteristics of anecdotal legend. One fact he did not mention, and which for me is a perfect symbol, is that the Nizam's heir-apparent, the Prince of Berar, lived in a palace called 'Bella Vista'.

Ronald Firbank (1886–1926) was born in Mayfair, the grandson of a self-made railway magnate, and died in Rome. On a substantial private income he travelled throughout Europe, North Africa, and the Caribbean, and was between times a conspicuous figure in London in the early Twenties. His idiosyncratic life has been much documented in recent years as the importance of his work is slowly recognised. His great idea for fiction was to omit anything he found a bore. The result is an open-ended *pointillisme* of calculated juxtapositions. Allusive, mobile and humorous, it appeals greatly to the imagination of McLuhan's television age. Firbank's influence on such disparate writers as Evelyn Waugh, Grahame Greene, William Burroughs, Noel Coward, Hunter Thompson, the entire black comedy school of modern America (the country which first took him up), and many more, has been wholly for the good, wholly in the interests of economy, speed, acumen and panache. Somebody once said that it was impossible to be as decadent as Ronald Firbank looked. It was one of his poses to eat very little and drink a great deal, which gave his face a flushed red-indian look. He was very affected, very shy, very self-conscious, but his persistence in the face of the literary establishment's patronising neglect reveals a surprising strength of character. All his novels are short. Many were published at his own expense. The story which I have called 'The Uncorked Governess' is a chapter from *The Flower Beneath The Foot*, a peculiar Ruritanian fantasy.

Lee Harwood (b.1939, Leicester) has so far had a chequered but rather unpretentious life. He read English at London University, took a variety of jobs to support his poetry, got married, worked for a period at the Better Books shop in London, and in 1971 became Writer-in-Residence at the Aegean School of Fine Arts, Paros, Greece, for the summer. He currently lives in Brighton where in the past he has been engaged as a bus conductor. 'Cable Street' was published in *The White Room*, 1968, by the Fulcrum Press, a company which has since gone out of business.

Nathaniel Hawthorne (1804–1864), though born on the Fourth of July, was noted for his withdrawn nature. The death of his father (a sea captain) when he was four, lameness resulting from an accident in boyhood, and an upbringing among women, confirmed this predisposition. At Bowdoin College, an establishment in Maine locally fashionable, he was a contemporary of Longfellow, for whose poetry he developed an exaggerated respect in later life. After graduation Hawthorne spent 12 years at home in virtual isolation, trying his skills as a writer. In 1828 he published privately a novel called *Fanshawe*, an error he attempted to correct soon after by destroying as many copies as he could find. The first edition of *Twice-Told Tales*, including 'Dr Heidegger's Experiment', appeared in 1837, but it was not until *The Scarlet Letter* (1850) that he achieved a reputation. When another college friend, Franklin Pierce, became President of the United States of America in 1853, Hawthorne was offered the consulship at Liverpool and Manchester which he took up in that year. His critical attitude towards the English draws attention to Hawthorne's own feelings of inadequacy and provincialism; this was however the most gregarious period of his life. In 1861 Hawthorne returned with his family to his home at Concord, Massachusetts, in which town's Sleepy Hollow Cemetery he is buried along with Ralph Waldo Emerson, Henry Thoreau and the father of Louisa M. Alcott. Throughout his life Hawthorne was fascinated by puritanism and the psychology of sin.

Mark Hyatt (1940–1972) was born in South London, the son of a rag and bone man, and left school at fourteen. For much of the time he worked as a barman in Soho nightclubs and was at one point a dustman. Some of his poetry was published by private presses. To my knowledge, 'Randel' has not been published before. He committed suicide in a cave in the Grampian Mountains. His son is studying at a monastery in Japan.

Anna Kavan (1901–1968), an Englishwoman, was born Helen Woods in Cannes and brought up in Europe, California and England. Nothing in her life seems fully to connect either with the outside world or with its own separate elements. She married twice, had a son (who was killed in World War II), was divorced twice. She attempted suicide from time to time. She entered clinics in England and Switzerland, the jumping off point for many of her stories. She never knew the love of her father (who reportedly committed suicide in her childhood) and became irrational in her pursuit of a surrogate for this, ending up with the solicitude of benign physicians. Her rich and glamorous mother also died early but somehow continued to oppress her daughter in a most frightful way. For her last thirty years Anna Kavan was addicted to heroin, injecting herself daily. But again this fact imposed no syndrome : she was always perfectly groomed for example and of exacting habits. Before the war she was taken away to Burma by her first husband, Donald Ferguson. After the failure of her second marriage, to a painter, she changed her name to 'Anna Kavan' by deed-poll. The early war years were spent in New York. She returned to work in psychiatric research among the British armed forces. In 1942 she joined the staff of Cyril Connolly's *Horizon* at its most manic depressive hour—Connolly was even then assembling his primer for aesthetes in abjection, *The Unquiet Grave,* and such a morbid proximity can have done nothing for a woman so prone to despair. She is the most pathetic of modern female writers and at the same time the bleakest and least effeminate. With her emotions salved by heroin and her application boosted by amphetamines and the blinds often down all day long, her pen was sufficiently detached to move across the cold and malevolent swampland of her dreams; it was through writing that Anna Kavan was able to establish for herself a precarious *gîte* on the outskirts of psychosis. Her painting was a less effective outlet for these awesomely trapped affections; the more gruesome pictures were destroyed after her death. A business in interior decoration provided the convenience of a distraction. She died in December, with a syringe in her hand, still full and unused. One report says that in her last months she was injecting every three hours. Scotland Yard's drugs squad, investigating the house, found 'enough heroin to kill the whole street'. 'Julia and the Bazooka' is a concentrate of her life, although not all its details are strictly autobiographical.

Sheridan Le Fanu (1814–1873), the son of a curate, took his degree in law at Trinity College, Dublin, but never practised at the Bar. His first short story was published in 1838 in the *Dublin University Magazine,* a journal independent of the university. At this time he had a notion of becoming an Irish Walter Scott, but upon realising that his market lay in England he gave his characters English names and settings. He was astute in business, buying three newspapers and merging them into Dublin's *Evening Mail* which survived until quite recent times. In 1844 Le Fanu married Susan Bennett, the well-connected daughter of a Dublin QC. They had two sons and two daughters. When her father died, Mrs Le Fanu inherited a large house on one of the sunless sides of Merrion Square (Oscar Wilde was born in this famous square in 1854) and it was within this house, after the death of his wife in 1858, that Le Fanu by degrees interned himself. Apart from purchasing the *Dublin University Magazine* in 1861 and editing it for a time, he circulated hardly at all, preferring to potter indoors at the study desk previously owned by his grand-uncle, the dramatist Richard Brinsley Sheridan. Le Fanu mostly wrote in bed at night, brewing endless cups of tea to sustain himself in an oppressively curtained bedroom. After midnight he might sleep for several hours, disconcerted by nightmares, then awake and write until dawn, thereafter sleeping until noon. He read such writers as Swedenborg, Jung Stillung, and Justinus Kerner, none of whom were likely to refresh the atmosphere, and by the end he was living in utter seclusion, receiving only his immediate family. 'Green Tea' was published in 1869 in *All The Year Round,* a weekly conducted by Charles Dickens (*A Tale of Two Cities* was written for it). In 1887 Richard Dowling described in his *Ignorant Essays* how a convent of Canadian nuns had been thrown into a great nervous anguish by the immoderate intake of green tea. Le Fanu's last book was called *Willing to Die.* A few days after its publication he was found dead of a heart disease.

Arthur Machen (1863–1947), in his autobiography *Far Off Things* (1922), counted it the greatest good fortune that 'when my eyes were first opened in earliest childhood they had before them the vision of an enchanted land'. This took place in the small Welsh village of Caerleon-on-Usk where his father was a clergyman: Machen remained in a Celtic Twilight dream throughout his life. Nonetheless he came to London in 1881 to work as a clerk. Poor, lonely, socially ill at ease, he found the metropolis full of enthralling horrors, a reaction similar to Thomas De Quincey's (who was among Machen's favourite writers, as were Poe and Hawthorne). Between the years 1881 and 1922, during which almost all his considerable body of work was produced, Machen earned exactly £635 from his books; this includes a massive twelve-volume translation of Casanova's *Memoirs* from the French. Apart from a privately printed poem of which only one copy is said to exist, his first publication was *The Anatomy of Tobacco* (1884), issued under the inelegant pseudonym of Leolinus Siluriensis. He became associated with the *fin-de-siècle cénacle* and two of his early books sported title-pages designed by Aubrey Beardsley. In 1901 Machen actually took to the stage by way of Frank Benson's Shakespearean Repertory Company, toured for a few years, married one of the actresses, then returned to his pursuit of letters which continued to be prolifically unsuccessful until September 29th, 1914. On that day *The Evening News* published 'The Bowmen.' This extremely short story relates how St George, leading a squad of archers from Agincourt, comes to the rescue of the British army in retreat from the Germans at Mons. Since this was published only a few days after the battle itself, the public fell upon the story in the hope that it might prove true. Overnight Arthur Machen became a celebrity. But the failure of St George to make an appearance on this occasion soon returned the author to the mystical half-light which had become his habitat. More books followed and Machen wandered on like Lovecraft's shadow out of time, gathering some reliquary interest in the process, until the strangely advanced year of 1947 when he passed away undramatically in Beaconsfield. 'The White Powder' is taken from *The Three Imposters* (1896).

Mohammed Mrabet (b.1940) is a traditional Moroccan storyteller of a kind now rare. But he is not an old man. His stories are not anthropological relics. He is both atavistic *and* modern. Paul Bowles, the expatriate American writer and composer and resident of Tangier, has taped many of Mrabet's narratives told in the Moghrebi language, and translated them directly into novels and short stories. The two printed here are from *M'Hashish* (meaning 'stoned'), a book unpublished in the United Kingdom. With reference to 'The Canebrake', Mrabet has spoken of his own grandfather who killed one of his wives for standing at the door of the house fully clothed, looking into the street. With reference to 'The Doctor from the Chemel'—the Rif Mountains are known as the Chemel in Morocco; a Nchaioui is the name for one who is chronically habituated to the use of cannabis.

Thomas Love Peacock (1785–1866) was, until his retirement in 1856, Chief Examiner of the East India Company, a distinguished post in which he had succeeded James Mill whose son, John Stuart Mill, was in turn Peacock's successor. Peacock's daughter, Mary Ellen, already a widow, married George Meredith in 1849. The marriage was a disaster and she died wretchedly in 1861 after a brief and unsuccessful fling on the continent with a painter called Henry Wallis (this marriage inspired, as it were, Meredith's famous sonnet sequence *(Modern Love)*). The elaborate display of erudition in Peacock's short satirical novels belies the fact that he was self-taught—on the other hand this handicap may have induced such a performance. 'The Dinner', one of many in his writings, appears in *Headlong Hall* (1816) which like all Peacock's best novels, has a negligible plot and absurd characters. Mr Panscope is based upon Coleridge; Mr Milestone upon Humphry Repton, the landscape gardener; Mr Gall to some degree upon Jeffrey, the editor of the *Edinburgh Review*; and Mr Mac Laurel represents the archetypal Scottish philosophical columnist. With reference to Squire Headlong's opening remarks, 'heeltaps' are those half-inches of liquor which tend to remain in the bottom of the glasses of tardy drinkers; 'skylight' was the space between these and the top of the glass; 'liberty-hall' would be the exhortation of a considerate host. The Greek quotation coming at the end of the story is from Homer and means 'A commotion and a din burst forth'. Apart from his love of learning, Peacock also appreciated the beautiful typographic effects of classical Greek—in fact his typography is always interesting. He died, as he had lived, near Chertsey.

Edgar Allan Poe (1809–49) was born in Boston, January 19th. Both his parents were actors of a vagabond type. Orphaned at two by the death of his mother, Poe was taken into the childless household of Mr and Mrs John Allan, a well-to-do Scots couple living in Richmond, Virginia. From 1815 to 1820 the Allans were in the United Kingdom and Poe went to school in Stoke Newington, North London. At 17 he entered the University of Virginia but was withdrawn after one term because of gambling debts. He left home for Boston where his first volume of poems was published when he was 18. Before he developed athlete's heart, Poe was a fine swimmer and jumper. This propulsive feature of his personality caused him to enlist in the army—Mr Allan obtained the boy's release and in 1830 sent him to West Point Military Academy (the painter Whistler is another unlikely alumnus of this institution). Poe disliked it, managed to be expelled the following year, and went to New York. In 1835 he was back in Richmond as editor of *The Southern Literary Messenger*, sacked for drunkenness in 1837 but not before he had married his cousin, Virginia Clemm, a girl of 13. His movements became no less erratic, although he continued to secure various attractive editorial posts and maintained the production of his tales and poems. In 1847 his wife died from tuberculosis —she had burst a blood vessel while singing and the recurrent haemorrhages proved fatal. Poe drank himself into illness. He seems to have loved her with an unhealthy rapture. She is said to have been the model for *Ligeia*, a story in which Poe's neurotic oscillation between worship and possession is revealed as a variety of vampirism (D. H. Lawrence regarded this as the key to Poe's work). Hereafter his vigour was soon dissipated and on October 3rd, 1849, friends found him ailing in a Baltimore tavern. Poe died in hospital four days later. Everything about his prose is 'incorrect'. T. S. Eliot saw it as 'slipshod writing, puerile thinking . . . haphazard experiments'. Yet it is this profound dysfunction at every level of Poe's work—theme, narrative, syntax—which gives rise to that virtiginous discomfort which readers experience quite independently of any particular item of content. Baudelaire, his devoted translator, wrote in a preface: 'Edgar Poe aime à agiter ses figures sur des fonds violâtres et verdâtres où se révèlent la phosphorescence de la pourriture et la senteur de l'orage.' 'The Cask of Amontillado' was published in 1846.

Peter Riviera (1941–76) was born in London and educated in England and Switzerland. After a short stay in Tunis, from which he was expelled in 1961, he went to live in Prague until the Russian Invasion, thereafter moving to Rome. In 1974 he took to travelling in the Middle East and died in Cairo two years later, suffering from leukemia but in comfortable circumstances owing to an inheritance. He made no great attempt to publish his writing and it never was in his lifetime, although he was despite appearances intensely serious about it and might have exploited several connections. The story included here is from his only completed book, 'an electric novel' which bears the title *The Swimming Pool of Sleeping Cars.* Peter Riviera was of an unconventional humour. Up on his roof garden he once mentioned that he had had a very potent dream the previous night. I asked about it and he said that in the dream he had copulated with a baby. 'Er . . . did it scream?' I replied. 'Oh no. Stillborn, of course.'

Terry Southern (b. Alvarado, Texas, 1924) spent much of his youth at universities. He started out at the Southern Methodist University, Dallas, then went on to the University of Chicago, and from there proceeded to the Northwestern University, Evanston, Illinois, from which he received a BA in 1948, and this was followed by two more years at the Sorbonne in Paris. His first and most famous book, *Candy,* was written in collaboration with Mason Hoffenberg and published by the Olympia Press, Paris, 1958. Since then, in addition to novels, he has written many screenplays; among them are *Dr Strangelove* (in collaboration with Stanley Kubrick), *The Loved One* (in collaboration with Christopher Isherwood), *Barbarella* and *Easy Rider*. His short stories, including the appetising one printed here, were collected under the title *Red-Dirt Marijuana and Other Tastes* (1967). The novels are less adroit: along with many other contemporary writers, Terry Southern's attempts at the full-length comic story have been made to appear ponderous by Hunter Thompson's *Fear and Loathing in Las Vegas*.

Hunter S. Thompson (b. Louisville, Kentucky, 1933) served in the United States Air Force, 1956–58. He was Caribbean correspondent for the *New York Herald Tribune* 1959–60; South American correspondent for the *National Observer*, 1961–63. In 1963 he married Sandra Dawn and produced a son, Juan. Later he became 'deeply involved with the Drug and Violence Subculture around San Francisco Bay' which led to the publication of his first book, *Hell's Angels*, a piece of developed journalism in the style of Tom Wolfe, but lacking vim. He made the transition from journalist to writer, from hack to star, with *Fear and Loathing in Las Vegas*, issued initially in two instalments by *Rolling Stone* magazine, 1971. This short book is a brilliantly flagrant exercise in controlled hysteria, with illustrations by Ralph Steadman that are equally frantic. Theoretically a documentary, it is in effect electrocuted and speeded up into more of a surreal comic novel which goes on getting faster and faster and funnier until it falls off its own last page. 'A Night on the Town . . .' comes in the first half and features the author's demented co-conspirator, the Samoan attorney, who is claimed to have actually existed in the form of a Chicano attorney called Oscar Acosta. By comparison Hunter Thompson's third book, *Fear and Loathing: On the Campaign Trail*, is wearisome.